I0028963

ASCENT®
CENTER FOR TECHNICAL KNOWLEDGE

Autodesk® InfraWorks® 2018 Fundamentals for Conceptual Design & Visualization

Learning Guide for the April 2017 Software Release
1st Edition

AUTODESK.
Authorized Publisher

ASCENT - Center for Technical Knowledge®
Autodesk® InfraWorks® 2018
Fundamentals for Conceptual Design & Visualization
1st Edition - April 2017 Software Release

Prepared and produced by:

ASCENT Center for Technical Knowledge
630 Peter Jefferson Parkway, Suite 175
Charlottesville, VA 22911

866-527-2368
www.ASCENTed.com

Lead Contributor: Michelle Rasmussen

ASCENT - Center for Technical Knowledge is a division of Rand Worldwide, Inc., providing custom developed knowledge products and services for leading engineering software applications. ASCENT is focused on specializing in the creation of education programs that incorporate the best of classroom learning and technology-based training offerings.

We welcome any comments you may have regarding this learning guide, or any of our products. To contact us please email: feedback@ASCENTed.com.

© ASCENT - Center for Technical Knowledge, 2017

All rights reserved. No part of this guide may be reproduced in any form by any photographic, electronic, mechanical or other means or used in any information storage and retrieval system without the written permission of ASCENT, a division of Rand Worldwide, Inc.

The following are registered trademarks or trademarks of Autodesk, Inc., and/or its subsidiaries and/or affiliates in the USA and other countries: 123D, 3ds Max, Alias, ATC, AutoCAD LT, AutoCAD, Autodesk, the Autodesk logo, Autodesk 123D, Autodesk Homestyler, Autodesk Inventor, Autodesk MapGuide, Autodesk Streamline, AutoLISP, AutoSketch, AutoSnap, AutoTrack, Backburner, Backdraft, Beast, BIM 360, Burn, Buzzsaw, CADmep, CAiCE, CAMduct, Civil 3D, Combustion, Communication Specification, Configurator 360, Constructware, Content Explorer, Creative Bridge, Dancing Baby (image), DesignCenter, DesignKids, DesignStudio, Discreet, DWF, DWG, DWG (design/logo), DWG Extreme, DWG TrueConvert, DWG TrueView, DWGX, DXF, Ecotect, Ember, ESTmep, FABmep, Face Robot, FBX, Fempro, Fire, Flame, Flare, Flint, ForceEffect, FormIt 360, Freewheel, Fusion 360, Glue, Green Building Studio, Heidi, Homestyler, HumanIK, i-drop, ImageModeler, Incinerator, Inferno, InfraWorks, Instructables, Instructables (stylized robot design/logo), Inventor, Inventor HSM, Inventor LT, Lustre, Maya, Maya LT, MIMI, Mockup 360, Moldflow Plastics Advisers, Moldflow Plastics Insight, Moldflow, Moondust, MotionBuilder, Movimento, MPA (design/logo), MPA, MPI (design/logo), MPI (design/logo), MPX, Mudbox, Navisworks, ObjectARX, ObjectDBX, Opticore, P9, Pier 9, Pixlr, Pixlr-o-matic, Productstream, Publisher 360, RasterDWG, RealDWG, ReCap, ReCap 360, Remote, Revit LT, Revit, RiverCAD, Robot, Scaleform, Showcase, Showcase 360, SketchBook, Smoke, Socialcam, Softimage, Spark & Design, Spark Logo, Sparks, SteeringWheels, Stitcher, Stone, StormNET, TinkerBox, Tinkercad, Tinkerplay, ToolClip, Topobase, Toxik, TrustedDWG, T-Splines, ViewCube, Visual LISP, Visual, VRED, Wire, Wiretap, WiretapCentral, XSI.

NASTRAN is a registered trademark of the National Aeronautics Space Administration.

All other brand names, product names, or trademarks belong to their respective holders.

General Disclaimer:

Notwithstanding any language to the contrary, nothing contained herein constitutes nor is intended to constitute an offer, inducement, promise, or contract of any kind. The data contained herein is for informational purposes only and is not represented to be error free. ASCENT, its agents and employees, expressly disclaim any liability for any damages, losses or other expenses arising in connection with the use of its materials or in connection with any failure of performance, error, omission even if ASCENT, or its representatives, are advised of the possibility of such damages, losses or other expenses. No consequential damages can be sought against ASCENT or Rand Worldwide, Inc. for the use of these materials by any third parties or for any direct or indirect result of that use.

The information contained herein is intended to be of general interest to you and is provided "as is", and it does not address the circumstances of any particular individual or entity. Nothing herein constitutes professional advice, nor does it constitute a comprehensive or complete statement of the issues discussed thereto. ASCENT does not warrant that the document or information will be error free or will meet any particular criteria of performance or quality. In particular (but without limitation) information may be rendered inaccurate by changes made to the subject of the materials (i.e. applicable software). Rand Worldwide, Inc. specifically disclaims any warranty, either expressed or implied, including the warranty of fitness for a particular purpose.

Contents

© 2017, ASCENT - Center for Technical Knowledge®

© 2017, ASCENT - Center for Technical Knowledge®

© 2017, ASCENT - Center for Technical Knowledge®

Preface

Note: This guide is based on the April 2017 release of the Autodesk® InfraWorks® software. There might be slight differences between the software used in this learning guide and other versions of the software.

The *Autodesk® InfraWorks® 2018: Fundamentals for Conceptual Design & Visualization* learning guide is designed for people using any of the following software packages:

- Autodesk® InfraWorks®
- Autodesk® Architecture, Engineering and Construction Collection

The learning guide provides you with a fundamental knowledge of the accelerated design process that uses data-rich 3D models with high-end visualizations. This enables you to create, evaluate, and better communicate 3D site plan proposals for faster approvals.

Topics Covered

- Navigate the Autodesk InfraWorks user interface

- Create new models from scratch

- Incorporate existing data sources into the model

- Add essential design elements to the model including:
  - Conceptual roads
  - Conceptual bridges
  - Conceptual buildings
  - Coverages and land areas for shaping terrain
  - Pipe networks
  - Conceptual railways
  - Water features (streams and bodies of water)
  - Vegetation, vehicles, and other city furniture

- Display features according to data behind the model

- Create new styles according to project requirements

- Analyze a model to ensure that project constraints are met

- Collaborate with other project team members

- Create high-impact visualizations of the project for better communication

- Generate videos by using storyboards

Note on Software Setup

This learning guide assumes a standard installation of the software using the default preferences during installation. Lectures and practices use the standard software templates and default options for the Content Libraries.

Students and Educators can Access Free Autodesk Software and Resources

Autodesk challenges you to get started with free educational licenses for professional software and creativity apps used by millions of architects, engineers, designers, and hobbyists today. Bring Autodesk software into your classroom, studio, or workshop to learn, teach, and explore real-world design challenges the way professionals do.

Get started today - register at the Autodesk Education Community and download one of the many Autodesk software applications available.

Visit www.autodesk.com/joinedu/

Note: Free products are subject to the terms and conditions of the end-user license and services agreement that accompanies the software. The software is for personal use for education purposes and is not intended for classroom or lab use.

© 2017, ASCENT - Center for Technical Knowledge®

Lead Contributor: Michelle Rasmussen

Specializing in the civil engineering industry, Michelle authors learning guides and provides instruction, support, and implementation on all Autodesk infrastructure solutions, in addition to general AutoCAD.

Michelle began her career in the Air Force working in the Civil Engineering unit as a surveyor, designer, and construction manager. She has also worked for municipalities and consulting engineering firms as an engineering/GIS technician. Michelle holds a Bachelor's of Science degree from the University of Utah along with a Master's of Business Administration from Kaplan University.

Michelle is an Autodesk Certified Instructor (ACI) as well as an Autodesk Certified Evaluator, teaching and evaluating other Autodesk Instructors for the ACI program. In addition, she holds the Autodesk Certified Professional certification for Civil 3D and is trained in Instructional Design.

As a skilled communicator, Michelle effectively leads classes, webcasts and consults with clients to achieve their business objectives.

Michelle Rasmussen has been the Lead Contributor for *Autodesk InfraWorks 360: Fundamentals* since its initial release in 2014.

© 2017, ASCENT - Center for Technical Knowledge®

In this Guide

The following images highlight some of the features that can be found in this Learning Guide.

Practice Files

The Practice Files page tells you how to download and install the practice files that are provided with this learning guide.

FTP link for practice files

Chapters

Each chapter begins with a brief introduction and a list of the chapter's Learning Objectives.

Learning Objectives for the chapter

Side notes

Side notes are hints or additional information for the current topic.

Instructional Content

Each chapter is split into a series of sections of instructional content on specific topics. These lectures include the descriptions, step-by-step procedures, figures, hints, and information you need to achieve the chapter's Learning Objectives.

Practice Objectives

Practices

Practices enable you to use the software to perform a hands-on review of a topic.

Some practices require you to use prepared practice files, which can be downloaded from the link found on the Practice Files page.

Chapter Review Questions

Chapter review questions, located at the end of each chapter, enable you to review the key concepts and learning objectives of the chapter.

© 2017, ASCENT - Center for Technical Knowledge®

Command Summary

The Command Summary is located at the end of each chapter. It contains a list of the software commands that are used throughout the chapter, and provides information on where the command is found in the software.

Autodesk Certification Exam Appendix

This appendix includes a list of the topics and objectives for the Autodesk Certification exams, and the chapter and section in which the relevant content can be found.

Icons in this Learning Guide

The following icons are used to help you quickly and easily find helpful information.

New in 2018	Indicates items that are new in the Autodesk InfraWorks 2018 software since the January 2017 version of the software.
Enhanced in 2018	Indicates items that have been enhanced in the Autodesk InfraWorks 2018 software since the January 2017 version of the software.

© 2017, ASCENT - Center for Technical Knowledge®

Practice Files

To download the practice files for this learning guide, use the following steps:

1. Type the URL shown below into the address bar of your Internet browser. The URL must be typed **exactly as shown**. If you are using an ASCENT ebook, you can click on the link to download the file.

    Address bar

    http://www.ASCENTed.com/getfile?id=sapientia

    File   Edit   View   Favorites   Tools   Help

2. Press <Enter> to download the .ZIP file that contains the Practice Files.

3. Once the download is complete, unzip the file to a local folder. The unzipped file contains an .EXE file.

4. Double-click on the .EXE file and follow the instructions to automatically install the Practice Files on the C:\ drive of your computer.

    Do not change the location in which the Practice Files folder is installed. Doing so can cause errors when completing the practices in this learning guide.

http://www.ASCENTed.com/getfile?id=sapientia

Stay Informed!

Interested in receiving information about upcoming promotional offers, educational events, invitations to complimentary webcasts, and discounts? If so, please visit:

www.ASCENTed.com/updates/

Help us improve our product by completing the following survey:

www.ASCENTed.com/feedback

You can also contact us at: *feedback@ASCENTed.com*

© 2017, ASCENT - Center for Technical Knowledge®

Navigating the User Interface

In this chapter you learn about Building Information Modeling (BIM) and how it is used in the Autodesk® InfraWorks® software. This includes investigating the software interface and terminology, learning how to navigate and work with a model, and becoming familiar with the basic zoom controls, bookmarks, and other predefined views.

Learning Objectives in this Chapter

- Locate basic features and commands in the Autodesk InfraWorks software interface.
- Navigate a model using the mouse, ViewCube, and bookmarks.
- Create new proposals in a model to provide additional design options.

1.1 Building Information Modeling

The Autodesk InfraWorks software is a powerful Building Information Modeling (BIM) program that streamlines site design and the design process for different types of infrastructure projects by using a 3D model. The BIM process supports the ability to coordinate, update, and share design data with team members throughout the design, construction, and management phases of a project's life cycle.

The Autodesk InfraWorks software creates data-rich models using information about the existing environment. Using these models supports more informed decision-making and an accelerated site design process. You can create multiple design alternatives in one model, enabling you to quickly estimate the budget, scope, and schedule with an appropriate level of detail from the beginning of a project. The high-impact visuals that are automatically created during the design process better communicate the design intent to stakeholders.

The Autodesk InfraWorks software coordinates with other software, such as the AutoCAD® Civil 3D® software and the Autodesk® Revit® software, to reduce rework and seamlessly enable coordination between project team members.

Launching the Software

The Autodesk InfraWorks software can be launched by double-clicking on (Autodesk InfraWorks) on the desktop (as shown in Figure 1–1) or from the Start menu.

Autodesk InfraWorks

Figure 1–1

© 2017, ASCENT - Center for Technical Knowledge®

When you open the software for the first time, you must sign in to the Autodesk 360 (A360) service. The Autodesk Account Sign In screen displays automatically, as shown in Figure 1–2. Enter your username and click **NEXT**. Enter your password and click **SIGN IN**.

Figure 1–2

1.2 Overview of the Interface

The Autodesk InfraWorks user interface is designed for intuitive and efficient access to commands and views. It includes the Home Screen and the Model View.

Home Screen

When Autodesk InfraWorks is initially launched, the Home Screen displays, as shown in Figure 1–3. This screen enables you to:

- Preview recent models.

- Access Model Builder.

- Open existing or create new models.

- Access the application's options.

- Toggle on and off available feature previews.

- Collaborate with others.

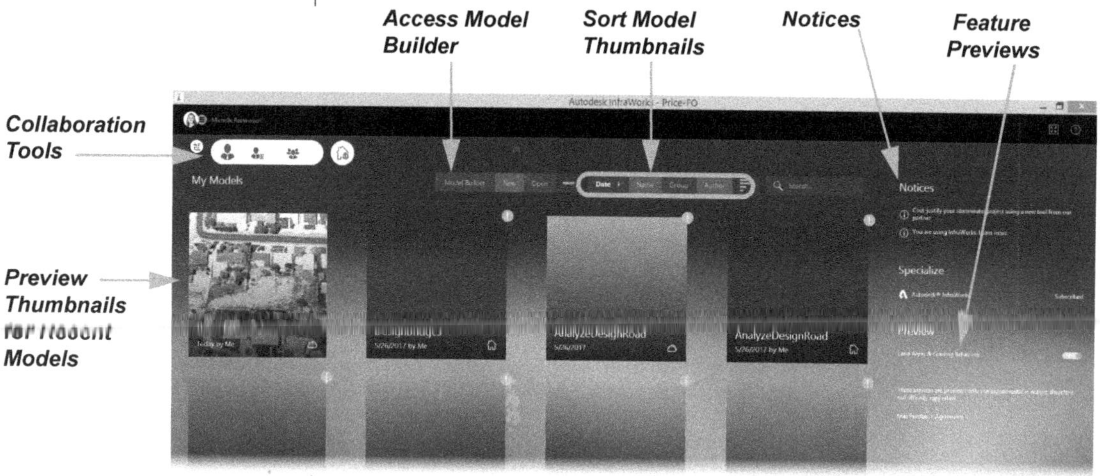

*A **Save** option is not available because the model is a database file (SQLite), which saves after every action. The **Duplicate** command, found under Settings and Utilities, enables you to save an existing model to a new file.*

Figure 1–3

- Various icons display on each preview thumbnail, as shown in Figure 1–4.

© 2017, ASCENT - Center for Technical Knowledge®

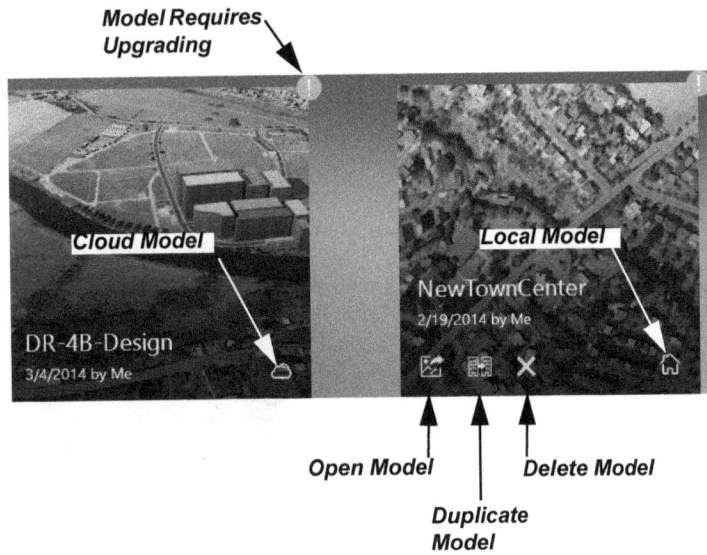

Figure 1–4

How To: Open a Model

1. In the Home Screen, sort the models according to your needs by clicking the required button at the top.
   - Sort models by Date, Name, Group, or Author, as shown in Figure 1–5.

Figure 1–5

2. Click on the preview thumbnail for the model you wish to work in.

- If the model you need to open is not visible on the Home Screen, click the **Open** button at the top. Then browse for the file location and click **Open**.

- If the model you need to work with was saved in an older version of the software, you can either **Upgrade** the model or **Create a Copy**, as shown in Figure 1–6.

All team members should sync their changes before any cloud model is upgraded.

Model Upgrade Needed

This model must be upgraded to your version of InfraWorks 360.

[Upgrade Model] [Upgrade a Copy] [Cancel]

Figure 1–6

Model View

The Model View displays when a model is created or opened from the Home Screen. Figure 1–7 shows the components in the model view user interface.

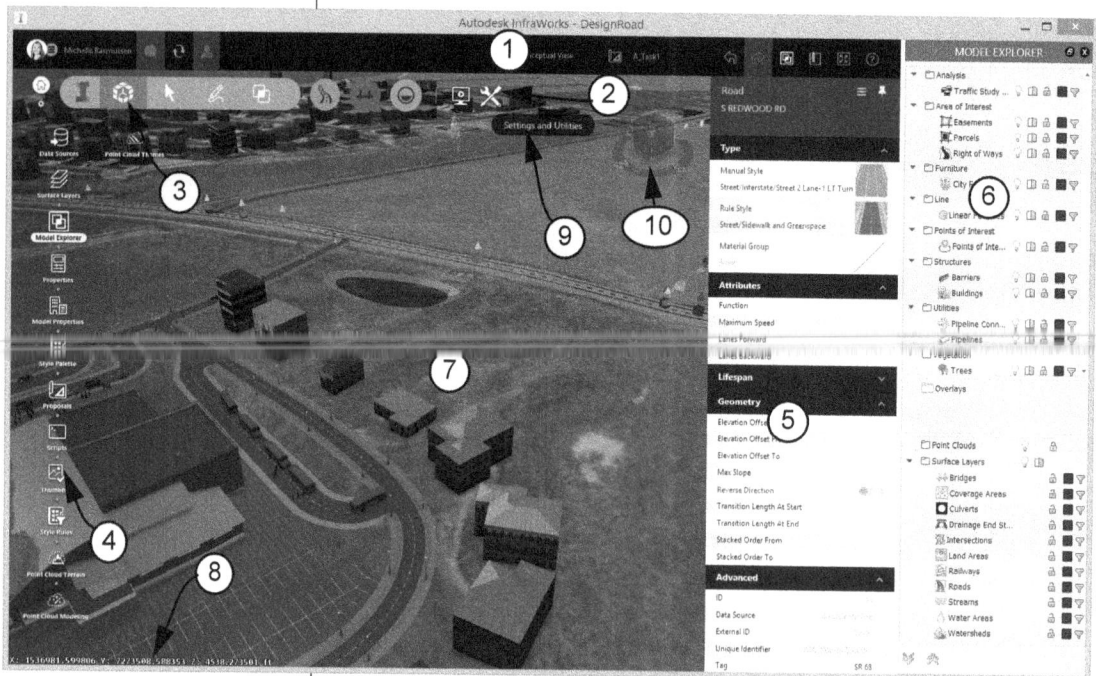

Figure 1–7

© 2017, ASCENT - Center for Technical Knowledge®

1. Utility Bar	5. Asset Card	9. Tooltips
2. In Canvas Tools	6. Model Explorer	10. ViewCube
3. Functional Tools	7. Model Window	
4. Expanded Tool Group	8. Model Coordinates	

1. Utility Bar

The Utility Bar (shown in Figure 1–8) provides a variety of frequently used tools.

- The Cloud Tools, shown on the left of the Utility Bar, provide options for discussing a design and sharing models with others over the Internet.

- The Common Tools, shown on the right of the Utility Bar, enable you to switch views and proposals, undo/redo commands, and select or edit model components.

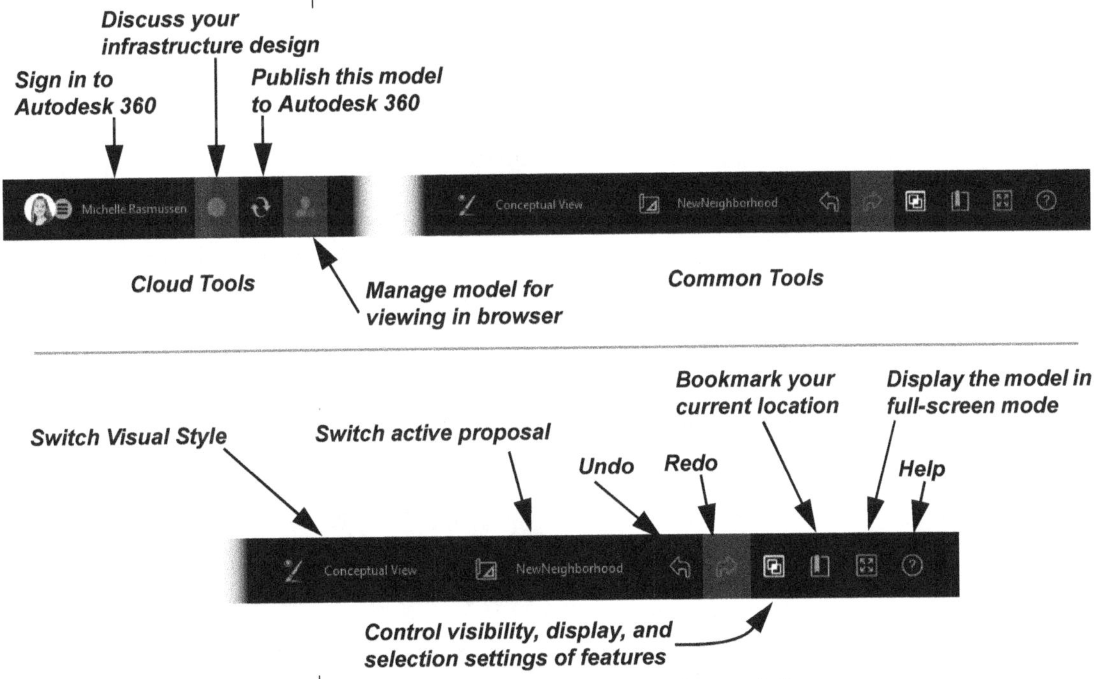

Figure 1–8

2. In Canvas Tools

The In Canvas tools provide quick access to all of the commands used for creating and editing models. Figure 1–9 shows the In Canvas tools collapsed. In their collapsed state, the In Canvas tools maximize the view of the model, while remaining available for use.

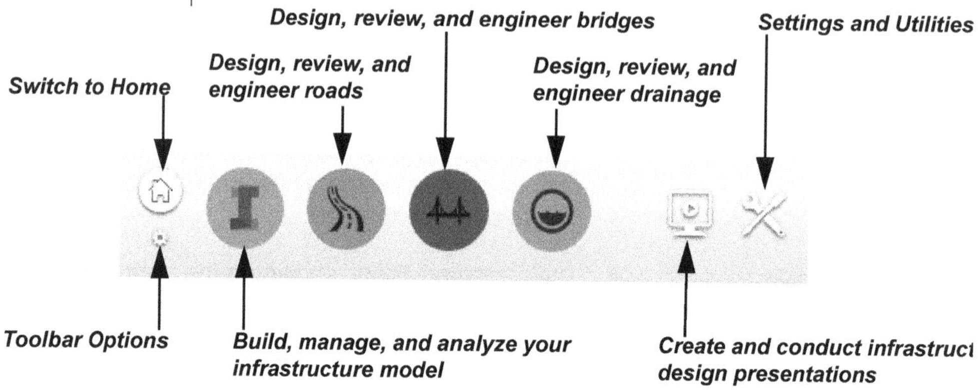

Design, review, and engineer bridges

Settings and Utilities

Design, review, and engineer roads

Design, review, and engineer drainage

Switch to Home

Toolbar Options

Build, manage, and analyze your infrastructure model

Create and conduct infrastructure design presentations

Figure 1–9

3. Functional Tools

The In Canvas tools are grouped together by function. When an In Canvas Tool is clicked, it expands and enables access to additional tools according to the type of operation they perform, as shown in Figure 1–10.

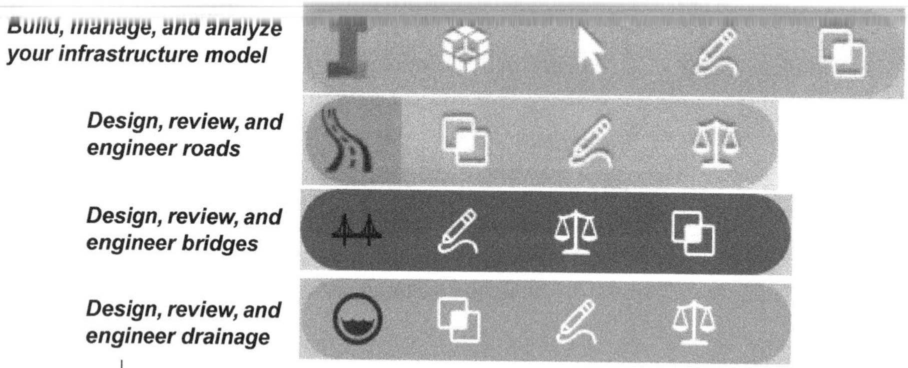

Build, manage, and analyze your infrastructure model

Design, review, and engineer roads

Design, review, and engineer bridges

Design, review, and engineer drainage

Figure 1–10

© 2017, ASCENT - Center for Technical Knowledge®

Each command in the Functional Tools is described as follows:

Icon	Name	Description
	Create and manage your model	Tools for importing existing data and managing the display of model features.
	Select model features	Tools for selecting features in the model.
	Create design features	Tools that enable you to create conceptual design features or engineering design features.
	Analyze your model	Tools for analyzing a model.
	Review and modify (Specific) designs	Tools for reviewing and modifying specific design elements that are only found in Autodesk InfraWorks Design tools.

4. Expanded Tool Group

When an In Canvas Tool or a Functional Tool is clicked, another set of tools are expanded down the left side of the model, as shown in Figure 1–11.

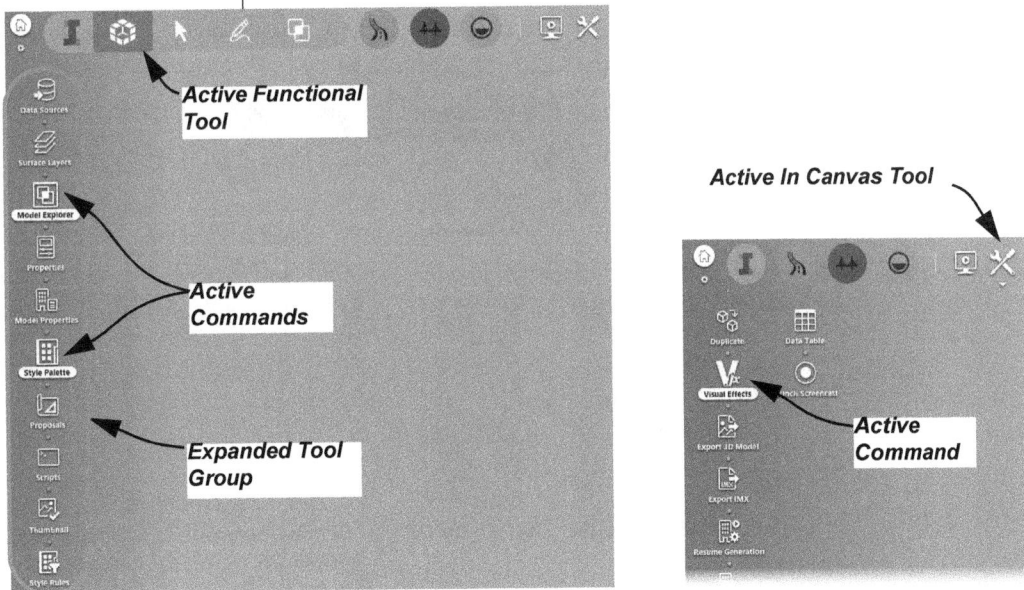

Figure 1–11

- When a Functional Tool is expanded, it changes color to indicate that it is active.

- Active commands are indicated by the highlighted label and icon, as shown in Figure 1–11.

- More than one expanded tool can be active at a time, as shown in Figure 1–11.

Toolbar Options

- Click ▣ (Toolbar Options) in the In Canvas tools, as shown in Figure 1–12, to change their appearance.

- Expanded Tools can be displayed with or without labels, as shown in Figure 1–12.

- Expanded Tools can be hidden automatically by toggling on Hide Tools, as shown in Figure 1–12.

- Toggling on *Shade Tools on Hover* causes a shadow to display behind the expanded tool group when you hover the cursor over the tools. When *Shade Tools on Hover* is toggled off, the shadow is constantly visible, as shown in Figure 1–12.

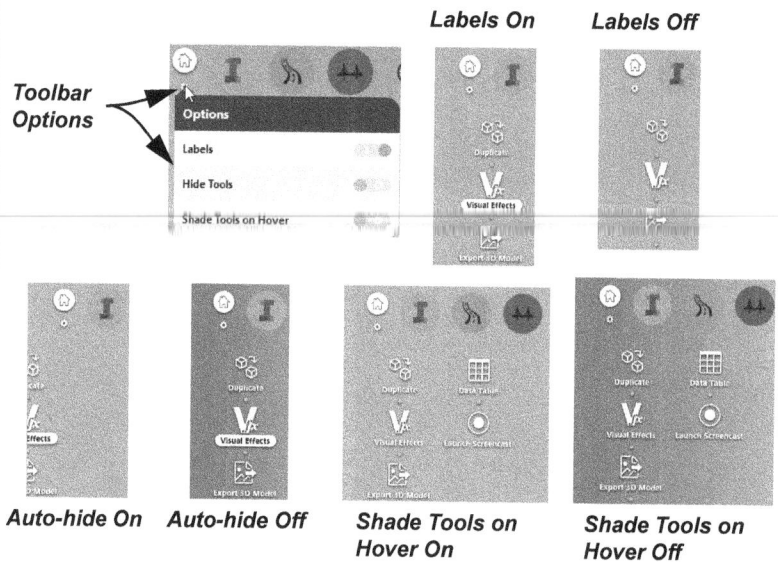

Figure 1–12

© 2017, ASCENT - Center for Technical Knowledge®

5. Asset Card

Asset Cards or Stacks are used to modify the model. They display when certain commands are active, or certain design features are selected in the model, as shown in Figure 1–13. Asset Cards offer relevant information for the currently selected feature. They enable you to do the following:

- View preview thumbnails for selected styles and colors.

- View and modify the properties of multiple features of the same type at the same time.

- Use the mini picker to change styles and colors of features.

- View warnings for attributes that violate specific parameters.

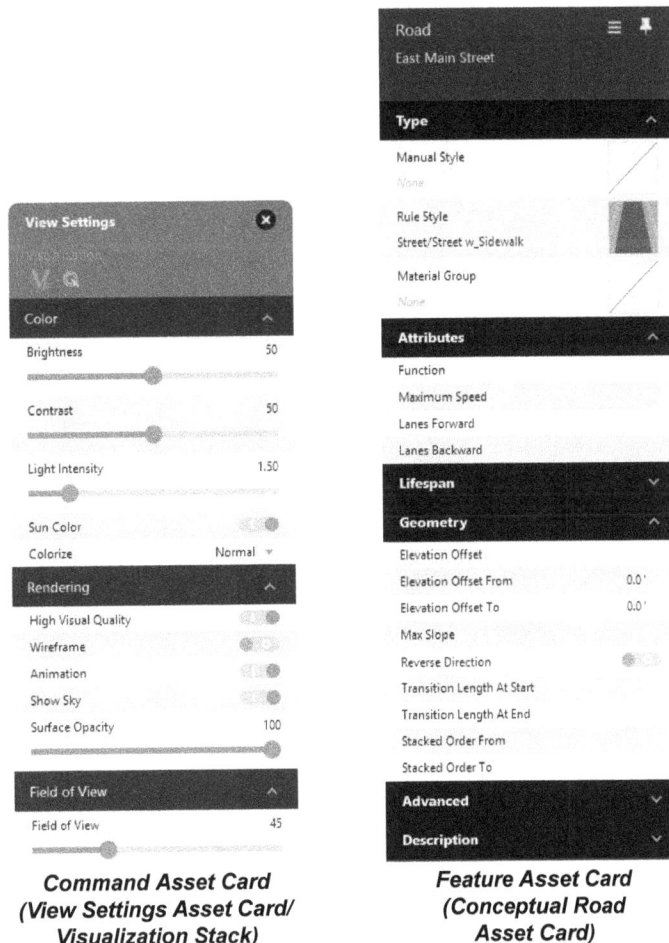

Command Asset Card
(View Settings Asset Card/
Visualization Stack)

Feature Asset Card
(Conceptual Road
Asset Card)

Figure 1–13

The contextual stacking of panels enables you to arrange and manage panels by doing the following:

- Maximize your model view by dragging panels to a second monitor.

- Show or hide specific attributes in a stack (customizable per asset type).

- Attach and detach individual panels to create stacks of information.

- Arrange panel sequences based on the information you need.

- Manage the display of information by collapsing and expanding individual panels.

- Hide or show panels using a menu on the top right of the stack.

- Reset the stack layout back to the default layout.

- Autohide the panels so that they only display when you are actively working with (hovering over) a stack area.

© 2017, ASCENT - Center for Technical Knowledge®

6. Model Explorer

The Model Explorer (shown in Figure 1–14) lists the layers that have been added to the model and enables you to hide or display individual model layers. Use any of the following methods to access the Model Explorer:

- In the In Canvas Tools, click ![icon] (Build, manage, and analyze your industry model) > ![icon] (Create and manage your model) > ![icon] (Model Explorer.

- In the Utility Bar, click ![icon] (Control visibility, display, and selectability of features).

- Press <Alt>+<3>.

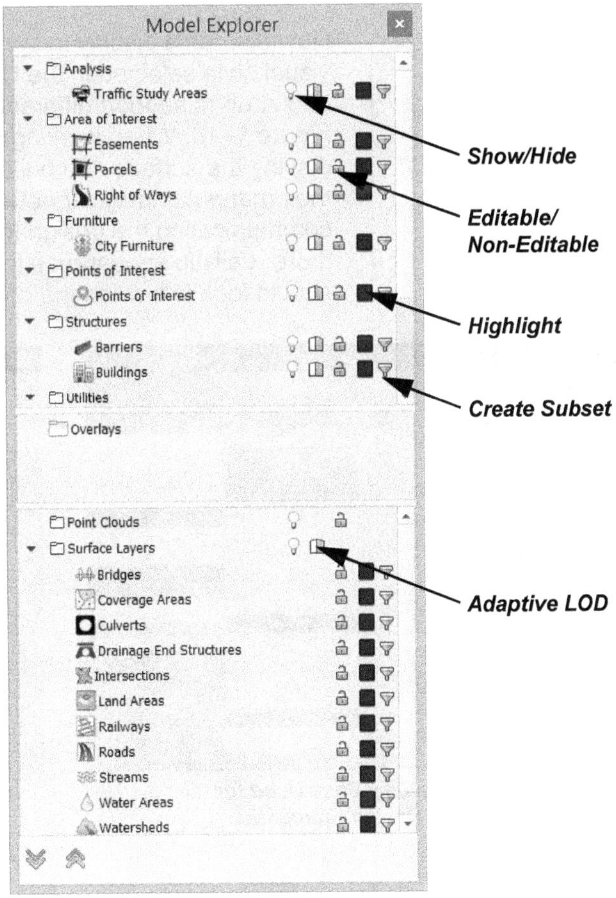

Figure 1–14

7. Model Window

The Model Window (shown in Figure 1–15) is the working area in which you create model elements.

Figure 1–15

How elements display in the Model Window depends on the visual style selected in the Utility Bar. Different view settings can be set up to support different work flows, as shown in Figure 1–16. When working on design roads, you might want to display the surface and buildings in wireframe in order to view their triangular irregular network (TIN). In contrast, when you are communicating the design to stakeholders, you might want a more realistic appearance to communicate what the design should look like when the construction is complete.

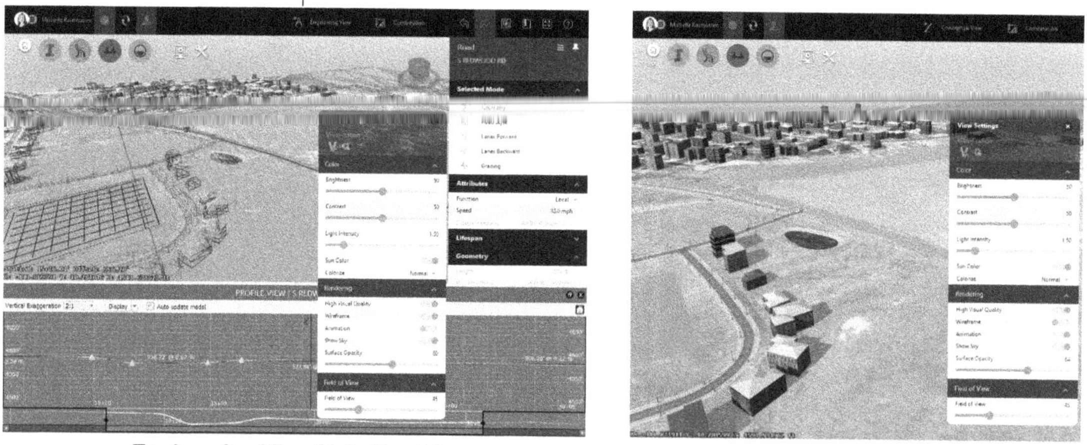

Engineering View Style Used for
Creating Design Elements

Conceptual View Style Used for
Communicating the Design

Figure 1–16

© 2017, ASCENT - Center for Technical Knowledge®

8. Model Coordinates

Each model is assigned a coordinate system that defines the project's location in the world. Once assigned, model coordinates display in the bottom left corner of the model window, as shown in Figure 1–17. The coordinates display the cursor's location in the model in the X, Y, and Z planes. They automatically update as the cursor moves around in the model.

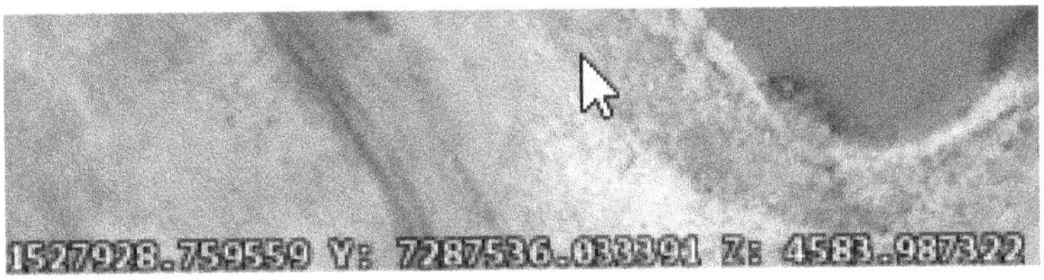

Figure 1–17

9. Tooltips

Tooltips display when you hover the cursor over a command or feature in the model. These tooltips are labels and short descriptions that display to help ensure that you are selecting the correct items. Figure 1–18 shows an example of a feature tooltip on the left and a command tooltip on the right. If Tooltips do not display as you hover over an item, you need to enable them.

When a model is created using the Model Builder, OpenStreetMap feature names display as tooltips (if available).

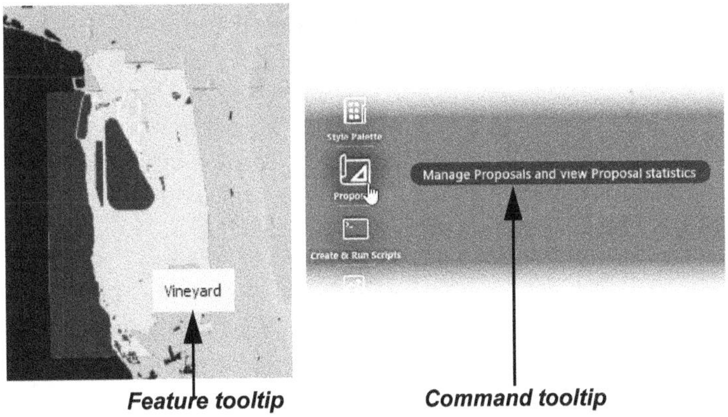

Feature tooltip   *Command tooltip*

Figure 1–18

To toggle tooltips on or off, in the Utility Bar, expand the View Style drop-down and click ⚙ (Configure current view), as shown in Figure 1–19. In the View Settings asset card, click 🔍 (Change navigation and application feedback settings) to open the *Interaction* stack. Under *Feedback*, click the **Tooltips** slider to toggle them on or off, as shown in Figure 1–20.

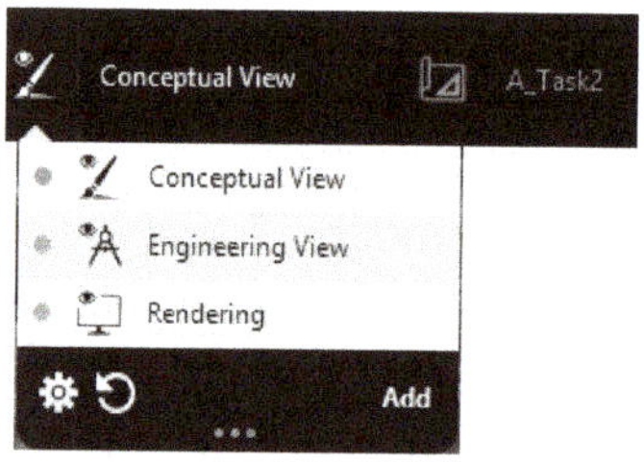

Figure 1–19

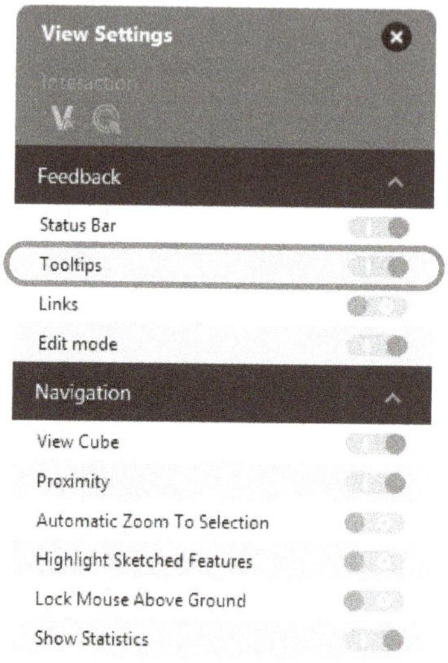

Figure 1–20

10. ViewCube

The ViewCube provides visual clues indicating the camera position in the model and the direction in which the camera is pointed. The ViewCube helps you to quickly move around the model by providing quick access to predefined views, as shown in Figure 1–21.

Figure 1–21

© 2017, ASCENT - Center for Technical Knowledge®

1.3 Navigating the Model

Navigation commands are critical for working efficiently in any drawing program. Sometimes you need to display the entire model, while other times you need to display more detail. When navigating the Autodesk InfraWorks model, you can change the camera position to obtain a better view of the design.

Mouse

The mouse is the main model navigation tool. A three-button mouse can be used to pan around the model, zoom in/out, and orbit the model in 3D, as shown in Figure 1–22.

Unlike AutoCAD-based software, holding the mouse wheel to Pan does not work in the Autodesk InfraWorks software.

Hold the mouse wheel to change the camera elevation.

Hold the right mouse button to Pan around.

Scroll the mouse wheel toward you to zoom out, and away from you to zoom in.

Hold the left mouse button to Orbit in 3D.

Figure 1–22

ViewCube

The ViewCube provides quick access to many different predefined views. As you move the cursor over it, each face or corner highlights. Once highlighted, you can click the face or corner to reorient the model to the highlighted predefined view, as shown in Figure 1–23. If you hover the cursor over the

ViewCube, ▲ (Home) and ▼ (Context Menu) both display, as shown in Figure 1–23.

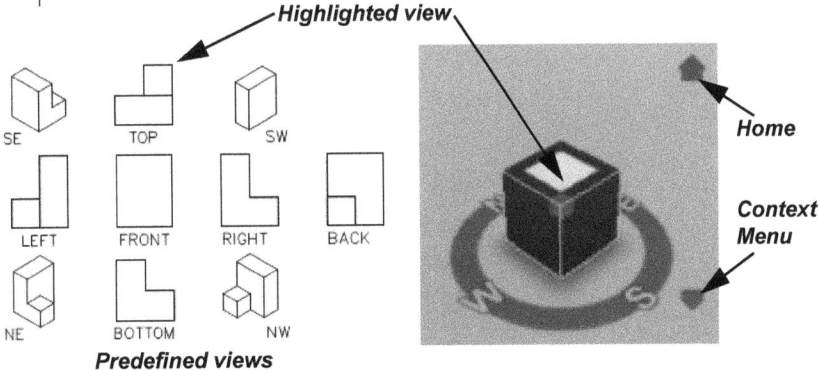

Highlighted view

SE   TOP   SW

LEFT   FRONT   RIGHT   BACK

NE   BOTTOM   NW

Predefined views

Home

Context Menu

Figure 1–23

Home View

The default Home view is a top view that displays the entire model or a view specified which you define. To quickly go back to the Home view, hover the cursor over the ViewCube and click ▣ (Home). Alternatively, you can press <Home> or <F4>.

How To: Change the Home View

1. Move the camera to the view that you want to use as the new Home view.
2. Click ▣ (Context Menu) or right-click on the ViewCube and select **Set current view as home**.

ViewCube Properties

The ViewCube Properties dialog box (shown in Figure 1–24) controls the ViewCube location, size, opacity, and whether it displays in the model.

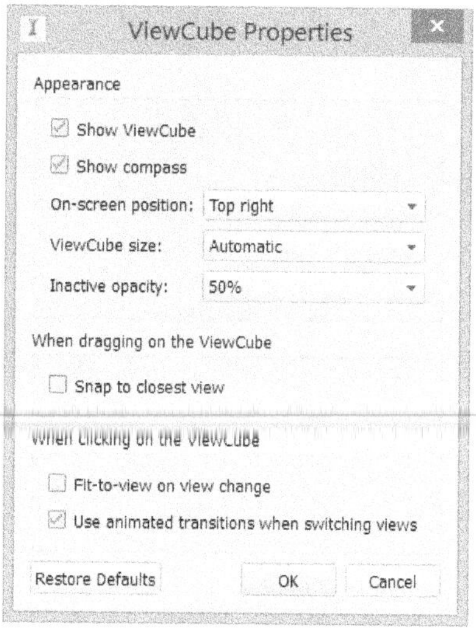

Figure 1–24

The ViewCube can display in any of the four corners of the model: top left, top right, bottom left, or bottom right. To open the ViewCube Properties dialog box, click ▣ (Context Menu) or right-click on the ViewCube and select **Properties**.

© 2017, ASCENT - Center for Technical Knowledge®

To toggle the ViewCube on or off, in the Utility Bar, expand the View Style drop-down and click ⚙ (Configure current view). In the View Settings asset card, click 🔍 (Change navigation and application feedback settings) to open the *Interaction* stack. Under *Navigation*, click the **ViewCube** slider to toggle it on or off, as shown in Figure 1–25.

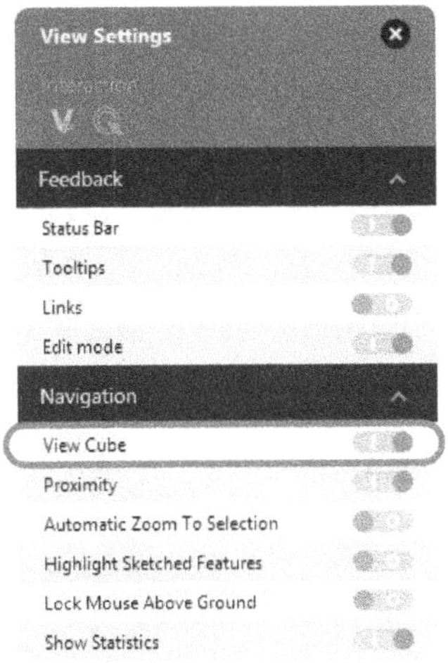

Figure 1–25

Bookmarks

Bookmarks are saved views that quickly reorient the view from one location of the model to another. You can create, preview, and search bookmarks. In addition, you can share bookmarks to show panoramic views on the web (however you can also disable this option for a specific view).

In the Utility Bar, when you click 🔖 (Bookmark your current location), a list of bookmarks with preview thumbnails displays, as shown in Figure 1–26.

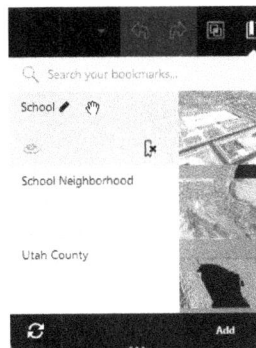

Figure 1–26

Hovering the cursor over a bookmark causes additional tools to display. The table below describes each tool available in the Bookmarks drop-down.

Icon	Description
✏	Enables you to rename a specific Bookmark.
👁	Disables the panorama view for the web for the specific Bookmark.
🔖x	Deletes the specific Bookmark.
🔄	Refreshes the preview thumbnails for all the Bookmarks according to what displays in the current proposal.
Add	Adds a new Bookmark for the current model view.

Other Navigation Tools

Lock Above Terrain

Designers are usually more concerned with what is happening above ground than below ground. To lock the camera position above the terrain:

1. In the Utility Bar, expand the View Style drop-down and click ⚙ (Configure current view).

2. In the View Settings asset card, click 🔍 (Change navigation and application feedback settings) to open the *Interaction* stack.

3. Under *Navigation*, click the **Lock Mouse Above Ground** slider to toggle it on or off, as shown in Figure 1–27.

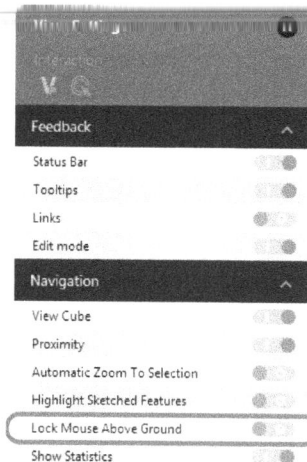

Figure 1–27

© 2017, ASCENT - Center for Technical Knowledge®

*Using <1> or <0> to
change the camera
elevation only works on
the numeric keypad of
the keyboard.*

Elevate/Lower Camera

To move the camera position in the Z-direction, press <Q> or
<1> to elevate the camera, or <E> or <0> (zero) to lower the
camera elevation.

Look Up/Down

The camera angle can be tilted up or down by pressing <S> to
look up, or <W> to look down.

Zoom to Selected

(Zoom to Selected) is used to zoom to a point of interest in
the model.

How To: To zoom in on a selected feature

1. Click ■ (Build, manage, and analyze your infrastructure

   model) > ▲ (Select model features).

   • Alternatively, in the Utility Bar, click ▲ (Select).

2. In the model, click on the feature to select it.

3. Click ✦ (Zoom selected), as shown in Figure 1–28.

Figure 1–28

• Alternatively, you can double-click in the model at the point of
  interest. Double-clicking inside the model to zoom in also
  rotates the view as it zooms.

1.4 Working with Proposals

A proposal is a design alternative in the model and should be created for each design alternative that you plan to explore or propose to the client. By default, every model has at least one proposal called the **Master**.

It is recommended that you only include base model information (existing conditions) in the master proposal. Then, create a new proposal for each new design alternative based on the master proposal. Everything in the current proposal is included in the new proposal.

For example, if you sketch new model elements in a proposal, any new proposals based on that proposal contain those model elements. By ensuring that the master proposal only contains the existing conditions, you can always create a clean proposal.

If you use pieces from multiple proposed designs, you can merge them to create one proposal that includes everything contained in the other proposals. You can then remove all but the required elements.

The Proposals list in the Utility Bar can be used to switch between proposals by expanding the ![icon] (Switch Active Proposal) drop-down list and selecting the proposal that you want active, as shown in Figure 1–29.

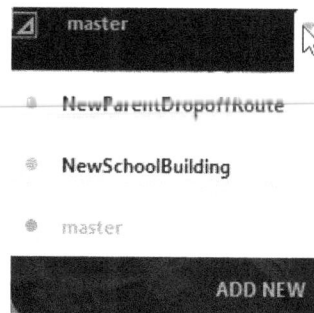

Figure 1–29

© 2017, ASCENT - Center for Technical Knowledge®

Proposals Palette

The Proposals palette contains statistics about the proposals you have created, as shown in Figure 1–30. The statistics include the number of items added or removed per feature type. You can also quickly display measurements for added features, such as length, area, and volume. To display statistics for specific features, expand Details under the feature type, and then expand the specific feature ID to display its measurements.

Proposal Switching Tool/ Current Proposal

Feature Statistics

Feature Type categories

Figure 1–30

Proposal Tools

The following tools can help you manage the proposals in the current model. They are located at the top of the Proposals palette. These tools are described as follows:

Icon	Description
✛ (Add new proposal)	Creates a new proposal based on the current proposal. It includes everything in the current proposal.
✕ (Delete Proposal)	Removes the current proposal from the model.
(Merge Proposals)	Combines a selected proposal's edit history with the edit history in the current proposal.
⊾ / ⌐ (View 2D/3D)	Displays sketched features as 2D linework when in 2D mode or as a 3D model when in 3D mode, as shown in Figure 1–31.

3D model   *2D linework*

Figure 1–31

How To: Create a New Proposal

1. Create a base model in the master proposal by importing data from various sources.

2. In the In Canvas tools, click ![icon] (Build, manage, and analyze your industry model)> ![icon] (Create and manage your model)> ![icon] (Proposals) to display the Proposals palette.

3. In the Proposals palette, select the proposal that you want to use as the base, as shown in Figure 1–32.

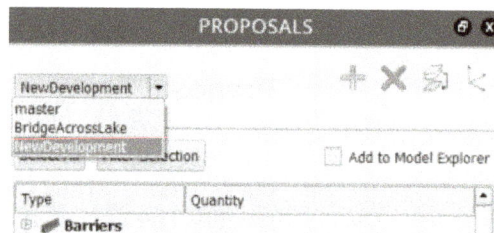

Figure 1–32

4. In the Proposals palette, click ![icon] (Add new proposal).
5. In the Add New Proposal dialog box, type a name for the proposal and click **OK**.

Alternatively, you can:

1. Select the proposal that you want to use as the base from the ![icon] (Switch Active Proposal) drop-down list to make it active.

2. Click remove **ADD NEW** from the ![icon] (Switch Active Proposal) drop-down list.

3. In the Add New Proposal dialog box, type a name for the proposal and click **OK**.

                    © 2017, ASCENT - Center for Technical Knowledge®

How To: Merge Proposals

1. In the In Canvas tools, click ![icon] (Build, manage, and analyze your industry model)> ![icon] (Create and manage your model)> ![icon] (Proposals) to display the Proposals palette.
2. Select the proposal into which you want to merge the features, as shown in Figure 1–33.

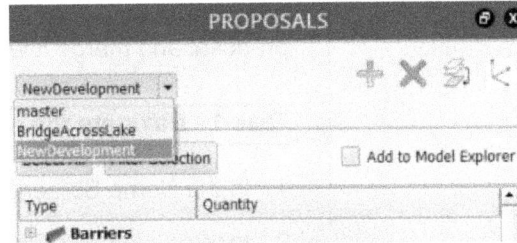

Figure 1–33

3. At the top of the Proposals palette, click ![icon] (Merge Proposals).
4. In the Merge Proposals dialog box, select the proposal that you want to merge into the current proposal, as shown in Figure 1–34. Click **OK**.

*To easily browse added or modified features, the Merge panel provides a **Zoom to Selected** option.*

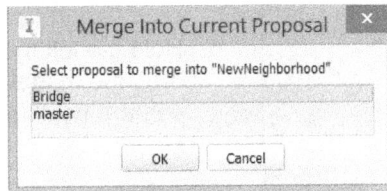

Figure 1–34

Practice 1a

Estimated time for completion: 30 minutes

Navigating the User Interface

Practice Objectives

- Navigate around a 3D model using preset views, manual orbiting tools, and the ViewCube.
- Manage proposals by creating new proposals and merging existing proposals.

In this practice you will access preset views, orbit the drawing, and return to a previous view. Additionally, you will create a new proposal and merge it with another proposal.

Task 1 - Navigate the model.

1. In the Home Screen, click **Open**.

2. In the *C:\InfraWorks Fundamentals Practice Files\ Introduction* folder, select **INTRO.sqlite**. Click **Open**.

3. In the Utility Bar, click ▥ (Bookmark) and select **Bridge**.

4. In the Utility Bar, select **Bridge** from the ▨ (Switch Active Proposal) drop-down list.

5. Scroll the middle mouse button toward you to zoom out.

6. Hold the left mouse button (Orbit) as you drag the mouse to orbit the model to display it as an elevation view with the camera south of the bridge, as shown in Figure 1–35.

Figure 1–35

© 2017, ASCENT - Center for Technical Knowledge®

7. Hold the right mouse button (Pan) as you drag the mouse to the left to pan the model to the intersection of the bridge road with Redwood Rd (the road that is running north and south), as shown in Figure 1–36.

Figure 1–36

8. In the Utility Bar, click ▣ (Bookmark) and select **New Neighborhood**.

9. In the Utility Bar, select **NewNeighborhood** from the ▣ (Active Proposal) drop-down list, as shown in Figure 1–37.

Figure 1–37

Task 2 - Create a new proposal.

1. In the In Canvas tools, click ■ (Build, manage, and analyze your industry model)> ▣ (Create and manage your model) > ▣ (Proposals).

2. In the Proposals palette, set the current proposal to the **master** proposal.

3. In the Proposals palette, click ✚ (Add new proposal).

4. In the Add New Proposal dialog box, for the proposal name type **Combination** and click **OK**. **Combination** is now the active proposal and includes everything that was in the master proposal.

Task 3 - Merge two proposals.

1. If you closed the Proposals palette, in the In Canvas tools, click ![icon] (Build, manage, and analyze your industry model)> ![icon] (Create and manage your model)> ![icon] (Proposals) to display the Proposals palette.

2. In the Utility Bar, click ![icon] (Bookmark) and select **Railway**.

3. At the top of the Proposals palette, click ![icon] (Merge Proposals).

4. In the Merge Proposals dialog box, select the **Bridge** proposal to merge it into the **Combination** proposal, as shown in Figure 1–38. Click **OK**.

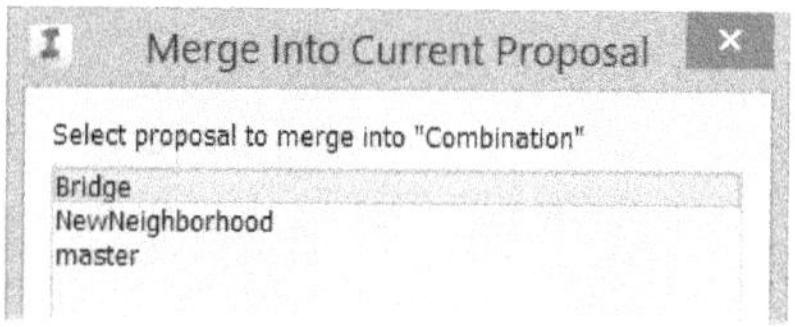

Figure 1–38

The bridge displays in the right side of the view.

5. At the top of the Proposals palette, click ![icon] (Merge Proposals).

6. In the Merge Proposals dialog box, select the **NewNeighborhood** proposal to merge it into the Combination proposal, as shown in Figure 1–39. Click **OK**.

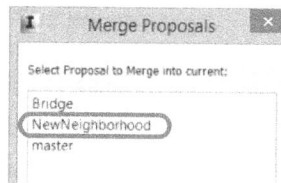

Figure 1–39

A new neighborhood with roads and buildings displays in the view.

© 2017, ASCENT - Center for Technical Knowledge®

Task 4 - Configure the view interaction settings.

1. In the Utility Bar, expand the View Style drop-down and click
   ⚙ (Configure current view), as shown in Figure 1–40.

2. In the View Settings asset card, click 🔘 (Change navigation and application feedback settings) to open the *Interaction* stack.

3. Under *Navigation*, click the **Lock Mouse Above Ground** slider to toggle it on, as shown in Figure 1–41. Ensure that **Tooltips** and **ViewCube** are also on.

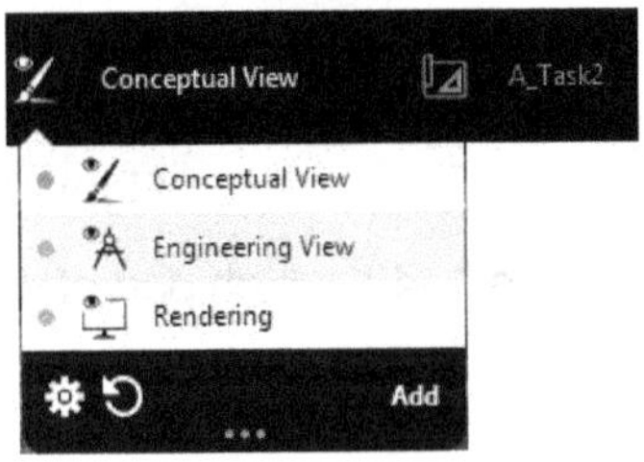

Figure 1–40

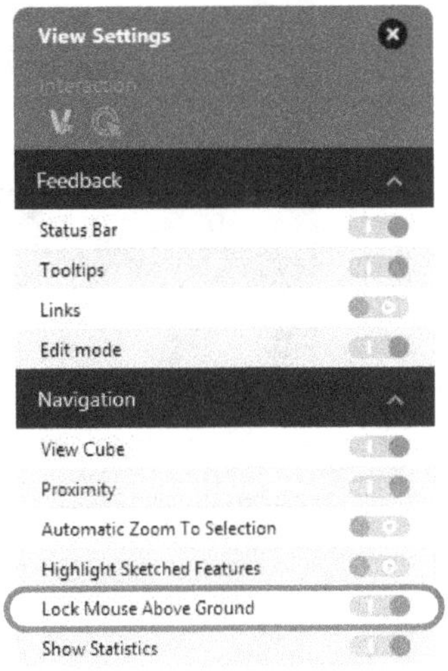

Figure 1–41

Chapter Review Questions

Use Figure 1–42 to answer Questions 1 and 2.

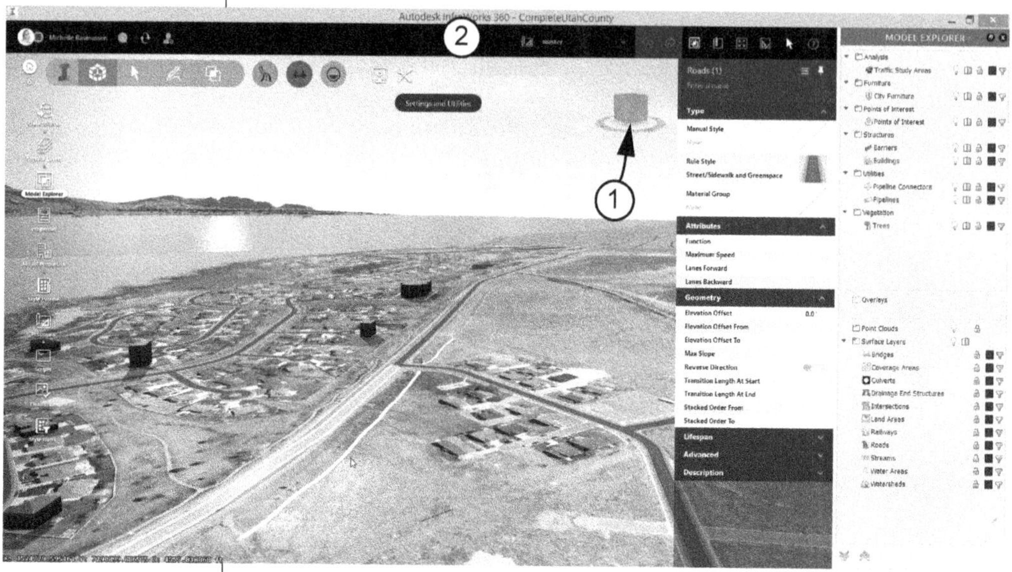

Figure 1–42

1. In Figure 1–42, which part of the user interface is indicated by number 1?

   a. In Canvas tools

   b. ViewCube

   c. Model Explorer

   d. Model Window

2. In Figure 1–42, what part of the user interface is indicated by number 2?

   a. ViewCube

   b. In Canvas tools

   c. Utility Bar

   d. Tooltips

3. Bookmarks are used to quickly change the view to a specific area of the model.

   a. True

   b. False

© 2017, ASCENT - Center for Technical Knowledge®

4. Which of the following should be used to display different design variations for the project?

   a. Bookmarks

   b. Proposals

   c. Coverages

   d. Model Explorer

5. How do you pan in a model?

   a. Click and drag the right mouse button.

   b. Click and drag the mouse scroll wheel.

   c. Scroll with the mouse scroll wheel.

   d. Click and drag the left mouse button.

Command Summary

Button	Command	Location
⚙	Application Options	• **Home Screen** • **In Canvas Tools:** Settings and Utilities
▯	Bookmark	• **Utility Bar**
▣	Close Current Model	• **In Canvas Tools**
N/A	Elevate Camera Down	• **Mouse:** Hold scroll wheel • **Shortcut Key**: <E> or <0> (zero)
N/A	Elevate Camera Up	• **Mouse:** Hold scroll wheel • **Shortcut Key**: <Q> or <1>
▮ / ⌂	Home	• **ViewCube** • **Keyboard:** <Home> or <F4>
N/A	Lock Above Terrain	• **View Settings>Interaction stack**
▣	Model Explorer	• **Utility Bar** • **In Canvas Tools:** Build, manage, and analyze your infrastructure model> Create and manage your model
N/A	Open	• **Home Screen**
N/A	Pitch Down	• **Shortcut Key**: <W>
N/A	Pitch Up	• **Shortcut Key**: <S>
▯	Proposals	• **Utility Bar** • **In Canvas Tools**: Build, manage, and analyze your industry model>Create and manage your model
N/A	Tooltips	• **View Settings>Interaction stack**
N/A	ViewCube	• **View Settings>Interaction stack**
N/A	Zoom In	• **Mouse:** Scroll Wheel • **Shortcut Key**: <+>
N/A	Zoom Out	• **Mouse:** Scroll Wheel • **Shortcut Key**: <->
🔍	Zoom Selected	• **Shortcut Key:** <F> • **In Canvas Tools:** Build, manage, and analyze your infrastructure model> Select model features • **In Model**: Double-click on point of interest

© 2017, ASCENT - Center for Technical Knowledge®

Chapter

2

Connecting to Data Sources

Firms that use existing GIS data during the project planning or bid phases of a project can offer a more complete analysis of the project and better proposals to stakeholders. In this chapter, you learn how to create a new model and then how to connect additional existing data sources. Finally, you configure the data sources to display correctly in the model.

Learning Objectives in this Chapter

- Create a new model using the Model Builder.
- Create a new model from scratch.
- Set the model coordinate system, units, and extents.
- Connect to select data source types to display the existing conditions in a model.
- Configure the connected GIS data for correct display.

2.1 Geographic Information Systems Overview

All Autodesk® InfraWorks® models begin by importing existing data from various sources. These sources include building outlines, roads, utilities, terrain, images, etc. Typically, the data you start with comes from a Geographic Information System (GIS). A GIS enables organizations to better store, manage, and analyze geographical data.

In its most simple definition, a GIS is the creation of a smart map in which data is attached to geographical elements. It attempts to explain or predict spatial distribution or variation in human activity and its connection to physical features on the earth's surface.

Most GIS sources include multiple files. The most basic GIS data source often includes a raster or vector file and a database file containing information referenced by the raster/vector features. For example, an ESRI Shape File includes the vector file (.SHP), a database file (.DBF), a projection file (.PRJ), etc., as shown in Figure 2–1.

Name	Type
BuildingFootprint.dbf	DBF File
BuildingFootprint.idx	IDX File
BuildingFootprint.prj	PRJ File
BuildingFootprint.sbn	SBN File
BuildingFootprint.sbx	SBX File
BuildingFootprint	AutoCAD Shape Source
BuildingFootprint.shp	HTML File
BuildingFootprint	AutoCAD Compiled Shape

Figure 2–1

Sample GIS Data

Many different agencies take advantage of the benefits of using GIS to analyze and manage their infrastructure and data. Uses of GIS data include:

- Cities store street centerline maps connected to pavement management system databases, ensuring the correct maintenance and repair of city roads.

© 2017, ASCENT - Center for Technical Knowledge®

- Utility companies store electronic maps indicating where pipes, manholes, and other utilities are buried to provide blue stake services to anyone needing a digging permit. If a utility is damaged due to a natural or man-made disaster, data connected to the utility maps can be used to quickly notify the affected residents about how long they are going to be without service.

- Retailers use GIS data to better analyze which customers buy certain goods. This enables them to send coupons and other marketing material directly to the customers that are most likely to buy their products. The data is also used to help them strategically locate merchandise in the store.

- GIS data is often created, managed, and stored by government agencies to help them track public infrastructure. During a project's planning phase, planners, developers, and civil engineers use GIS data to help select the best location for the proposed project. During this phase of the project, existing GIS data is collected from various agencies.

Model Builder

AUTODESK
INFRAWORKS 360

To use this feature, access to the Internet is required.

The easiest way to find GIS data, is to use the Model Builder. The Model Builder creates a new model and includes existing datasets from the following sources:

Data Type	Source
Elevation	Terrain data for the United States and its territories uses 10 and 30 meter DEMs from the National Elevation Dataset (NED). The rest of the globe (between -60 degrees latitude) uses SRTM 90m DEM data processed by CIAT-CSI.
Imagery	Satellite imagery from Microsoft® Bing® Maps is draped over the model terrain.
Roads and Highways	OpenStreetMap's (OSM) Highway and Railway datasets are readily available. They are used to create roads and railway features in the model. If feature names are available from OSM, they appear as tooltips and provide a hyperlink to the source feature that opens in the default web browser.
Buildings	The building data is also from the OpenStreetMap dataset.

How To: Create a New Model Using Model Builder

Use the mouse to zoom and pan in the map.

1. In the Home Screen, click **Model Builder**.
2. In the Model Builder dialog box, type the project address in the *Search by Location* field or zoom in on the project area using the map in the right pane, as shown in Figure 2–2.

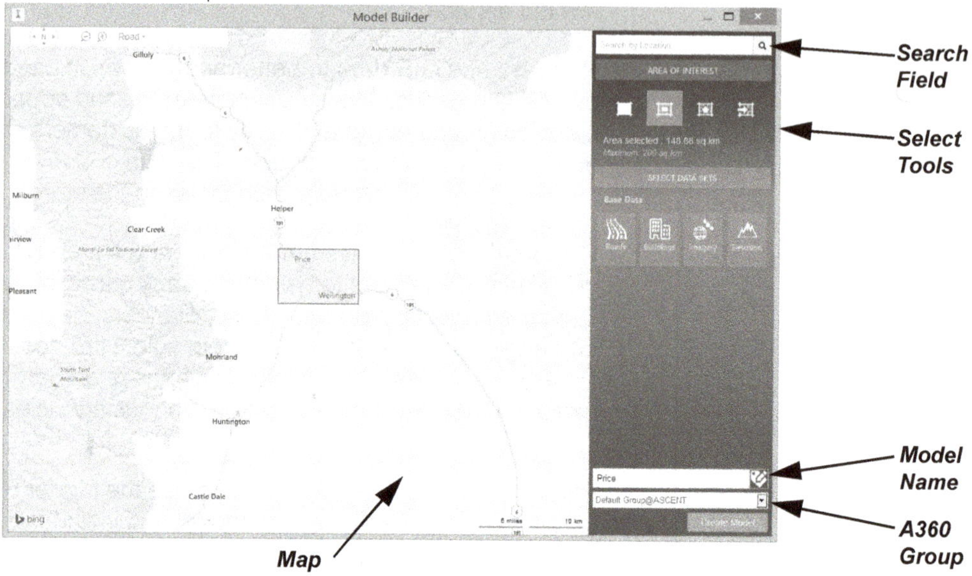

Map

Search Field

Select Tools

Model Name

A360 Group

Figure 2–2

3. Use one of the Select tools to define the Area of Interest (AOI) to include in the model (Note: There is a 200 sq KM maximum area limit). You can chose between the following:

   - Select current map extents.
   - Draw a rectangle to select an AOI.
   - Draw a polygon to select an AOI.
   - Import a polygon to select an AOI.

4. Type a name for the model.
5. Select a group to share the model with through the Cloud.
6. Click **Create Model**. The model is created in the background and stored in A360. Click **Close** in the Model Builder message box.
7. Close the Model Builder.

You are notified by email when the model is ready.

8. In the Home screen, click on the newly created model to open it.
9. In the message box that displays, click **Download**.

© 2017, ASCENT - Center for Technical Knowledge®

Finding GIS Data

The second easiest way to find GIS data for your project site is to perform an Internet search for the city, state, and/or country where the project is located. Include the keywords **GIS data** in your search. Several agencies recognize the value that GIS data brings to a project and the importance of sharing it due to the exhausting cost of its collection.

The data for this course was downloaded from the AGRC (found at gis.utah.gov/) and the Utah County Government GIS site (www.utahcounty.gov/).

A large number of Internet sites provide free GIS data to the public, such as *www.GISDepot.com* and *www.USGS.gov.* There are also private and government organizations around the world that collect GIS data and act as a central resource for GIS data, which you can purchase or download for free. Ensure that when you download the data sources, you include all of the connected file types and download them to the same directory.

Geographic Coordinate Systems

When working with GIS data, note that it can be created in many different geographic coordinate systems. A geographical coordinate system is a mathematical equation that takes the earth's features (formed on a sphere) and projects them onto a flat sheet of paper. Cartographers first developed coordinate systems to help them map locations on Earth by assigning numbers or letters for ease in plotting them on a map. One or two numbers represent the horizontal position (*x, y* or *latitude* and *longitude*), and one number represents the vertical position (*z* or *elevation*).

Several coordinate systems have been developed over the centuries to assist in plotting elements on the Earth's surface. They include cylindrical, conical, and azimuthal, as shown in Figure 2–3. In each of the projection types, there are two ways to line up the projection plane.

- One is to make it tangent to the earth's surface so that there is only one line or point where the distances are 100% accurate.

- Another is to make it secant to the earth's surface. This provides two lines where distances are 100% accurate. The distances between the secant lines are within civil engineering error tolerances.

Tangent

Secant

Cylindrical   **Conical**   **Azimuthal**

Figure 2–3

Setting Coordinate Systems and Model Extents in the Autodesk InfraWorks software

When a model is created using the Model Builder, the coordinate system is automatically set to LL84 (WGS84 datum, Latitude-Longitude; Degrees).

When a new model is created using the Autodesk InfraWorks software, the coordinate system and model extents can be set immediately. Setting the model extents focuses the model on the project area and reduces the size of the model file. The minimum and maximum X- and Y-values can be entered into the software.

© 2017, ASCENT - Center for Technical Knowledge®

Setting the coordinate system indicates which mathematical equation is going to be used for setting the coordinates of your project, and which values display in the bottom left corner of the model area, as shown in Figure 2–4.

Model coordinates (X, Y, and Z) at the cursor location

X: 1529473.217353 Y: 7267597.802425 Z: 5270.229904 ft

Figure 2–4

When you import data from other sources, the Autodesk InfraWorks software automatically transforms the data to your project's coordinate system and can trim the data at the project extents (minimum and maximum X,Y values). Over 6,000 coordinate systems are stored in the software.

When starting a new project, you might not know the coordinates for the model extents. In this situation or if you used Model Builder to create the model, you can set the model extents and/or coordinate system after you import the data. In the In

Canvas Tools, click ✖ (Settings and Utilities),> ▦ (Model Properties).

You can import the model extents from any of the following formats: .ADF, .ASC, .BT, .DB, .DEM, .DOQ, .PNG, .SDF, .SQLITE, .SHP, .TIF, and .SID. This is helpful if you often work in the same geographical areas, or if you plan to set the model limits to the extents of an aerial image or .DEM file.

Design Standards

Design Standards are used to set the horizontal and vertical design control for creating design roads. It is important to set the design standard if you plan to create design roads. Different design standards should be used depending on the location of the project and the units in which the project is being designed.

The Autodesk InfraWorks Roadway Design tools provide the opportunity to control curve radii, grades, and other parameters associated with road geometry.

How To: Start a New Model with the Correct Coordinate System

1. In the Home Screen, click **New**.
2. Type a filename in the *Name* field and a description in the *Description* field.
3. Set where to store the file:
   - If you select *Autodesk 360*, then you also need to select the group with which to share it.
   - If you select *My Computer*, then you also need to set the directory path.
4. Click **Model Extents**, as shown in Figure 2–5.

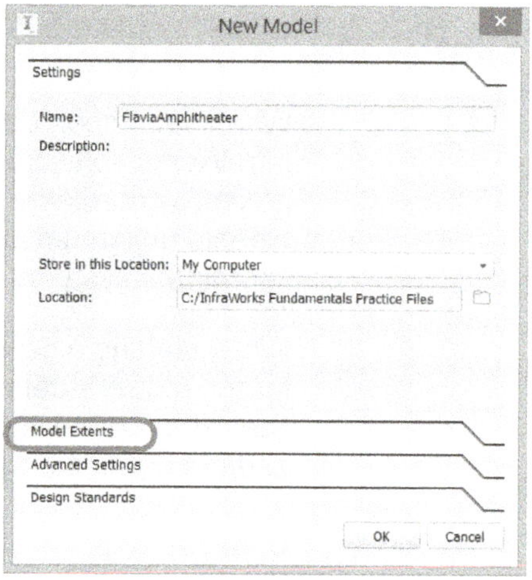

Figure 2–5

5. Select the **Define Model Extents** option to set the minimum and maximum X- and Y-values to set the model extents.
6. Click **Advanced Settings**.

7. In the *Coordinate Systems* area, click (Choose coordinate system) in the *UCS* coordinate system field. Select a category in the left pane, and then double-click on the project coordinate system in the right pane, as shown in Figure 2–6.

© 2017, ASCENT - Center for Technical Knowledge®

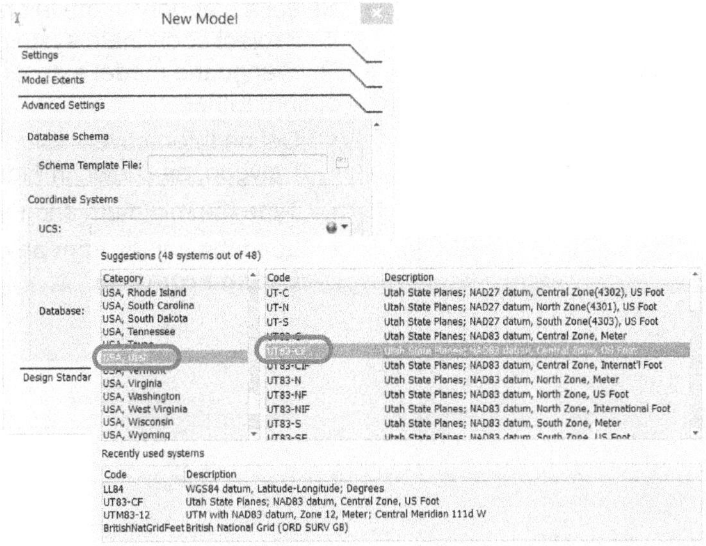

Figure 2–6

8. Repeat Step 7 for the *Database* coordinate system field.
9. Click **Design Standards**.
10. In the *Road Standards* drop-down list, select the appropriate standards for your project. Then, select which side of the road traffic travels on to indicate **Driving Direction**, as shown in Figure 2–7.

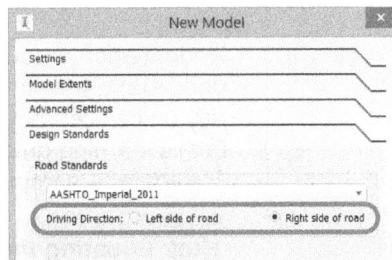

Figure 2–7

11. Click **OK** to create the model.

How To: Set the Coordinate System of an Existing Model

1. In the In Canvas tools, click ✖ (Settings and Utilities)> (Model Properties).
2. In the Model Settings dialog box, in the *Coordinate Systems* area, in the *UCS* field, click 🌐 (Choose coordinate system).

If Model Builder was used to create the model, the model extents are defined during the creation process.

3. Select a category in the left pane, and then double-click on the project coordinate system in the right pane.
4. To change the model extents, clear the **Use Entire Model** option. Either:
   - Define Interactively using a bounding box (BBox) or Polygon, as shown in Figure 2–8, or
   - Type the minimum and maximum X- and Y-values, or
   - Load the values from an external file by clicking **Load Extent From File**.

Extent

Define Interactively: BBox   ▼

☐ Use Entire Model   BBox

   Polygon

	X	Y
Minimum:	1834326.0	7024081.6
Maximum:	1838770.9	7027403.7

Load Extent From File...

Figure 2–8

5. Click **Save**.

Metadata

Most GIS sources provide metadata in the form of an HTML or PDF file. This metadata file contains information on the contents of the file, coordinate system used in the file, limitations of the file, and the kind of data contained in each of the database fields.

Understanding how the GIS data was created helps you to understand how the data can be used, and how much you can rely on its accuracy. Metadata for all of the GIS source files used in this learning guide is located in the class files folder under *Metadata*. A sample metadata file is also shown in Appendix A

Hint: Locating the Information About the Database Fields

If the metadata file does not describe each of the fields in the database connected to the geographic features, you can use the AutoCAD® Map 3D software or the AutoCAD® Civil 3D® software to determine the information. Connect to the data using the **Planning** and **Analysis** tools and open the data table.

© 2017, ASCENT - Center for Technical Knowledge®

Units

The assigned coordinate system indicates which units are used for the model (feet or meters). However, those units do not display automatically. The default units that display in the model are meters. Once changed, the new units remain the display units for all the models opened in the Autodesk InfraWorks software until it is changed.

> **Hint: Imperial Units - Feet verses US Survey Feet**
>
> If you are using imperial units, you can display them in feet or US Survey feet. The difference between the two measurements is only 2 parts per million. However, that difference is measured from the origin and results in a difference of two feet for every 189 miles from the origin point. Therefore, it is important to use the same units as the coordinate system.

How To: Set the Display Units for the Model

1. In the Home Screen, click 🔧 (Application Options).
   - Alternatively, if you already have a model open, in the In Canvas tools, click ✖ (Settings and Utilities)> 🔧 (Application Options).
2. In the Application Options dialog box, in the left pane, select **Unit Configuration**. On the right, select the required default units for the model, as shown in Figure 2–9.

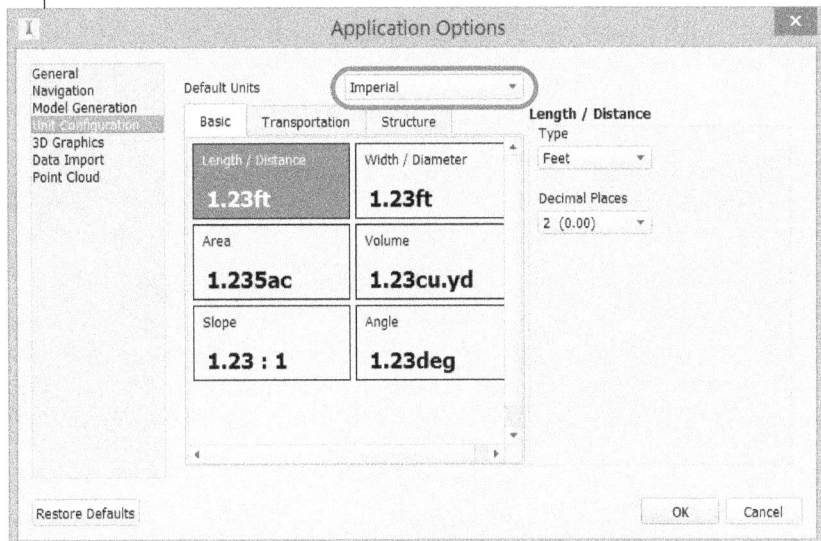

Figure 2–9

3. Click **OK**.

Practice 2a

Create a New Model From Scratch

Estimated time for completion: 5 minutes

Practice Objectives

- Create a new model from scratch.
- Set the coordinate system and units for the model.

In this practice you will create a new model from scratch while simultaneously setting the coordinate system for the model.

Task 1 - Create a new model.

1. In the Home Screen, click **New**.

2. Set the following, as shown in Figure 2–10:

   - *Name*: **FlaviaAmphitheater**
   - *Location:* **C:\InfraWorks Fundamentals Practice Files**

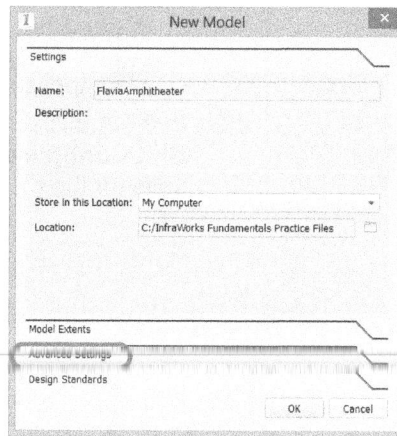

Figure 2–10

3. Click **Advanced Settings**.

4. Under Coordinate Systems, click   (Choose coordinate system). For the *Category*, select **USA, Utah**. Under code, double-click on the **UT83-CF** coordinate system, as shown in Figure 2–11.

© 2017, ASCENT - Center for Technical Knowledge®

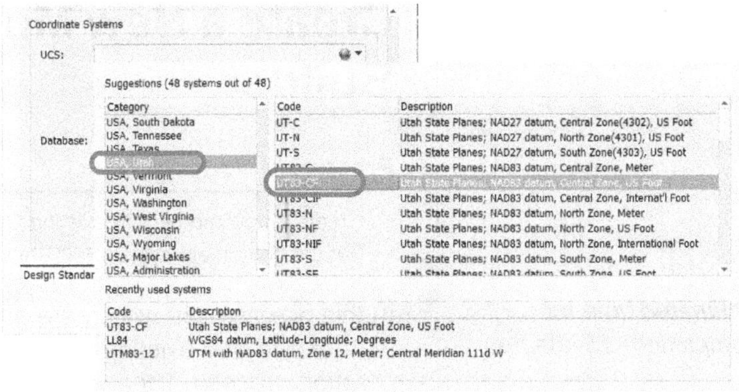

Figure 2–11

5. Repeat the previous step for the *Database* coordinate system field.

6. Click **OK** to create the model.

7. In the In Canvas tools, click ✗ (Settings and Utilities)> ⚙ (Application Options).

8. In the Application Options dialog box, select **Unit Configuration**. Expand the *Default Units* drop-down list and select **Imperial,** as shown in Figure 2–12.

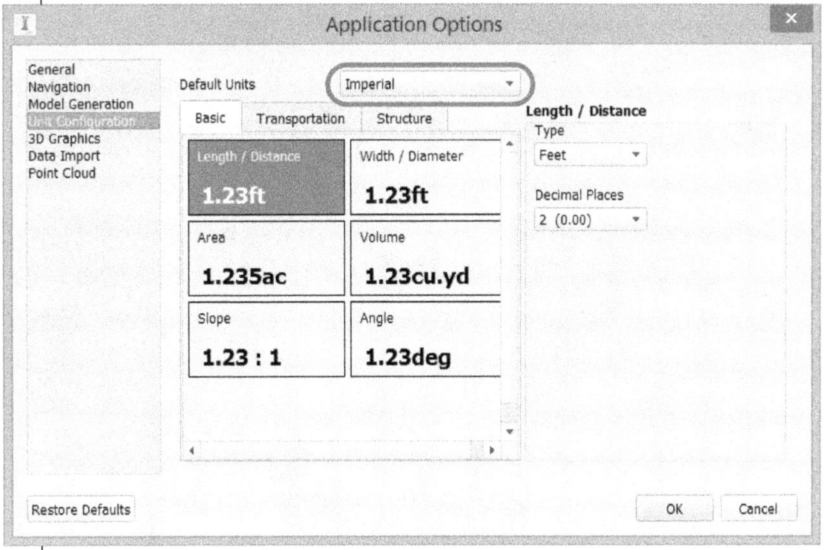

Figure 2–12

9. Click **OK**.

Practice 2b

Create a New Model Using Model Builder

Practice Objectives

- Create a new model with existing GIS data.
- Set the coordinate system and units for the model.

In this practice you will create a new model using the Model Builder and add existing GIS data to it automatically during the creation process. Then you will change the coordinate system and units for display.

Estimated time for completion: 15 minutes

AUTODESK INFRAWORKS 360

To complete this practice, access to the Internet is required.

Task 1 - Create a new model.

1. In the Home Screen, click **Model Builder**.

2. In the Model Builder dialog box, under Area of Interest, click
   ▣ (Draw a rectangle to select an AOI). Zoom in on the state of Utah and select the area indicated in Figure 2–13.

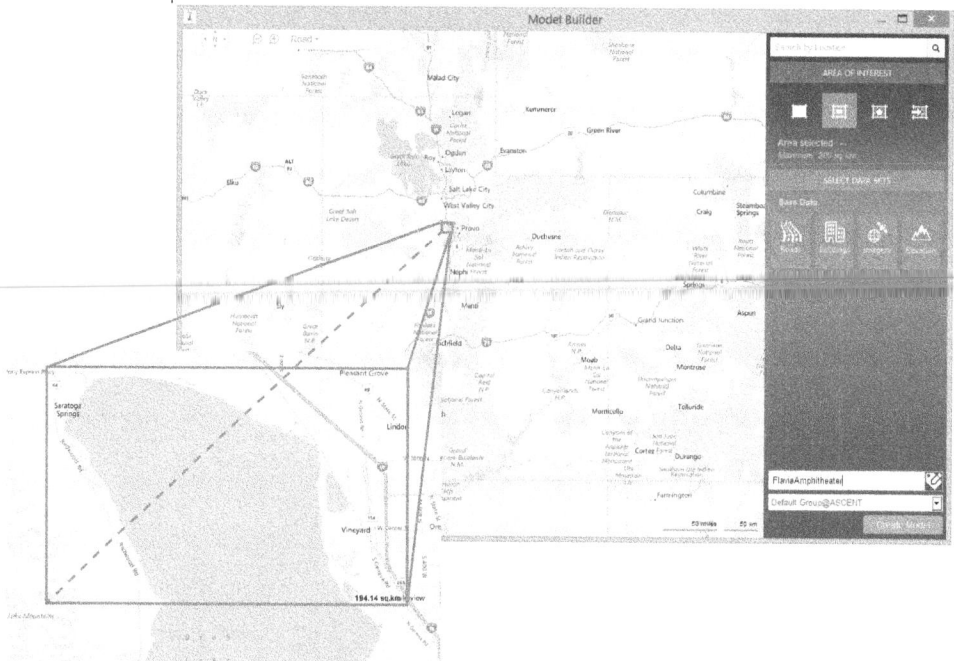

Figure 2–13

© 2017, ASCENT - Center for Technical Knowledge®

3. In the *Name* field, type **FlaviaAmphitheater**. Click **Create Model**, as shown in Figure 2–13. Close the Model Builder dialog box.

It might take a few minutes before the model displays on the Home screen.

4. In the Home Screen, select the **FlaviaAmphitheater.sqlite** model that was just created in the cloud.

5. In the In Canvas Tool, click ✖ (Settings and Utilities)> ▦ (Model Properties)

6. Under Coordinate Systems, click 🌐 (Choose coordinate system). For the *Category*, select **USA, Utah**. In the right pane, double-click on the UT83-CF coordinate system, as shown in Figure 2–14.

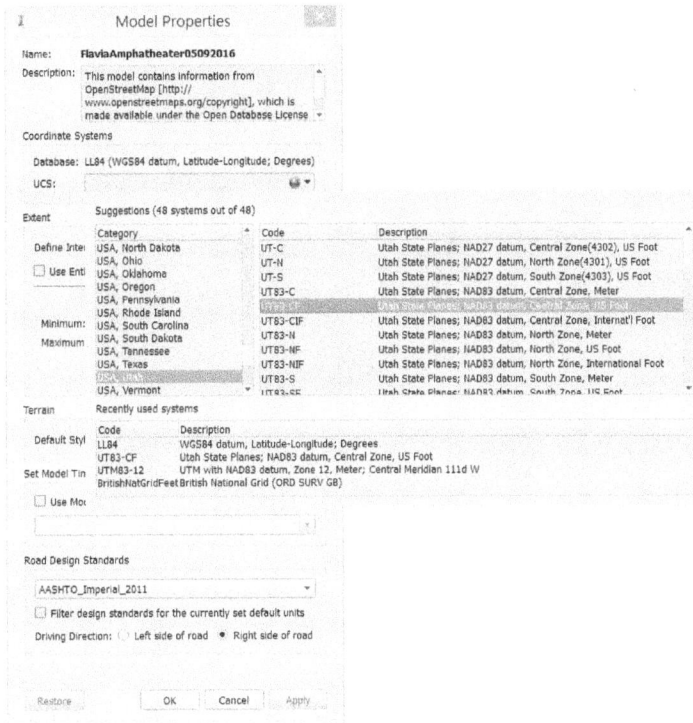

Figure 2–14

7. Click **OK** to update the model.

8. In the In Canvas tools, click ✖ (Settings and Utilities)> ⚙ (Application Options).

9. In the Application Options dialog box, select **Unit Configuration**. Expand the Default Units drop-down list and select **Imperial**, as shown in Figure 2–15.

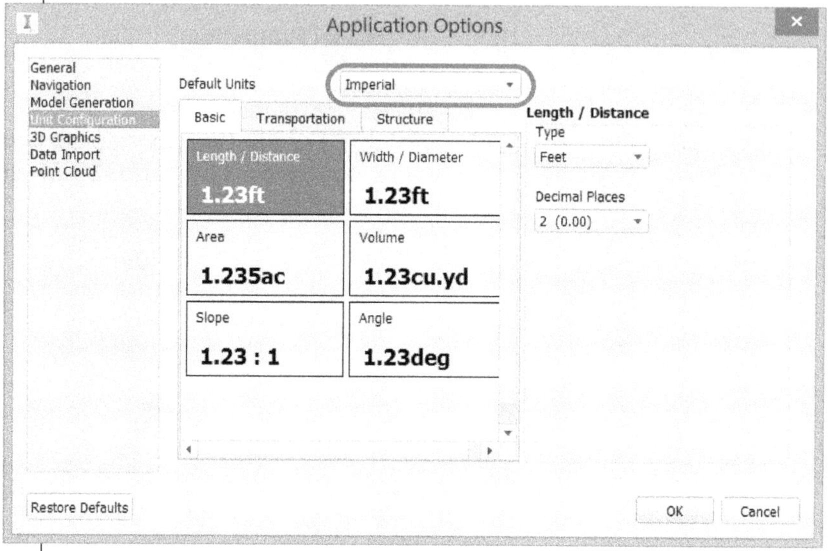

Figure 2–15

10. Click **OK**.

© 2017, ASCENT - Center for Technical Knowledge®

2.2 Connect to Data Sources

External GIS data is imported into the model as layers using the Model Builder or the Data Sources explorer, as shown in Figure 2–16. The Data Sources explorer opens when a new, empty model is created. If you close it before you have finished adding data, you can reopen it using the In Canvas tools.

In the Data Sources explorer, connected data is listed in the top area, while information about the data is listed in the bottom area. Two categories of data sources can be used in the model:

- ⬜ ▾ (File Data Source)

- 🗄 (Database Data Source)

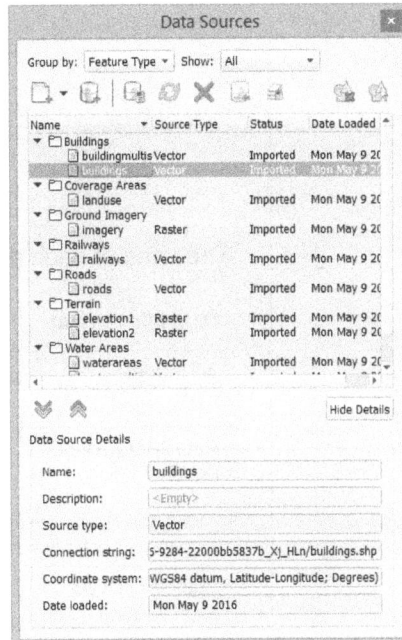

Figure 2–16

File Data Sources

A File Data Source can be a raster or a vector file. Several different file data sources can be imported into the Autodesk InfraWorks model, as shown in Figure 2–17. For each file data source type, multiple file formats can be used. To add a file data source, click ⬜ ▾ (Add file data source) in the Data Sources explorer.

Figure 2–17

The uses of each data file format are described as follows:

Data File Format	Use and Accepted File Extensions
3D Model	Importing local 3D models (.3DS, .DAE, .DXF, .FBX, or .OBJ).
AutoCAD Civil 3D DWG	Importing AutoCAD Civil 3D objects which include corridors, surfaces, pipes, and pipe networks.
	To use this file format, you must have the AutoCAD Civil 3D 2017 software installed.
AutoCAD DWG (3D Objects)	Importing local or cloud-based 3D objects, including 3D solids, surfaces, and meshes.
	To use this file format, you must have the Autodesk Navisworks (Manage 2017 or Simulate 2017) software installed.
AutoCAD DWG as 2D Overlay	Importing local or cloud-based 2D line data from AutoCAD files (.DWG, .DXF).
	To use this file format, a connection to the Internet and an A360 account are required.
Autodesk IMX	Importing local AutoCAD Civil 3D design elements, such as surfaces, pipes, alignments, profiles, and corridor shapes (.IMX).

© 2017, ASCENT - Center for Technical Knowledge®

Autodesk Revit	Importing Autodesk Revit files (.RVT, .RFA). To use this file format, you must have the Autodesk Navisworks (Manage 2017 or Simulate 2017) software installed.
CityGML	Importing cloud-based virtual 3D city models (.CITYGML, .GML, or .XML). To use this file format, a connection to the Internet and an A360 account are required.
DGN 3D Model	Importing cloud-based or local 2D and 3D line work from Bentley v7 or v8 software (.DGN). To use this file format, you must have the Autodesk Navisworks (Manage 2017 or Simulate 2017) software installed.
IFC	Importing cloud-based or local Industry Foundation Classes (IFC) models. To use this file format, you must have the Autodesk Navisworks (Manage 2017 or Simulate 2017) software installed.
LandXML	Importing local terrain or surface models (.XML or .LANDXML).
Point Cloud	Importing local 3D laser scans (.RCS or .RCP). Note: Point clouds must be imported into Recap first to be configured. If you do not do this step, the point cloud does not render.
Raster	Importing local terrain or surface data from raster or vector-based data as well as imagery (.ADF, .ASC, .BT, .DDF, .DEM, .DT0, .DT1, .DT2, .GRD, .HGT, .DOG, .ECW, .IMG, .JP2, .JPG, .JPEG, .PNG, .SID, .TIF, .TIFF, .WMS, .XML, .VRT, .ZIP, or .GZ).
SDF	Importing local Autodesk Spatial Data Files 3.0 (.SDF).
SHP	Importing local ESRI Shape Files (.SHP). Note: It is important to ensure that you have all of the files that are associated with a shape file that is stored in the same location as the shape file (.PRJ, .SHX, .SBN, .DBF, .IDX, .SBX, etc.).
SketchUp Files	Importing cloud-based or local SketchUp (up to 2016) files (.SKP). To use this file format, you must have the Autodesk Navisworks (Manage 2017 or Simulate 2017) software installed.
SQLite	Importing SQLite 3.6 files (.SDX, .SQLITE, or .DB).

How To: Connect to File Data Sources

1. Open the Data Sources explorer using the In Canvas tools by clicking ![icon] (Build, manage, and analyze your industry model)> ![icon] (Create and manage your model)> ![icon] (Data Sources).

2. In the Data Sources panel, expand ![icon] ▾ (Add file data source) and select the file format, as shown in Figure 2–18.

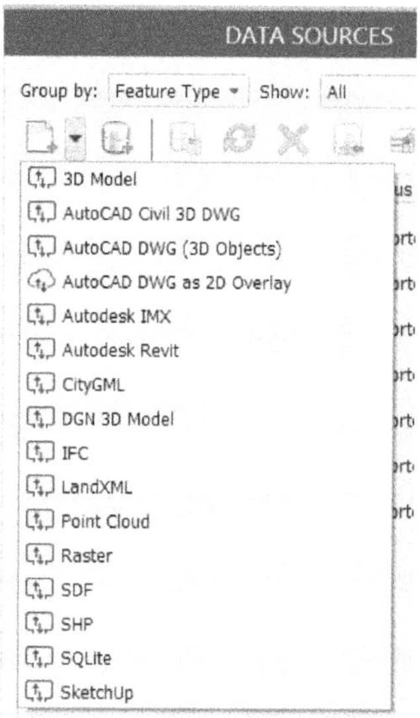

DATA SOURCES

Group by: Feature Type ▾ Show: All

- 3D Model
- AutoCAD Civil 3D DWG
- AutoCAD DWG (3D Objects)
- AutoCAD DWG as 2D Overlay
- Autodesk IMX
- Autodesk Revit
- CityGML
- DGN 3D Model
- IFC
- LandXML
- Point Cloud
- Raster
- SDF
- SHP
- SQLite
- SketchUp

Figure 2–18

Hold <Shift> or <Ctrl> to select multiple files from the directory.

3. Browse to the directory in which the file is located. Select the required file(s) and click **Open**.

© 2017, ASCENT - Center for Technical Knowledge®

Hint: Cloud Vs Local Import

When importing files, the Autodesk InfraWorks software converts the files into a usable format. This conversion is usually completed in the cloud. You can modify the application options to enable local processing of supported formats.

If you want to use the Autodesk Navisworks software (rather than the cloud) to process files, in the In Canvas tools, click

 (Settings and Utilities)> (Application Options). On the Data Import page, select **Navisworks based Local Import**, as shown in Figure 2–19.

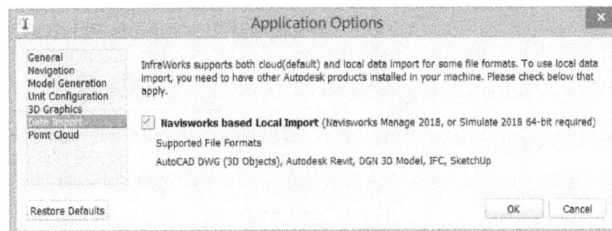

Figure 2–19

Database Data Sources

A Database Data Source can be a vector, ODBC, or OpenGIS raster file. Seven different database types can be added to the Autodesk InfraWorks model. To connect to a database, click

 (Add database data source) in the Data Sources explorer. Select the database type in the expanded Connection type drop-down list (as shown in Figure 2–20) and fill in the required fields.

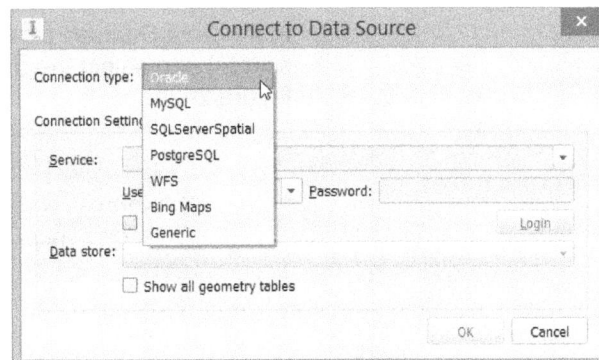

Figure 2–20

The types of database data source are described as follows:

Database	Use and Accepted File Extensions
Oracle	Imports Oracle Express, Standard, and Enterprise Editions (Oracle 10g, Release 2, or Oracle 11g, Release 2). Note: The Oracle Client or Instant Client must be installed and configured before the file can be connected.
MySQL	Imports MySQL 5.5. Note that to connect to your MySQL data source, you need to copy **libmySQL.dll** into the *\Autodesk\InfraWorks 2014* folder.
SQL Server Spatial	Imports Microsoft SQL Server 2008 R2, 2012, or 2014, which supports Express, Standard, and Enterprise Editions.
PostgreSQL	Imports PostGIS 1.50 and PostgreSQL 9.0
WFS	Imports WFS 1.1.0.
Bing Maps	Imports imagery which can be one tile at ground resolution of 78,271.5170 m/pxl, up to 19 tiles at ground resolution of 0.2986 m/pxl.
Generic	Imports a number of generic database types, such as ArcSDE 3.7, TIGER, DGN, UK.NTF, etc. Note: ArcSDE connections require a script that is unique to each instance.

How To: Connect to Database Data Sources

1. Open the Data Sources explorer using the In Canvas tools by clicking ![icon] (Build, manage, and analyze your industry model)> ![icon] (Create and manage your model)> ![icon] (Data Sources).

2. In the Data Sources panel, click ![icon] (Add database data source) and select the database type, as shown in Figure 2–21.

Figure 2–21

3. Fill in all of the required login information for the selected database and click **OK**.

© 2017, ASCENT - Center for Technical Knowledge®

Practice 2c

Import GIS Data

Practice Objective

- Connect to existing GIS data.

Estimated time for completion: 10 minutes

In this practice, you will connect additional data to the model that you obtained from the local government agencies. This data includes a more accurate DEM file, a higher resolution aerial image, and various shape files that contain roads, water bodies, buildings, etc. You can choose to add data to the blank canvas of the model created in Practice 2a, or you can add more accurate data to the model created using Model Builder in Practice 2b. However, the model created for this exercise includes predefined bookmarks to help you navigate the model more efficiently.

1. Open **CreateModel.sqlite** from the *...\ModelExplorer* folder.

2. Ensure that the **Master** proposal is active.

3. In the In Canvas tools, click ▮ (Build, manage, and analyze your infrastructure model) > 🖼 (Create and manage your model> 🗄 (Data Sources).

The data already in the model came from Model Builder.

4. In the Data Sources palette, take note of the data that is already connected to the model. Zoom in and view the data in the model a little closer.

5. In the Data Sources palette, double-click on any of the data sources. You should receive an error because you cannot modify data source connections that came from Model Builder. Click **OK**.

6. In the Data Sources panel, expand 🗋 (Add file data source) and select **Raster**, as shown in Figure 2–22.

Group by: Feature Type ▾ Show: All

- 3D Model
- Autodesk AutoCAD Civil 3D DWG
- Autodesk IMX
- Autodesk Revit
- CityGML
- DGN 3D Model
- DWG 3D Model
- IFC
- LandXML
- Point Cloud
- Raster
- SDF

Figure 2–22

7. Browse to *C:\InfraWorks Fundamentals Practice Files\DEMs*. Press <Ctrl>+<A> to select all of the DEM files[1] in the list, and click **Open**.

8. In the Data Sources explorer, continue adding files using the following information. Figure 2–23 shows the Data Sources palette once all of the data has been added.

File Path	File Path	Files to Select
Raster	*C:\InfraWorks Fundamentals Practice Files\Images*[2]	All
SHP	*C:\InfraWorks Fundamentals Practice Files\ShapeFiles*[3]	All

Figure 2–23

1.((AGRC), Utah Automated Geographic Reference Center, 2007)
2.((AGRC), Automated Geographic Reference Center, 2012)
3.(Department, GIS Division of the Utah County Information Systems, 2013)

© 2017, ASCENT - Center for Technical Knowledge®

2.3 Configure and Display Data Sources

Although the source data has been connected, it does not display in the model because the data must be configured first. Configuring the data is important because it enables you to:

- Set the coordinate system in which the source data is located.

- Map database fields located in the source data database file to the properties specified in the model template.

The more database fields you can map to your model, the more analysis can be done with the model. You can also add more accuracy to the model if database fields specify elevations, heights, and other numerical information about the raster or vector to which they pertain.

Data Source Configuration

Once a data source has been imported, it is configured in the Data Sources explorer by either double-clicking on the data source, or selecting the data source and clicking 🖳 (Configure Data), as shown in Figure 2–24.

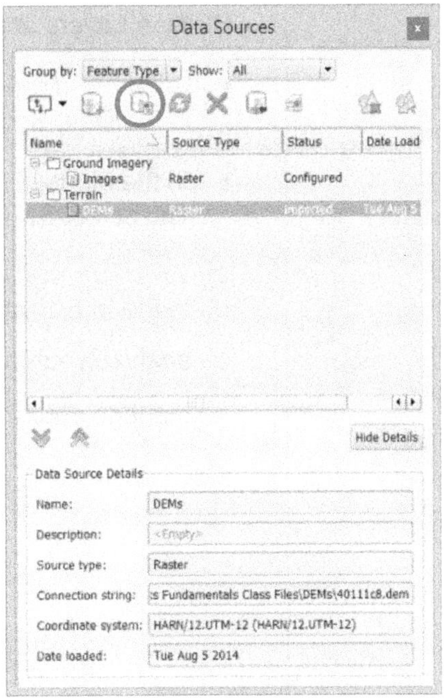

Figure 2–24

Hint: Terrain Data

It is essential that terrain data be added to the model first, since all other data sits on top of the terrain. Without a terrain surface, other data cannot be displayed. Additionally, only one terrain surface can display at any one time. If multiple terrain surfaces exist in a model, the visibility of the surfaces can be determined by setting the display order in the Surface Layers dialog box. Use the arrows at the top of the box to set the display priority, as shown in Figure 2–25.

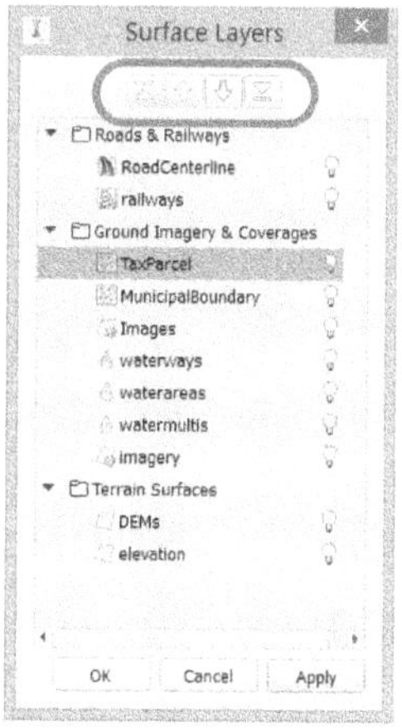

Figure 2–25

Surface Layers are available in multiple places:

- Click ⬛ (Manage the order and visibility of surface data) in the Data Sources palette.

- In the Model Explorer palette, right-click on *Surface Layers* and select **Surface Layers**.

- In the In Canvas tools, click ⬛ (Build, manage, and analyze your infrastructure model) > ⬛ (Create and manage your model> ⬛ (Surface Layers).

© 2017, ASCENT - Center for Technical Knowledge®

Data Source Details

When a data source is selected, in the Data Sources explorer, details about the source display in the Data Source Details panel. The Data Source Details include the name, description, source type, connection string (indicating where the source file is located), coordinate system, and date that the source was loaded into the model.

If a data source file is moved to a new location, the connection to the file is lost and errors might occur when working with features from that data source. Therefore, avoid moving files once you have connected them to an Autodesk InfraWorks model unless doing so is absolutely necessary.

If the data source files must be moved, you must re-associate them from the new location.

How To: Reassociate Moved Data Sources

1. Select the data source in the Data Sources explorer, and click

   ▢ (Manage paths of file data sources).
2. In the File Data Source Reconnection dialog box, click

   ▢ (Browse) under the New column, as shown in Figure 2–26. Locate and select the file.

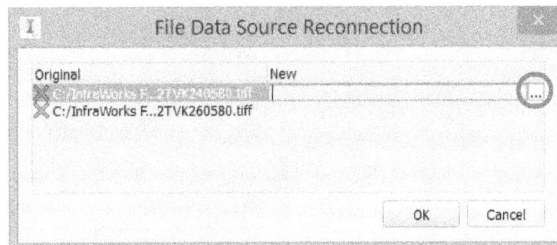

Figure 2–26

- This must be done for every proposal in which the data source is located.
- If more than one file is listed under the source data and both are located in the same directory, the paths for the additional files in the File Data Source Reconnection dialog box should automatically be populated.

General Information

In the *General* area at the top of the Data Source Configuration dialog box, every layer includes a *Name*, *Description*, *Source*, and *Type* field, as shown in Figure 2–27. The *Description* and the *Type* are usually the only two fields required to input information in the *General* area.

Figure 2–27

The *Type* field is the most important field in the *General* area. It determines the table and other settings that become available for the data source. Once the type has been configured in a model, it cannot be changed. The available configuration types are as follows:

• Barriers	• Pipelines
• Building	• Points of Interest
• City Furniture	• Project Sites
• Coverage Areas	• Railways
• Culverts	• Right of Ways
• Drainage End Structures	• Roads
• Easements	• Streams
• Land Areas (Only available with A360)	• Terrain
• Parcels	• Traffic Study Areas
• Parking Areas	• Trees
• Parking Rows	• Water Areas
• Pipeline Connectors	• Watersheds

© 2017, ASCENT - Center for Technical Knowledge®

Common Tab

There are multiple ways to set styles in the Autodesk InfraWorks software.

Note that each data type has different fields available on the various tabs.

The *Common* tab (shown in Figure 2–28) maps database fields to specific model properties and sets the styles to display the data source features.

Figure 2–28

How To: Select a Style for Data Source Features

1. In the *Style* field, click (Style Chooser), as shown in Figure 2–28. Select the required style in the Select Style dialog box, as shown in Figure 2–29.

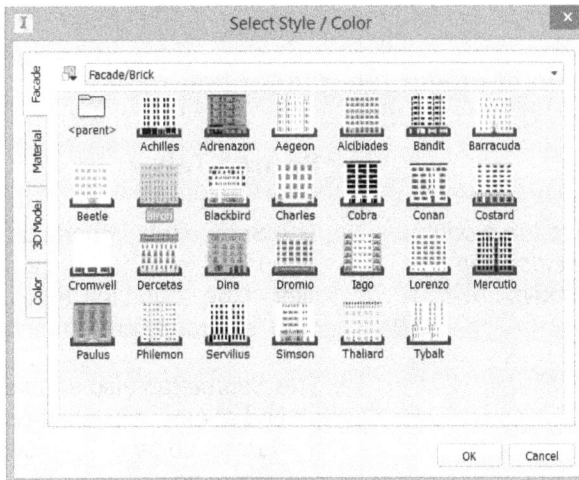

Figure 2–29

2. Click **OK**.

Geo Location Tab

The *Geo Location* tab (shown in Figure 2–30) sets the source data's original geographic coordinate system. It is important to ensure that the *Coordinate System* field is correct because it is used to project the source data to the model coordinate system. If the wrong coordinate system is selected, the features display in the wrong location in the model.

If required, you can change the coordinate system using the Coordinate System drop-down list. Additional commands in the *Geo Location* tab enable you to manually set the insertion point, scale and rotation factors, or interactively place the data source.

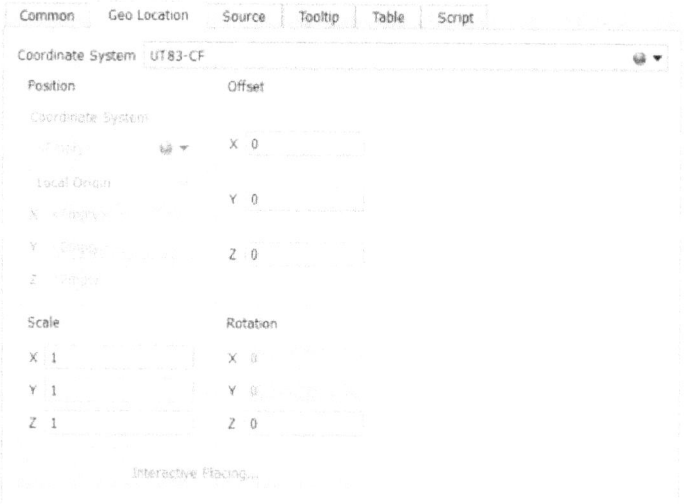

Figure 2–30

Source Tab

Clipping to the model extents helps keep the file size down.

The *Source* tab, imports a subset of the original data by creating a source filter. The source filter can be a property filter or location filter. If the option to **Clip to model extent** is selected, the source data is automatically trimmed to the model extents.

The *Source* tab also enables you to control whether features are placed at a set elevation according to a property, or draped on the terrain surface. The following three options are available for the elevation.

© 2017, ASCENT - Center for Technical Knowledge®

Option	Description
Don't drape	Features are not assigned an elevation. Instead they are imported at the elevation at which they were originally created.
Drape	Feature elevations are automatically taken from the terrain surface elevations.
Set Elevation	Enables you to select a field in the data table to be used to set the elevation.

If you are importing a source file that consists of polylines, you can select the option to **Convert closed polylines to polygons**, as shown in Figure 2–31.

Figure 2–31

Tooltip Tab

The *Tooltip* tab temporarily labels a model element by displaying a selected property when the cursor hovers over a feature. Figure 2–32 shows the name of a city when the cursor hovers over any part of the city. Additionally, hyperlinks can be added to link features to a specific web page or other files.

Tooltips are automatically added to data obtained from Model Builder.

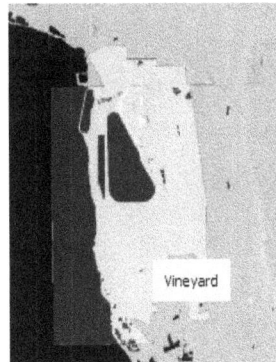

Figure 2–32

How To: Add a Tooltip to a Data Source

1. In the *Tooltip* tab, select the *Html* tab, and click 🖻 (Insert Property).
2. In the Select Property dialog box, select the property that you want to display, as shown in Figure 2–33.

Figure 2–33

3. Click **OK**.

Table Tab

The *Table* tab maps (connects) fields from the original GIS data source database to the list of properties for the current data type. You must map any key fields that you plan to use later for stylizing and analyzing the model. In the example shown in Figure 2–34, the current market value (**MKT CNTVAL**) is mapped to the *User Data* property for a parcel coverage. This data can be used to display the coverage, with various fill patterns or colors, according to the property value.

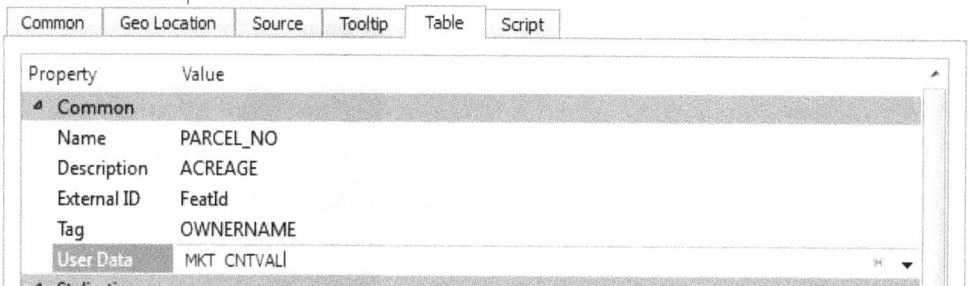

Figure 2–34

© 2017, ASCENT - Center for Technical Knowledge®

Script Tab

The *Script* tab specifies advanced import settings using JavaScript. The example script (shown in Figure 2–35) varies the style for streets based on their values for the *Elevation* property.

```
1  function Process() {
2      ROADS.ELEV_FROM = SOURCE.ElevStart;
3      ROADS.ELEV_TO = SOURCE.ElevEnd;
4      ROADS.LANES_BACKWARD = SOURCE.LanesTo;
5      ROADS.LANES_FORWARD = SOURCE.LanesFrom;
6      ROADS.NAME = SOURCE.Name;
7      if ((ROADS.ELEV_FROM > 0) || (ROADS.ELEV_TO > 0)){
8          ROADS.RULE_STYLE = "DefaultStreetStyles:Bridge0";
9      if ((ROADS.ELEV_FROM > 0) || (ROADS.ELEV_TO > 0)){
10          ROADS.RULE_STYLE = "DefaultStreetStyles:Tunnel0";
11      } else {
12          ROADS.RULE_STYLE = "DefaultStreetStyles:Street0";
13      }
14  }
```

Figure 2–35

Converter Tab

The *Converter* tab (shown in Figure 2–36) is only available for terrain data source types. You can convert vector data, such as contours, into raster data by converting it to a grid and setting the grid size. The grid sizes must be between 0.5 and 500 meters. If the grid is too small, the model generation slows down. If the grid is too large there is a loss of detail in the terrain layer.

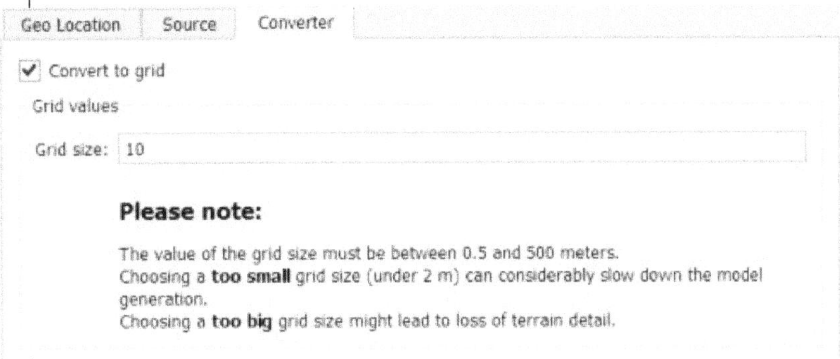

Geo Location   Source   Converter

✔ Convert to grid

Grid values

Grid size: 10

Please note:

The value of the grid size must be between 0.5 and 500 meters.
Choosing a **too small** grid size (under 2 m) can considerably slow down the model generation.
Choosing a **too big** grid size might lead to loss of terrain detail.

Figure 2–36

Expressions

Expressions are required when mapping a database field that does not directly match a property in the model. For example, the source data might list the number of floors or stories in a building, but not the actual roof height. To display the building with an accurate roof height, you need to create an expression in the *Roof Height* field that multiplies the number of floors by an average floor height.

How To: Create an Expression

1. In the Data Source Configuration dialog box, select the tab containing the field that you want to calculate (e.g., *Common*, *Table*, etc.).
2. In the field next to the property that you want to calculate, click ⋈ (Expression Editor), as shown in Figure 2–37.

Note: If ⋈ *(Expression Editor) is not displayed, select the field to make it display.*

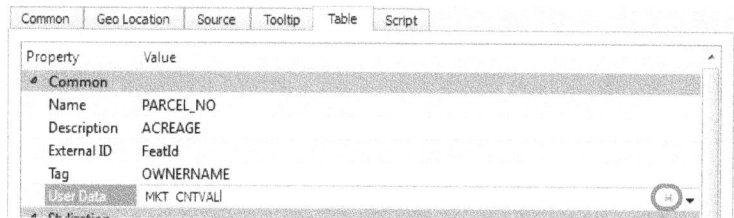

Common	Geo Location	Source	Tooltip	Table	Script

Property	Value
Common	
Name	PARCEL_NO
Description	ACREAGE
External ID	FeatId
Tag	OWNERNAME
User Data	MKT_CNTVALI

Figure 2–37

3. In the Expression Editor, create a simple numeric expression, as shown in Figure 2–38:

   - Select a property in the expanded Property list.
   - Select an operation in the expanded Operator list.
   - Enter the value by which to modify the property.

Figure 2–38

4. Click **OK**.

© 2017, ASCENT - Center for Technical Knowledge®

Model Explorer

Using the Model Explorer, you can hide/display, lock/unlock, and highlight layers that have been added to the model, such as shape files, raster images, and DEM files. You can also filter the data that displays to focus on a specific attribute, or to only display data in a specific area. To display the Model Explorer, in the In Canvas tools, click ![Build icon] (Build, manage, and analyze your industry model)> ![Create icon] (Create and manage your model)> ![Model Explorer icon] (Model Explorer) or in the Utility Bar, click ![Control icon] (Control visibility, display, and selectability of features).

In the Model Explorer, layers are listed on the left with icons on the right identifying their display and select-ability status, as shown in Figure 2–39.

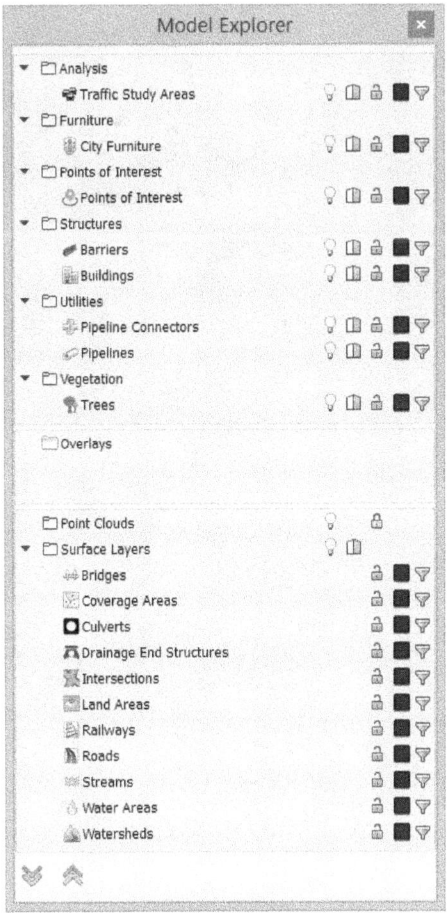

Figure 2–39

The icons in the Model Explorer are described as follows.

Icon	Purpose
(Display/Hide Layers)	Indicates whether the layer displays in the model. Yellow indicates that the layer is displayed in the model, while gray indicates that the layer is hidden.
(Level of Detail)	Specifies the level of detail displayed for various layers according to the zoom distance. Higher levels display more detail while lower levels display less detail.
	By default, *Level of Detail* is set to **Adaptive**, which displays objects that are closer with more detail and objects that are further away with less detail.
(Selectable/ Unselectable)	Makes items in the layer selectable when the lock is in the open position. When the lock is in the closed position, the layer cannot be selected.
(Highlight)	Highlights the layer features in the model.
	Note: The highlight is only used for identification. Highlighting a layer does not mean it has been selected for editing.
(Create Subset)	Filters the layer to only display the number of features that you specify.

© 2017, ASCENT - Center for Technical Knowledge®

Practice 2d

Estimated time for completion: 45 minutes

Configure Source Data for Display

Practice Objectives

- Display connected GIS data in the model.
- Set the model extents for the new model.

In the previous practice, you imported multiple data sources. In the Data Sources palette, the data is separated into three categories: *No Feature Type*, *Ground Imagery*, and *Terrain*. All of the DEM files are under the **Terrain** layer and can be configured at the same time. All of the Aerial Images are under **Ground Imagery** and can also be configured at the same time. However, all of the shape files are listed in the *No Feature Type* category and must be configured individually.

Task 1 - Configure terrain source data.

In this task you will configure the new DEM files for display.

1. Continue working in the same model as the last practice or open **CreateModel.sqlite** from the practice files *…/ModelExplorer* folder. Switch to the **D_Task1** proposal.

2. If the Data Sources explorer is not displayed, in the In Canvas tools, click (Build, manage, and analyze your infrastructure model) > (Create and manage your model)> (Data Sources).

3. In the Data Sources explorer under *Terrain*, double-click on the **DEMs**[1] layer to configure all of the DEMs at the same time.

---

1. ((AGRC), Utah Automated Geographic Reference Center, 2007)

4. Note that *Type* is set to **Terrain** automatically. In the *Geo Location* tab, ensure that the *Coordinate System* is set to **Harn/12.UTM-12**, as shown in Figure 2–40.

The Coordinate System was set automatically because a projection file was included with the DEM file.

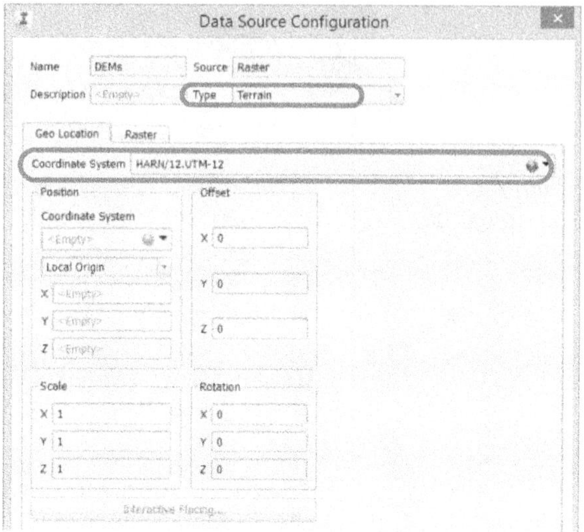

Figure 2–40

5. On the *Raster* tab, select the **Clip to Model Extent** option, as shown in Figure 2–41.

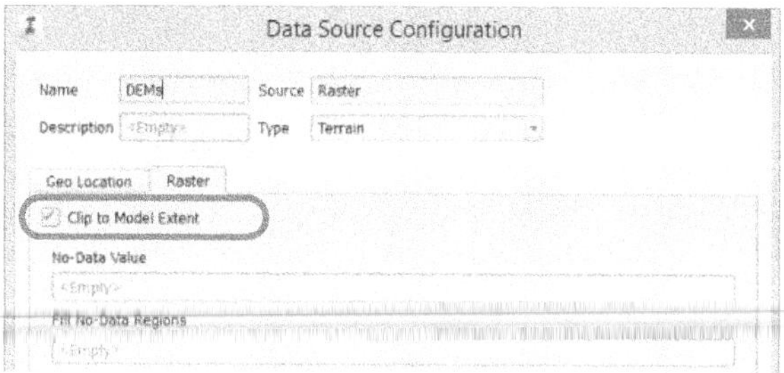

Figure 2–41

You might not notice a difference unless you started from the blank model created in Practice 2a.

6. Click **Close & Refresh** to display the terrain in the model.

Task 2 - Configure image source data.

In this task, you will configure a higher quality image for display in the project area.

1. Continue working in the same model as the last task. Switch to the **D_Task2** proposal.

2. On the Utility Bar, click ▣ (Bookmark your current location) and select **Image Quality**.

© 2017, ASCENT - Center for Technical Knowledge®

3. In the Data Sources explorer under *Ground Imagery*, double-click on the **Images** layer to open the Data Source Configuration dialog box.

4. Ensure that *Type* is set to **Ground Imagery**[1]. In the *Geo Location* tab, ensure that the *Coordinate System* is set to **UTM83-12**, as shown in Figure 2–42.

The coordinate systems often vary for different data sources, depending on who created them and when.

Figure 2–42

*Since nothing changed in the Data Source Configuration dialog box, you could have also selected **Images** and clicked* ⟳ *(Refresh data source).*

5. On the *Raster* tab, ensure that the option is selected to **Clip to Model Extents.**

6. Click **Close & Refresh** to display the images in the model. The quality of the new image is much better than the one inserted by the Model Builder, as shown in Figure 2–43.

Figure 2–43

---

1. ((AGRC), Automated Geographic Reference Center, 2012)

Task 3 - Add tags to data sources.

In this task, you will take advantage of tags as you configure data sources for display.

1. Continue working in the same model as the last task. Switch to the **D_Task3** proposal.

2. On the ViewCube, click 🏠 (Home) to view the entire model.

3. In the Data Sources explorer, double-click on the **MunicipalBoundary**[1] layer to open the Data Source Configuration dialog box.

4. Set the *Type* to **Coverage Areas**. In the *Geo Location* tab, ensure that *Coordinate System* is set to **UT83-CF**.

5. In the *Source* tab, set the *Draping Options* to **Drape** and select the **Clip to model extent** option, as shown in Figure 2–44.

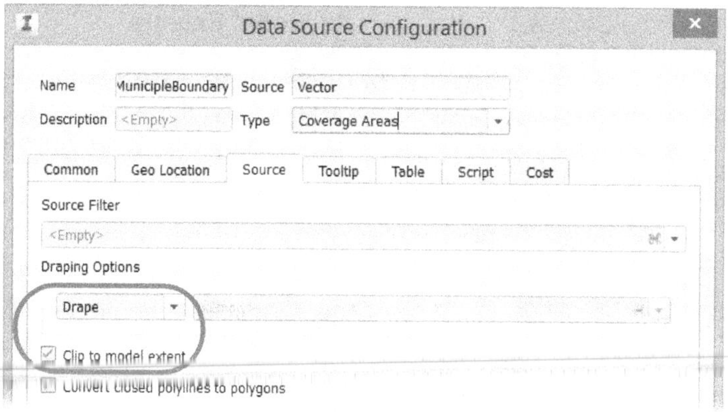

Figure 2–44

6. In the *Common* tab, in the *Rule Style* field, click ✎ (Style Chooser)

7. In the Select Style / Color window, in the *Coverage* tab, select **Boundary** for the style, as shown in Figure 2–45. Click **OK**.

The Boundary style was created for these practices. Therefore, it does not exist outside of the CreateModel.sqlite model.

---

1. (Department, GIS Division of the Utah County Information Systems, 2013)

© 2017, ASCENT - Center for Technical Knowledge®

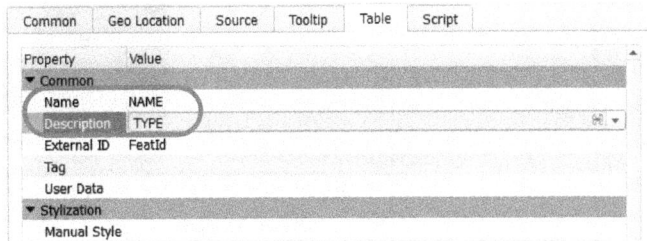

Figure 2–45

8. In the *Table* tab, set the following parameters, as shown in Figure 2–46:
   - *Name:* **NAME**
   - *Description:* **TYPE**

Figure 2–46

9. In the *Tooltip* tab, select the *Html* tab and click in the content area. Click ⎙ (Insert Property).

10. In the Select Property dialog box, expand the drop-down box and select **Name**, as shown in Figure 2–47. Click **OK**.

If green text does not display in the Tooltip script area (as shown below), the Tooltips will not work.

Figure 2–47

11. Click **Close & Refresh** to display the city boundaries in the model.

12. In the model, hover the cursor over the various land areas that surround the lake. As you move the cursor over each city in the model, note that the area is highlighted and the city name displays as a tooltip, as shown in Figure 2–48.

Note: This feature might not display depending on the version of software that you are using.

Figure 2–48

13. In the Data Sources explorer, double-click on the **TaxParcel**[1] layer to open the Data Source Configuration dialog box. Set the following parameters, as shown in Figure 2–49:

- *Type:* **Coverage Areas**
- *Geo Location* tab, *Coordinate System:* **UT83-CF**
- *Source* tab, *Draping Options:* **Drape**
- *Source* tab: **Clip to model extent**
- *Table* tab, *Name:* **PARCEL_NO**
- *Table* tab, *Description:* **ACREAGE**
- *Table* tab, *Tag:* **OWNERNAME**
- *Table* tab, *User Data:* **MKT_CNTVAL**

Figure 2–49

1. (Department, GIS Division of the Utah County Information Systems, 2013)

© 2017, ASCENT - Center for Technical Knowledge®

14. In the *Tooltip* tab, select the *Html* tab. Click 🖉 (Insert Property).

15. In the Select Property dialog box, expand the drop-down box and select **TAG**, as shown in Figure 2–50. Click **OK**.

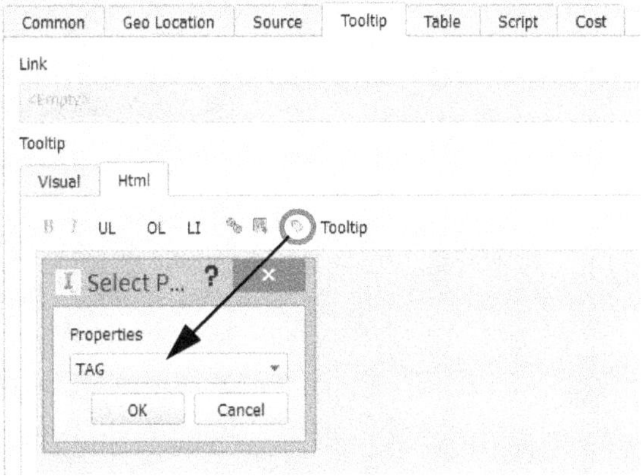

Figure 2–50

16. Click **Close & Refresh** to display the parcel boundaries in the model. Note: Because a style was not set, it will display as though nothing has changed in the model. However, when you move the cursor over the terrain, the parcels of land highlight as shown in Figure 2–51.

Figure 2–51

Task 4 - Display data sources using expressions.

In this task, you will take advantage of expressions as you configure data sources for display.

1. Continue working in the same model as the last task. Switch to the **D_Task4** proposal.

2. On the ViewCube, click (Home) to view the entire model.

3. In the Data Sources explorer, double-click on the **RoadCenterline**[1] layer to open the Data Source Configuration dialog box. Set the following parameters:
   - *Type:* **Roads**
   - *Geo Location* tab, *Coordinate System*: **UT83-CF**
   - *Source* tab, *Draping Options*: **Drape**
   - *Source* tab: **Clip to model extent**

4. In the *Common* tab, in the *Elevation Offset* field, click (Expression Editor).

5. In the Expression Editor, expand Properties>*Numeric* and double-click **ROADLEVEL**, as shown in Figure 2–52.

Figure 2–52

1. (Department, GIS Division of the Utah County Information Systems, 2013)

© 2017, ASCENT - Center for Technical Knowledge®

6. In the *Expression* area, after **ROADLEVEL**, type ***12,** as shown in Figure 2–53.

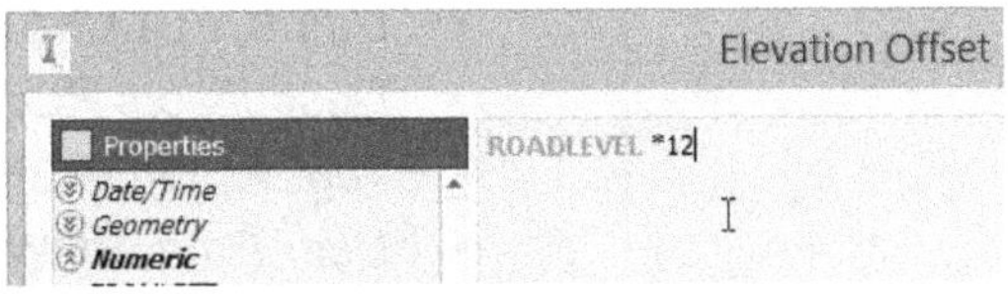

The ROADLEVEL field has three values: -1, 0, and 1. Multiplying it by 12 sets the elevation to 12 feet above or below ground level (used for overpasses or underpasses), or drapes on the terrain for zero values.

Figure 2–53

7. Click **OK**.

8. In the *Common* tab, in the *Rule Style* field, click (Style Chooser).

9. In the Select Style window, in the *Road* tab, for the style select **Sidewalk and Greenspace**, as shown in Figure 2–54. Click **OK**.

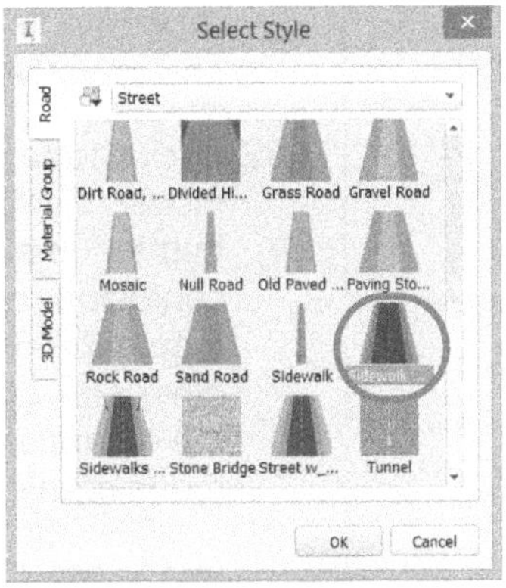

Figure 2–54

In the next step, you will map the data fields in the connected data base file to the fields created by the Autodesk InfraWorks data scheme. This step is important if you plan to use the database information to label or analyze the model. In this case, you will map the *Roadclass* database field to the *Description* field so that you can use that information to set Style Rules later.

10. On the *Table* tab, set the following parameters, as shown in Figure 2–55:

   - *Name:* **FULLNAME**
   - *Description:* **ROADCLASS**
   - *Tag:* **ALTROADNAM**
   - *User Data:* **ROW_WIDTH**

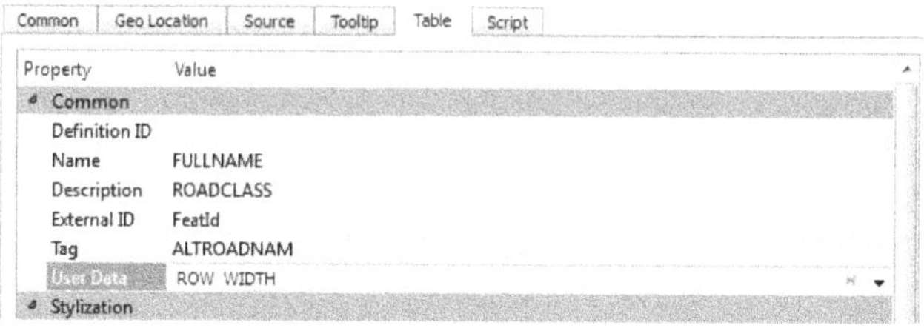

Figure 2–55

11. In the *Tooltip* tab, select the *Html* tab, and click (Insert Property). In the Select Property dialog box, select **NAME** and click **OK**.

12. Click **Close & Refresh** to display the road centerlines in the model. If you started the model using Model Builder, it is likely that roads already existed in the model which causes confusion regarding which roads to display, as shown in Figure 2–56. In cases like this, it is best to remove one or the other sets of roads. Since we plan to use the information in the database to set road styles later, we need to remove the roads created in Model Builder.

Figure 2–56

These are the roads added by Model Builder.

13. In the Data Sources explorer under *Roads*, select **roads** and click (remove data source).

© 2017, ASCENT - Center for Technical Knowledge®

14. In the Data Sources explorer, double-click on the **BuildingFootprint**[1] layer to open the Data Source Configuration dialog box. Set the following parameters:

   - *Type:* **Buildings**
   - *Geo Location* tab, *Coordinate System*: **UT83-CF**
   - *Common* tab, *Roof Height*: **20**
   - *Source* tab, *Draping Options*: **Drape**
   - *Source* tab: **Clip to model extent**

15. Click **Close & Refresh** to display the buildings in the model, as shown in Figure 2–57. Use the mouse and/or ViewCube to view the model from different angles.

Figure 2–57

Task 5 - Set the model extents.

The model that you have configured includes several cities. The project you will create is a multi-use development on the west side of the lake. The development will connect to the east side of the lake using a bridge. To focus on the area of interest and trim the data to this area, you will set the model extents.

1. (Department, GIS Division of the Utah County Information Systems, 2013)

1. In the model, move the cursor around and note how the coordinates change in the bottom left corner of the model area, as shown in Figure 2–58. The minimum and maximum X,Y values required for the model determine the values you will set for the model extents.

Model coordinates (X, Y, and Z) at the cursor location

X: 1529473.217353 Y: 7267597.802425 Z: 5270.229904 ft

Figure 2–58

2. In the In Canvas tools, click ✖ (Settings)> 🔲 (Model Properties).

3. In the Model Properties dialog box, clear the **Use Entire Model** option. Set the following parameters, as shown in Figure 2–59:

Field	X	Y
Minimum	1532500	7267000
Maximum	1543000	7274500

Alternatively, you could have chosen to define the extents using a bounding box or polyline.

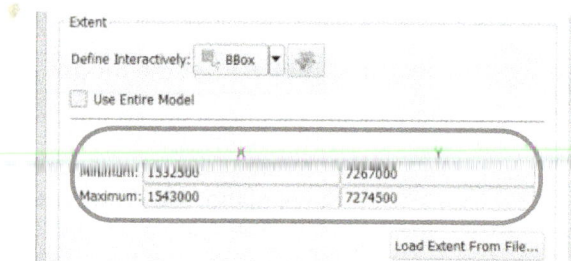

Figure 2–59

4. Click **Apply** and **OK**. The model will adjust to its new extents, as shown in Figure 2–60.

© 2017, ASCENT - Center for Technical Knowledge®

Note that the model does not need to be saved as it has been automatically saved while you were working.

Figure 2–60

Task 6 - Hide model elements.

In this task you will hide and lock a specific layer to help focus on the project area.

1. In the Utility Bar, click ⬛ (Bookmark your current location). Select **Project Area** to return to the previously-saved view where the project will be focused. Note: When you hover the cursor over an area, a parcel is highlighted instead of the city outline.

2. In the Utility Bar, click ⬛ (Control visibility, display, and selectability of features). Note: The Surface Layers are combined to make it easier to control all of them at the same time. This includes the DEM files, images, and other GIS data that was imported into the model.

3. In the Model Explorer panel, right-click on **Surface Layers** and select **Surface Layers** (as shown in Figure 2–61) to manage the surface layers separately.

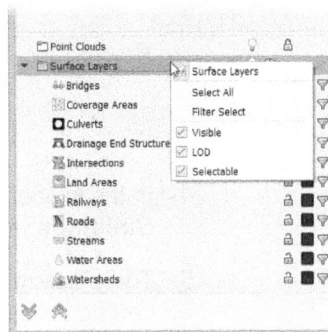

Figure 2–61

4. In the Manage Surface Layers dialog box, click 💡 to the right of the **TaxParcels** layer to toggle it off, as shown in Figure 2–62.

Figure 2–62

5. Click **Apply** then **OK**.

6. Move the cursor over the model and note that the city is highlighted rather than the parcel.

Task 7 - Lock the existing GIS layers.

1. In the Utility Bar, click 🔳 (Bookmark your current location) and select **Buildings**.

2. In the Utility Bar, click 🔳 (Edit).

3. In the model, select one of the buildings. Note that the bottom of the building has gizmos that enable you to edit it, as shown in Figure 2–63. Press <Esc> to clear the selection of the building.

Figure 2–63

4. In the Model Explorer panel, click 🔒 to the right of the **Buildings** layer.

5. Try to select a building in the model. Note that the buildings can no longer be selected.

6. Close the model.

© 2017, ASCENT - Center for Technical Knowledge®

Chapter Review Questions

1. Why is the source data not displayed once it has been imported into the model?

   a. By default, it is toggled off in the Model Explorer.

   b. It needs to be configured before it can be displayed.

   c. The graphics card is not powerful enough to display the data.

   d. It might be hidden under another data source.

2. How can you determine whether the GIS data is usable for your project's needs? (Select all that apply)

   a. Communicate with the owner of the GIS data source.

   b. Download and read the metadata included with the GIS data source.

   c. Connect to the data in the AutoCAD Map 3D or AutoCAD Civil 3D software to preview the data and its data table before importing it into the Autodesk InfraWorks model.

   d. There is no way of determining its usability.

3. Which of the following types is not available as an option when configuring data sources?

   a. Barriers

   b. Bridges

   c. Buildings

   d. Railways

4. Which configuration tab would you use to drape data on a terrain surface?

   a. *Common*

   b. *Geo Location*

   c. *Source*

   d. *Script*

5. Which configuration tab would you use to display feature attributes in the model as you hover the cursor over them?

   a. *Common*

   b. *Source*

   c. *Table*

   d. *Tooltip*

6. Why is it important to set both the model coordinate system and the data source coordinate system?

   a. So that the software can automatically re-project the data sources for you and make everything line up with the correct insertion point, scale factor, and rotation value.

   b. So that the correct units (feet or meters) display in the model.

   c. So that the visual styles for the data sources all coordinate with the project.

   d. You only have to set one or the other, not both.

© 2017, ASCENT - Center for Technical Knowledge®

Command Summary

Button	Command	Location
⚙	Application Options	• **Home Screen** • **In Canvas Tools:** Settings and Utilities
🗄	Data Sources	• **In Canvas Tools:** Build, manage, and analyze your infrastructure model> Create and manage your model
N/A	Deselect	• **Shortcut Key:** <Esc>
◣	Edit	• **Utility Bar**
🔒	Layer Lock/ Unlock	• **Palette:** Model Explorer
💡	Layer On/Off	• **Palette:** Model Explorer
🔲	Model Explorer	• **Utility Bar** • **In Canvas Tools:** Build, manage, and analyze your infrastructure model> Create and manage your model
🗄	Model Properties	• **In Canvas Tools:** Settings and Utilities
N/A	New Model	• **Home Screen**
N/A	Select All	• **Shortcut Key:** <Ctrl>+<A>
▱ / ▱	Surface Layers	• **Palette:** Data Sources and Model Explorer (Right-click Surface Layers) • **In Canvas Tools:** Build, manage, and analyze your infrastructure model> Create and manage your model

© 2017, ASCENT - Center for Technical Knowledge®

Stylize Data Sources

Model features are thought of as a single category. However, it might occasionally be necessary to display features in the same data source differently. For example, an interstate typically has more lanes than a local road. Additionally, a local road often has a sidewalk and lamp posts running along side, while an interstate does not have these design elements. In this chapter, you learn how to use scripts, expressions, and style rules to display data sources according to information connected to the model (i.e., in database fields). You also learn how to override style rules to manually change the display of specific features. If the required style is not available, it might be necessary to create a custom style to suit the project's needs. You learn how to create and share styles from one project to another.

Learning Objectives in this Chapter

- Display a data source according to specific data in the database that is connected to the feature.
- Change the style of selected features to override any style rules being used.
- Create/edit styles in catalogs.
- Share style catalogs with other users.

3.1 Using Multiple Styles to Display Features

You have learned how to select one style for an entire data source during the data configuration process. In the *Common* tab of the Data Configuration dialog box (shown in Figure 3–1), you used 🖊 (Style Chooser) in the *Rule Style* field to select one style for the entire data source.

Figure 3–1

Alternatively, you can set the style for a data source subset by clicking ⬚ (Expression Editor) in the *Rule Style* field (shown in Figure 3–2).

Figure 3–2

Create Filter Expressions

To automatically stylize a feature based on the connected database data, you must create an expression. The Create Filter Expression dialog box enables you to create two types of filter expressions:

- Location Filters

- Property Filters

© 2017, ASCENT - Center for Technical Knowledge®

Location Filters

In the Create Filter Expression dialog box, click **Spatial**. The five types of location boundaries available are described as follows:

Disjoint	Selects all features that do not overlap the shape you draw.
Inside	Selects all features that do not overlap the shape you draw.
Intersects	Selects all features that intersect with the shape you draw.
Overlaps	Selects all features that overlap any part of the shape you draw.
Within	Selects all features within the shape you draw but are not touching the edges of the shape.

Property Filters

In the Create Filter Expression dialog box, click **Properties**, and select a property from the list. The available properties vary according to the database fields that are connected to the data source. After selecting a property, you need to set the values in the data field that you want to use to define the style. An operator is required to help filter the list of values. Some of the available comparison operators are shown in Figure 3–3.

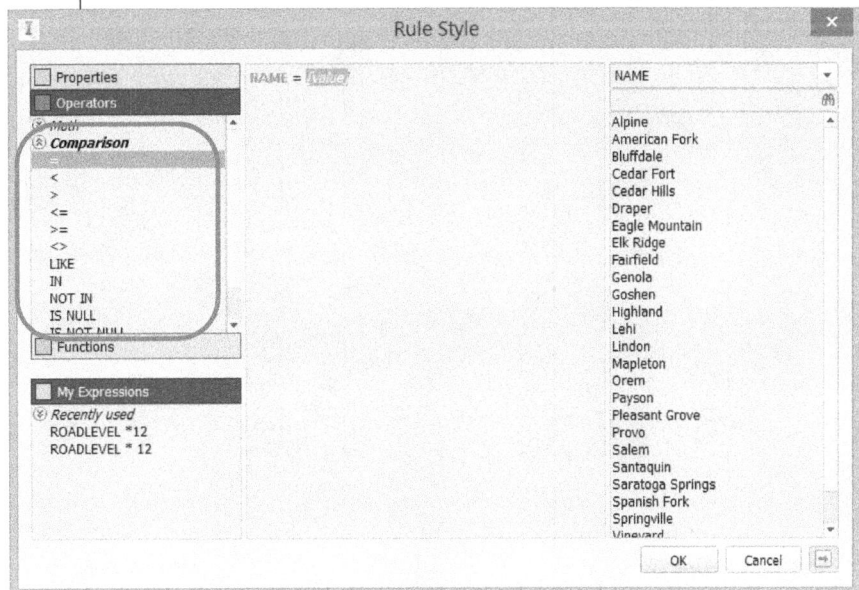

Figure 3–3

Find Available Values

It is important to determine which values are available in each property to determine which operator to use. You can determine the available values in a property by clicking ⬚ (Show/Hide the Values pane) in the Create Filter Expression dialog box. If you have selected a numeric property, you can use operators, such as **greater than**, **less than**, or **equal to**, to refine the selection. If a text property is selected, you must use a text operator, such as **Like**, **Not Like**, or **Null**. These and other operators are accessed by clicking **Operators** in the Create Filter Expression dialog box.

How To: Find Available Values

1. In the Create Filter Expression dialog box, click
   ⬚ (Show/Hide Values Pane) to display the Values pane.
2. In the Values pane, select a property to retrieve from the drop-down list, as shown in Figure 3–4. The list of available values displays.

If required, you can filter the list of values by entering keywords into the Filter the list of values text box.

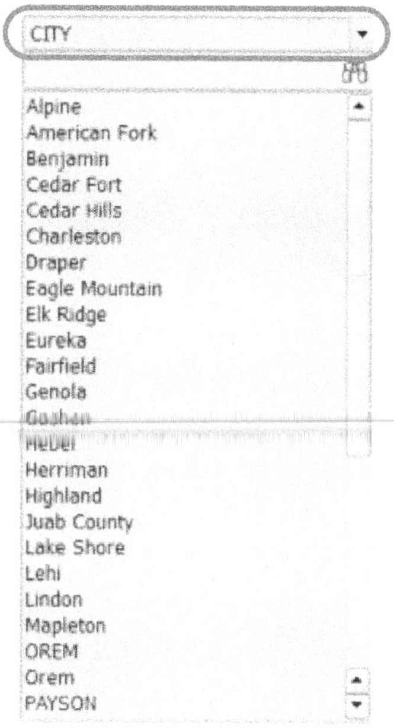

Figure 3–4

3. Select a value from the list and double-click on it to populate the value in the expression editor, as shown in Figure 3–5.

© 2017, ASCENT - Center for Technical Knowledge®

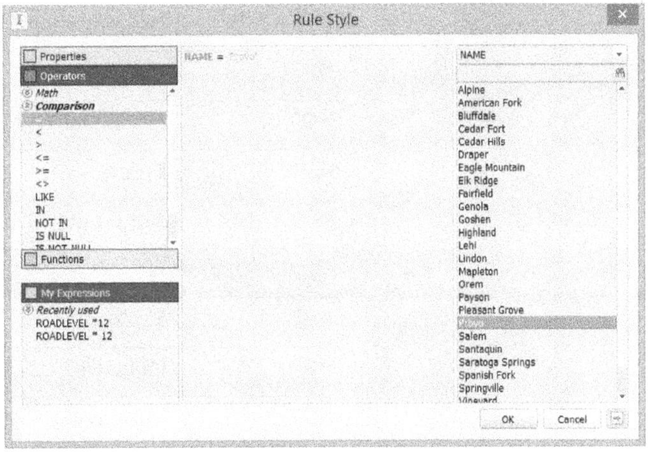

Figure 3–5

Operators

There are four groups of operators: **Math**, **Comparison**, **Logical**, and **Other**. The available operators are described as follows:

Math Operators

+	Add	Sums numerical properties.
-	Subtract	Subtracts numerical properties.
*	Multiply	Multiplies numerical properties.
/	Divide	Divides numerical properties.

Comparison Operators

=	Equal To	Text or numerical properties hold an exact value.
<	Less Than	Numerical properties are less than an exact value.
>	Greater Than	Numerical properties are greater than an exact value.
<=	Less Than or Equal To	Numerical properties are less than or equal to an exact value.
>=	Greater Than or Equal To	Numerical properties are greater than or equal to an exact value.
<>	Not Equal To	Does not equal a specific value.
LIKE	Matching	Text matches a pattern.

NOT LIKE	Not Matching	Text does not match a pattern.
IN	Equal To Any	Matches any value in a list.
NOT IN	Not Equal To Any	Does not match any value in a list.
IS NULL	Empty	Returns if property is empty.
IS NOT NULL	Not Empty	Returns if property has any value.

Logical Operators

AND	Exclusive	Must meet all conditions.
OR	Inclusive	Matches any one of the conditions.
NOT	Selective	Negates the expression.

Other

()	Group	Group the Selection in Parentheses.

How To: Create a Filter Expression

1. In the Create Filter Expression dialog box, expand Properties and select the property containing the appropriate values, as shown in Figure 3–6.

Figure 3–6

2. Select an appropriate operator, as shown in Figure 3–6.

3. In the Create Filter Expression dialog box, click

   (Show/Hide Values Pane) to display the Values pane.

© 2017, ASCENT - Center for Technical Knowledge®

4. In the Values pane, in the drop-down list, select the required property, as shown in Figure 3–7.

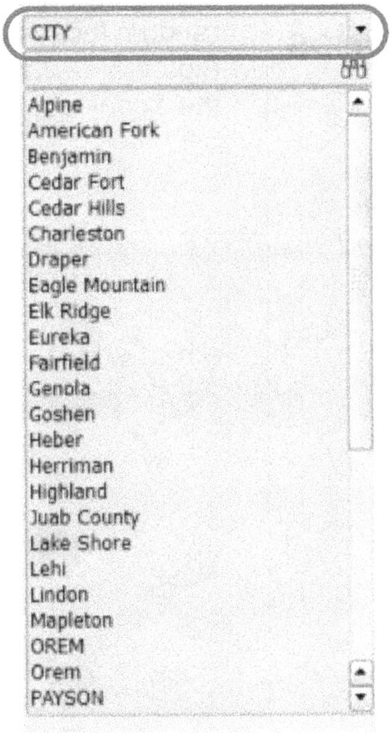

Figure 3–7

5. Select the value from the list and double-click on it to populate the value in the expression editor, as shown in Figure 3–8.

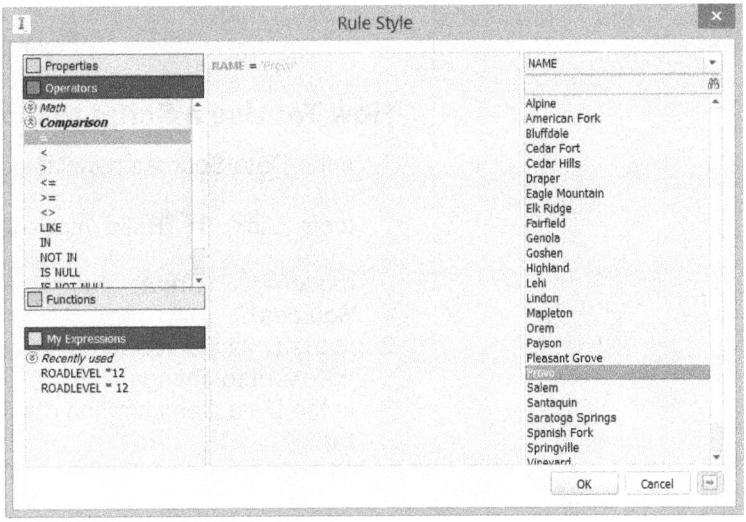

Figure 3–8

Using Scripts to Set Multiple Feature Styles

Custom scripts for an Autodesk InfraWorks model can be created by anyone with a knowledge of JavaScript.

Scripts can be used to assign multiple styles simultaneously for one data source. For example, this can happen when you import a building's data source into the model. The buildings use random facade and roof colors from a default script, as shown in Figure 3–9. JavaScript® is used to create scripts that are used in the *Script* tab, in the Data Configuration dialog box.

Figure 3–9

How To: Use a Script to Modify Feature Styles

1. If the Data Sources panel is not displayed, in the In Canvas tools, click (Build, manage, and analyze your industry model)> (Create and manage your model)> (Data Sources).
2. In the Data Sources explorer, double-click on the layer that you want to change.
3. In the Data Configuration dialog box, in the *Script* tab, click **Edit**.

© 2017, ASCENT - Center for Technical Knowledge®

4. Using JavaScript, make the required changes. Figure 3–10 shows a script that varies the road styles based on the property value for *Elevation*.

```
1  function Process() {
2      ROADS.ELEV_FROM = SOURCE.ElevStart;
3      ROADS.ELEV_TO = SOURCE.ElevEnd;
4      ROADS.LANES_BACKWARD = SOURCE.LanesTo;
5      ROADS.LANES_FORWARD = SOURCE.LanesFrom;
6      ROADS.NAME = SOURCE.Name;
7      if ((ROADS.ELEV_FROM > 0) || (ROADS.ELEV_TO > 0)){
8          ROADS.RULE_STYLE = "DefaultStreetStyles:Bridge0";
9      if ((ROADS.ELEV_FROM > 0) || (ROADS.ELEV_TO > 0)){
10         ROADS.RULE_STYLE = "DefaultStreetStyles:Tunnel0";
11     } else {
12         ROADS.RULE_STYLE = "DefaultStreetStyles:Street0";
13     }
14 }
```

Figure 3–10

5. Click **Close & Refresh** to display the changes in the model.

Create Style Rules

You can also use style rules to modify how features display in the model according to data connected to each feature. Style rules override anything that was set during the data configuration process. Each feature class is stylized separately and has a tab in the Style Rules dialog box. In the example shown in Figure 3–11, the *Roads* class tab is active and six rules are listed.

Figure 3–11

Each class of features is stylized separately using expressions. Expressions can use values from source data fields or a location to stylize features. Once an expression has been created, a style is assigned to the rule.

How To: Create a New Style Rule

1. In the In Canvas tools, click ![icon] (Build, manage, and analyze your industry model)> ![icon] (Create and manage your model)> ![icon] (Style Rules). Select the required tab.

2. At the top of the Style Rules dialog box, click ![icon] (Add a new Rule).

3. In the Add Rule Style dialog box, type a name, as shown in Figure 3–12. Click **OK**.

Figure 3–12

4. In the Style Rules dialog box, select the new rule and click ![icon] (Edit properties).

5. In the Rule Editor, in the *Expression* area, click ![icon] (Edit), as shown in Figure 3–13.

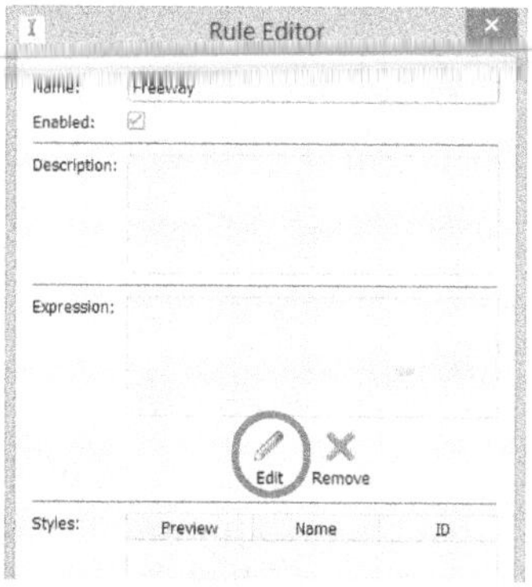

Figure 3–13

6. In the Create Filter Expression dialog box, define the required expression and click **OK**.

© 2017, ASCENT - Center for Technical Knowledge®

7. In the Rule Editor dialog box, in the *Styles* area, click ✛ (Add an existing style), as shown in Figure 3–14.

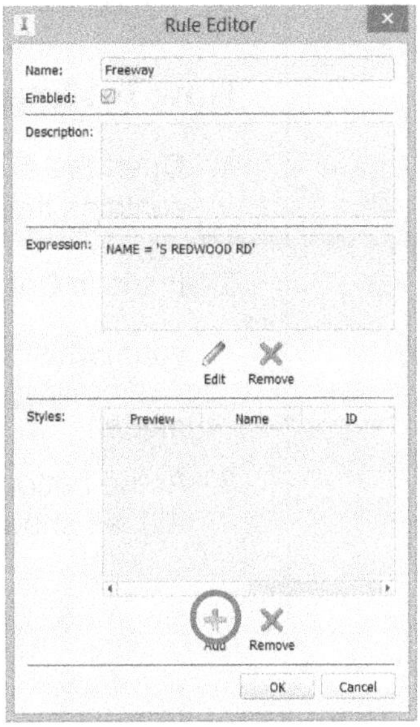

Figure 3–14

8. In the Select Style dialog box, in the *Road* tab, select a style, as shown in Figure 3–15. Click **OK**.

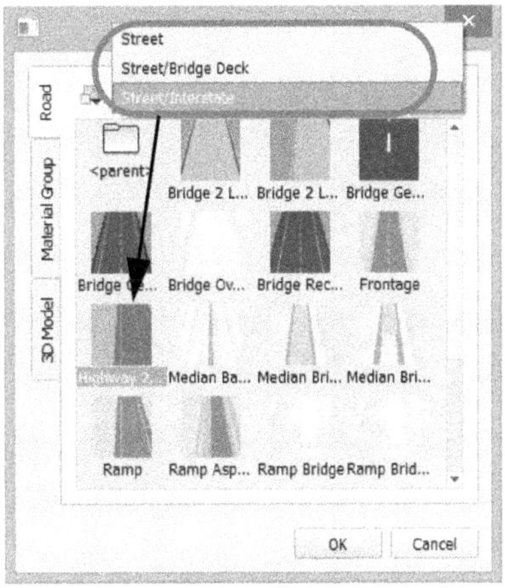

Figure 3–15

9. In the Rule Editor, click **OK** to return to the Style Rules dialog box.

10. In the Style Rules dialog box, click ⏵ (Run Rules) to display the results of the style change.

Reuse/Share Style Rules

If the same rules are used repeatedly to stylize different models, it is possible to save the rules in an .XML file. The .XML file can be reused in other proposals in the same model, or imported into other models.

How To: Export Style Rules

1. Open the Autodesk® InfraWorks® model and proposal that contains the style rules that you want to reuse.

2. In the In Canvas tools, click ▮ (Build, manage, and analyze your industry model)> 🛠 (Create and manage your model)> 📋 (Style Rules) and review the rules.

3. At the bottom of the Style Rules dialog box, click ⇨ (Export All), as shown in Figure 3–16.

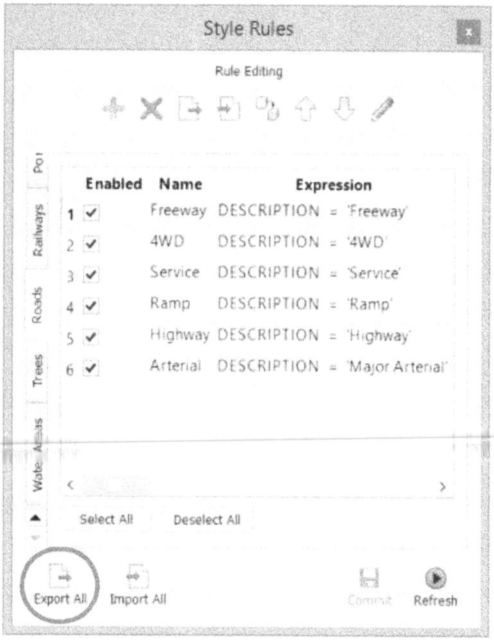

Figure 3–16

4. Select the path and enter a filename for the Style Rules (*.rules.json) file. Click **Save**.
5. Close the Style Rules dialog box.

© 2017, ASCENT - Center for Technical Knowledge®

How To: Import Style Rules

Rules in the saved file that have the same name as an existing rule in the model cannot be imported. Therefore, it is important to delete or change the names of any existing rules if you want to use the imported rules.

1. Open the Autodesk InfraWorks model to which the style rules are to be imported.

2. In the In Canvas tools, click ⬛ (Build, manage, and analyze your industry model)> ◈ (Create and manage your model)> 🗺 (Style Rules). Review any existing rules.

3. At the bottom of the Style Rules dialog box, click ⬗ (Import All), as shown in Figure 3–17.

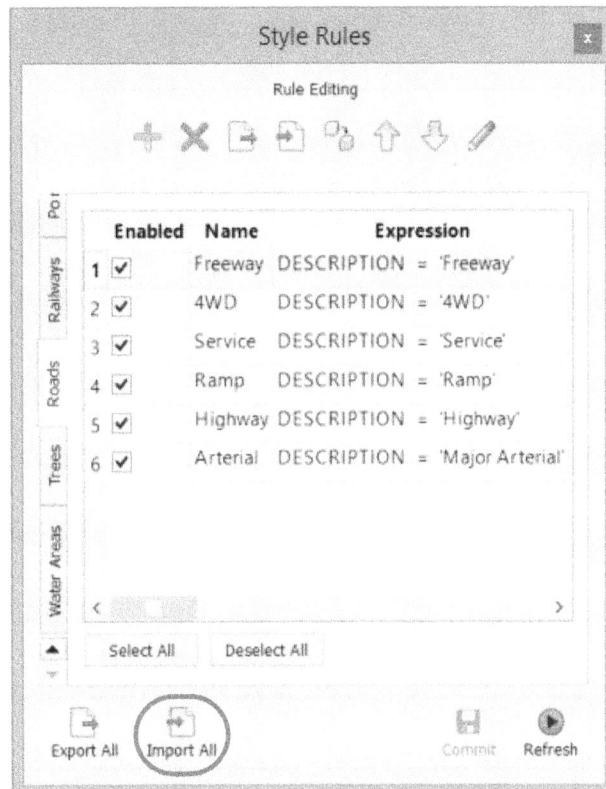

Figure 3–17

4. Select the path and filename for the Style Rules (*.rules.json) file that contains the required style rules. Click **Open**.

5. Close the Style Rules dialog box.

3.2 Overriding Style Rules

There always seems to be at least one exception to every rule. For example, it is common to stylize roads according to their road classification. However, if the road has a bridge on one of its sections, it might be necessary to override the road classification style given to that section with a bridge style, as shown in Figure 3–18.

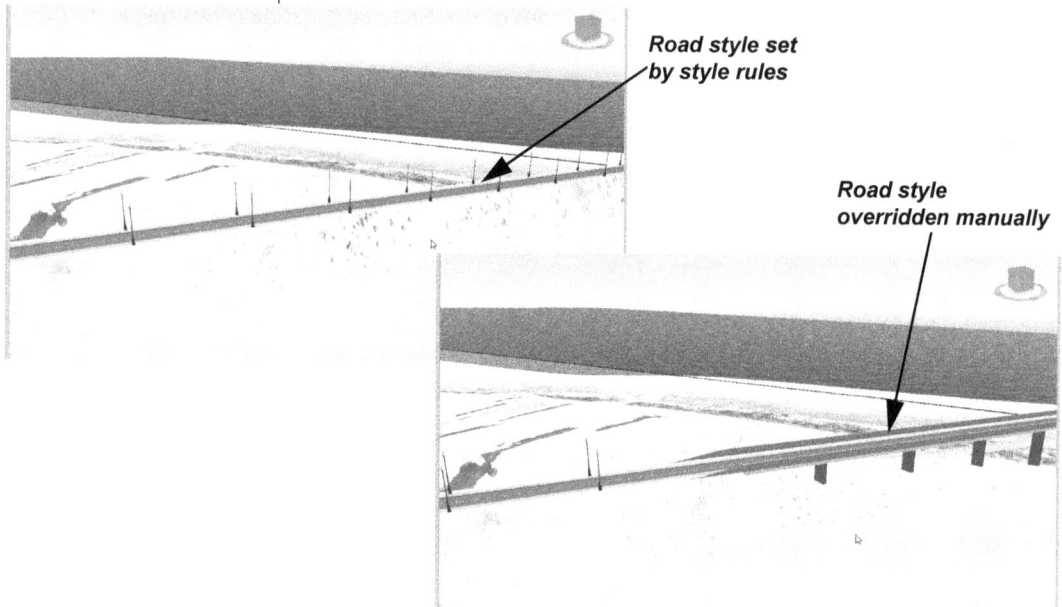

Figure 3–18

How To: Change a Style Using the Style Palette

1. In the In Canvas tools, click ▮ (Build, manage, and analyze your industry model)> ▥ (Create and manage your model)> ▦ (Style Palette) and select the appropriate tab for the feature you are changing.
2. Select the style from the preview area and drag and drop it onto the feature to apply the style, as shown in Figure 3–19.

© 2017, ASCENT - Center for Technical Knowledge®

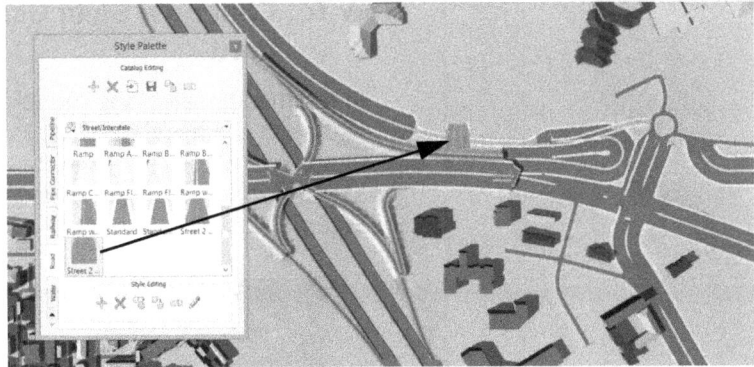

Figure 3–19

3. Close the Style Palette.

How To: Change a Style Using Feature Properties

1. In the model, select the model feature, right-click on the feature, and select **Properties**.
2. In the Properties palette, change the style in the *Manual Style* field, as shown in Figure 3–20.

You can remove a style override by deleting the Manual Style from the Properties palette and updating the model.

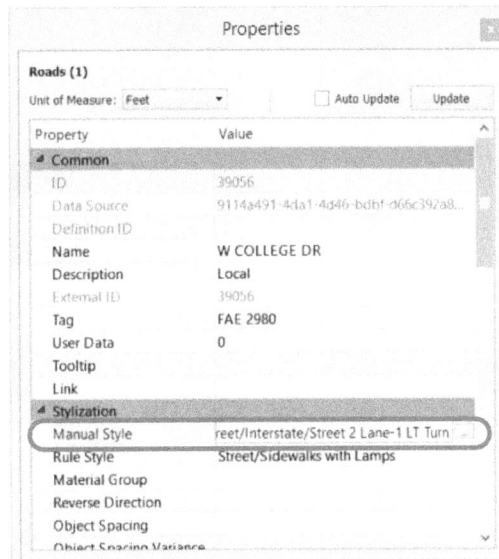

Figure 3–20

3. Click **Update** to display the change in the model.

How To: Change a Style Using a Feature's Asset Card

1. In the model, select the model feature.
2. In the feature asset card, click on the Manual Style thumbnail and select a frequently used style or click **More Styles** to select a style from the Select Style Dialog box, as shown in Figure 3–21.

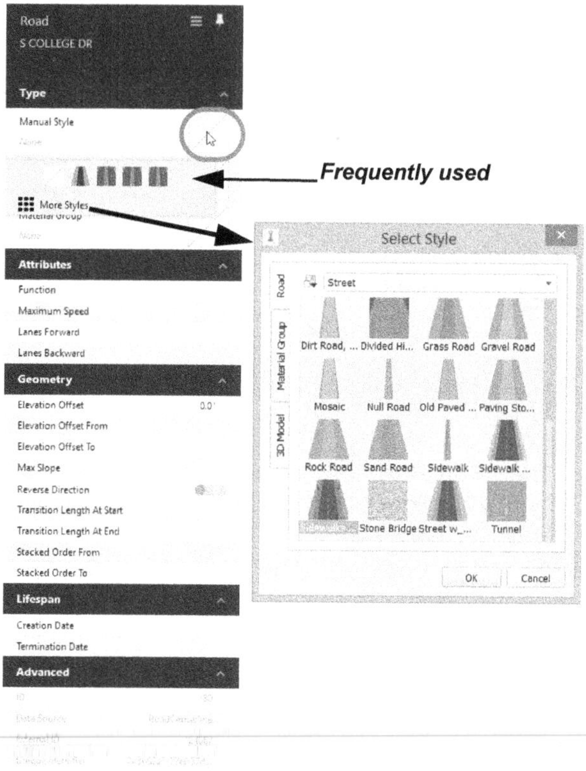

Figure 3–21

3. Click **OK**.

© 2017, ASCENT - Center for Technical Knowledge®

Practice 3a

Stylize Data Sources

Practice Objective

- Change the visual style assigned to a model feature using scripts, style rules, and style overrides.

Estimated time for completion: 20 minutes

Task 1 - Use scripts to change the display of model features.

A default script is currently being used in the model to randomly set the color of the buildings. Additionally, all of the buildings in the model are currently the same height. A JavaScript expert has created a script for you that will randomize the building styles and heights throughout the model. In this task, you will use this script to automatically modify the building styles.

1. In the Home Screen click **Open**.

2. In the *C:\InfraWorks Fundamentals Practice Files\Styles* folder, select **Styles.sqlite** and click **Open**.

3. In the Utility Bar, click ▣ (Bookmark your current location) and select **Buildings**. Ensure that **A_Task1** is the current proposal.

4. If the Data Sources panel is not already displayed, in the In Canvas tools, click ▣ (Build, manage, and analyze your industry model)> ▣ (Create and manage your model)> ▣ (Data Sources).

5. In the Data Sources explorer, double-click on the **BuildingFootprint** layer.

6. In the **Start** menu on your computer, launch Notepad.

7. In the Notepad window, expand the **File** menu and select **Open**.

8. In the *C:\InfraWorks Fundamentals Practice Files\Styles* folder, select **BuildingScript.txt** and click **Open**.

9. Press <Ctrl>+<A> to select all of the contents of the file. Press <Ctrl>+<C> to copy the file contents.

10. Return to the Autodesk InfraWorks software.

11. In the Data Configuration dialog box, in the *Script* tab, click **Edit**.

12. Place the cursor anywhere inside the script area and press <Ctrl>+<A> to select all of the content of the script.

13. Press <Delete> to remove the content of the script.

14. Press <Ctrl>+<V> to paste the contents from the text file into the script area.

*If the buildings do not change styles randomly according to the script, you might need to remove the **BuildingsFootprint** layer from the Data Sources explorer and re-import the buildings.*

15. Click **Close & Refresh** to display the changes in the model. Note that each building now has a different facade (including color and windows), a different height, and a different roof style.

16. Close the Data Sources panel.

Task 2 - Use style rules to change the display of the model features.

The roads in this model are currently only using one style. However, there are a number of different types of roads and many of them follow a similar pattern according to their road class. The **RoadCenterline.shp** file[1] lists each road's classification in a database field called *ROADCLASS*. When the layer was imported and configured, the *ROADCLASS* field was mapped to the *Road Description* property in the *Table* tab, in the Data Source Configuration dialog box. In this task you will use this property to set the styles for the road centerlines.

*If you did not complete the previous task, set the **A_Task2** proposal to current in the Utility Bar.*

1. In the Utility Bar, click ▢ (Bookmark your current location) and select **Road Styles**.

2. In the In Canvas tools, click ▢ (Build, manage, and analyze your industry model)> ▢ (Create and manage your model) > ▢ (Style Rules) and select the *Roads* tab.

You might have to scroll down in the Rule Editing tabs to locate the Road tab. There are several road rules already created.

3. At the top of the Style Rules dialog box, click ✛ (Add a new Rule).

1.(Department, GIS Division of the Utah County Information Systems, 2013)

© 2017, ASCENT - Center for Technical Knowledge®

4. In the Add Rule Style dialog box, type **Freeway**, as shown in Figure 3–22. Click **OK**.

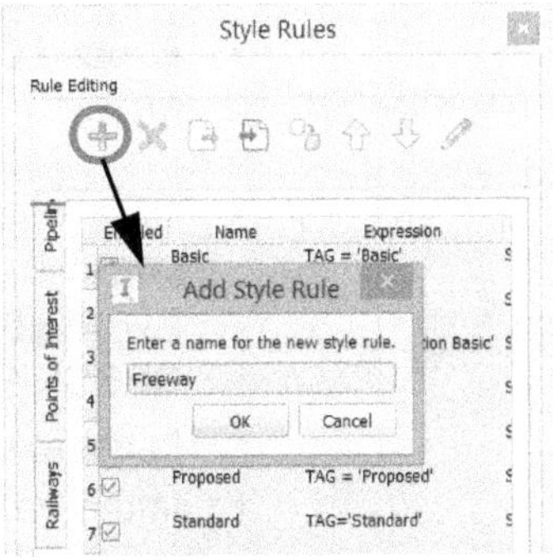

Figure 3–22

5. In the Style Rules dialog box, double-click on **Freeway** to edit the rule.

6. In the Rule Editor, in the expression area, click ✎ (Edit) as shown in Figure 3–23.

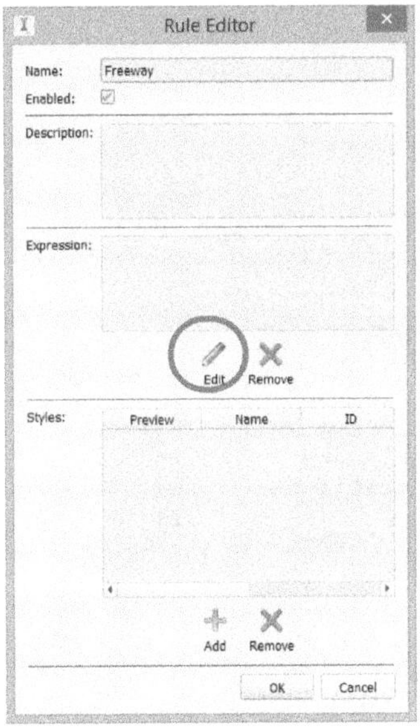

Figure 3–23

7. In the Create Filter Expression dialog box:
    - Expand **Properties**, and under **Common**, double-click on **DESCRIPTION**.
    - Expand **Operators**, and under **Comparison**, double-click on **=**.
    - Click ⬚ (Show/Hide Values Pane) to display a list of possible properties.
    - Expand the Properties drop-down list, and select **DESCRIPTION**.
    - In the expression area, select **[value]**.
    - In the Values pane, double-click on **Freeway**.
    - Click **OK**, as shown in Figure 3–24.

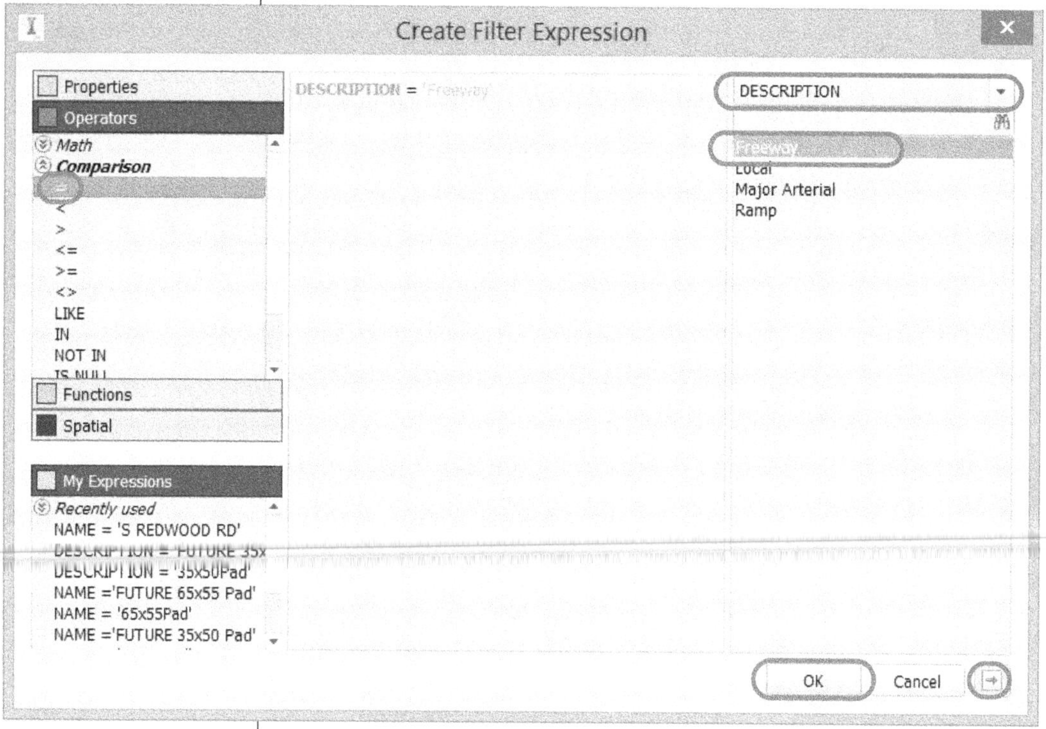

Figure 3–24

8. In the Rule Editor dialog box, in the *Styles* area, click ✚ (Add an existing style), as shown in Figure 3–25.

© 2017, ASCENT - Center for Technical Knowledge®

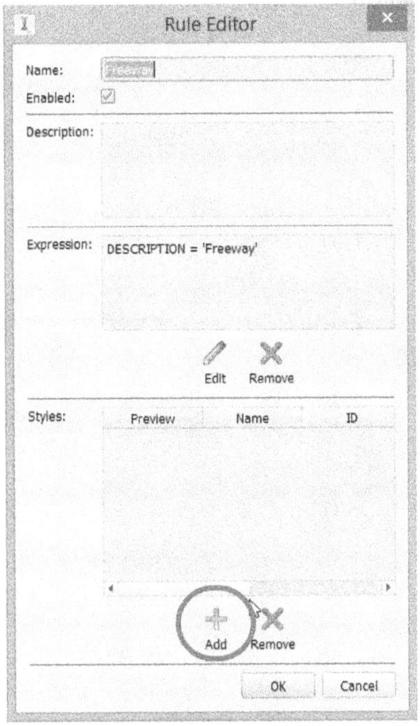

Figure 3–25

9. At the top of the Select Style dialog box, in the *Road* tab, expand the drop-down list and select **Street/Interstate**. In the *Preview* area, select **Highway 2 Lane Forward** and click **OK**, as shown in Figure 3–26.

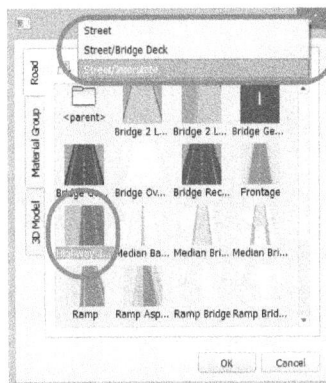

Figure 3–26

10. In the Rule Editor, click **OK** to return to the Style Rules dialog box.

11. In the Style Rules dialog box, click ▶ (Run Rules) to display the results of the style change.

12. Repeat Steps 4 to 10 to add the following rules and styles.

Name	Expression	Style
Ramp	DESCRIPTION =Ramp	Street/Interstate/Ramp Asphalt
Major Arterial	DESCRIPTION =Major Arterial	Street/Interstate/Street 2 Lane-1 LT Turn
Local	DESCRIPTION =Local	Street/Old Paved Road, Grass Shoulder

13. In the Style Rules dialog box, click ▶ (Run Rules) to display the results of the style changes.

14. Close the Style Rules dialog box.

Task 3 - Override the style rules.

Stylizing the road centerlines according to the road class helps create a more realistic model. In this model, part of the frontage road has been given the wrong styles and does not match what is actually there. In this task, you will override a style rule to give the road the correct style.

*If you did not complete the previous task, set the **A_Task3** proposal to current in the Utility Bar.*

1. In the Utility Bar, click ▢ (Bookmark your current location) and select **Road Styles**.

2. In the In Canvas tools, click ▮ (Build, manage, and analyze your industry model)> ▦ (Create and manage your model)> ▦ (Style Palette) and select the *Road* tab.

© 2017, ASCENT - Center for Technical Knowledge®

3. At the top of the Style Palette, expand the drop-down list and select **Street/Interstate**. Click and drag **Street 2 Lane-1 LT Turn** from the Style Palette to the model and drop it on the segment of frontage road that was styled incorrectly, as shown in Figure 3–27.

Figure 3–27

4. Close the Style Palette.

3.3 Create and Share Styles

Although many styles come with the Autodesk InfraWorks software, you might need to create additional styles for your project. You can do so by creating a new catalog of styles or by adding a new style to an existing catalog.

Catalogs

A catalog is a collection of styles that are sorted by feature category. The catalog is listed in a drop-down list at the top of the Style Palette. You can manage style catalogs using the tools at the top of the Style Palette, as shown in Figure 3–28.

Figure 3–28

Catalog Editing Tools

The Catalog Editing tools at the top of the Style Palette only affect the style catalogs. The tools control how the styles are grouped together.

Icon	Description
(Add New Style Catalog)	Creates a style catalog. It is added to the Style Palette and becomes the active catalog. The catalog is stored in an .XML file in a specified location.
(Delete Selected Style Catalog)	Removes the current style catalog from the Style Palette. Note: Style catalogs can be re-imported if required. The catalogs are saved externally in an .XML file, which is not deleted when the catalog is removed from a model.

© 2017, ASCENT - Center for Technical Knowledge®

(Import Style Catalog From File)	Imports a style catalog from a specified file. The catalog is added to the Style Palette and becomes the active catalog.
(Export Selected Style Catalog)	Creates an external file of the current style catalog. The copy is stored in a specified location.
(Copy Selected Style Catalog)	Makes a copy of the current style catalog, which becomes the active catalog. The copy is stored in a specified location.
(Rename Selected Style Catalog)	Enables you to enter a new name for the current style catalog.

Styles

Styles are used to make a model look more realistic. Each style category contains unique settings that must be set to create a style.

The quickest way to create new styles is to create a new style based on an existing style. You can also create new styles from scratch or from 3D models. If you plan to make changes to an existing style, it is recommended that you copy the style first, and then make changes to the copy.

> **Hint: Creating Styles for a Model**
>
> The Autodesk InfraWorks Online Help has additional information on creating specific styles. To open the Autodesk InfraWorks Online Help, press <F1>.

Style Editing Tools

The Style Editing tools at the bottom of the Style Palette only affect the currently selected style. Using these tools enables you to copy and edit the available styles.

Icon	Description
(Add New Style)	Creates a style in the current catalog. A blank style entry displays in the preview area. Double-click on the style to specify the style components.
(Delete Selected Style)	Removes the selected style from the current style catalog.

⬚ (Copy Selected Style to Another Catalog)	Makes a copy of the selected style and moves the copy to another style catalog in the current feature category.
⬚ (Copy Selected Style Locally)	Makes a copy of the selected style in the current style catalog.
⬚ (Rename Selected Style)	Enables you to enter a new name for the selected style.
✏ (Edit Selected Style)	Opens the Style Editor, in which you can change the properties of the selected style.

Material Styles

Defining a material style enables you to create a fill pattern for any other style. Selecting a **Color** material style type enables you to use a color from the palette, or to create a custom color using HSV or RGB values. You can use a custom image by selecting the **Texture** material style type. If you use a custom image file to create the fill pattern, you can set the size of the image to control the size of the pattern in the model. The Define New Material dialog box is shown in Figure 3–29.

Figure 3–29

© 2017, ASCENT - Center for Technical Knowledge®

Barrier Styles

Barriers are often used to control traffic of various types, such as vehicular, bike, or pedestrian traffic. Defining a barrier style enables you to change the barrier segment length, the barrier height, the material for the barrier faces, and the spacing between each barrier. Changing the thickness changes the buffer along the polyline representing the barrier. The Configure Barrier dialog box is shown in Figure 3–30.

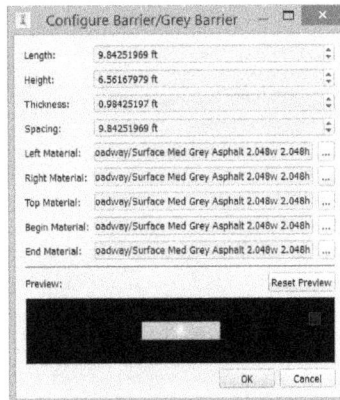

Figure 3–30

Coverage Styles

Coverages can represent parking areas, empty lots, parks, etc. Defining a coverage style enables you to select the material used to fill the interior area, and to select a material and width for the outline. The Configure Coverage dialog box is shown in Figure 3–31.

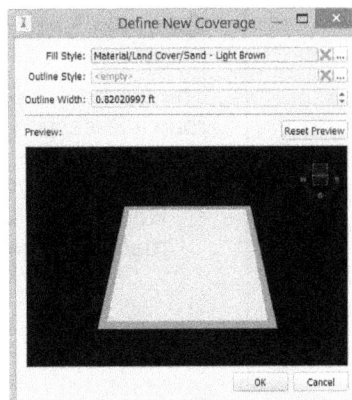

Figure 3–31

Road Styles

Road styles are more complex than most other styles. Defining a road style enables you to define the types of materials used by different parts of the road and the number of default travel lanes that are available. It also enables you to add barriers and other safety features to a road, such as lighting, park strips, and sidewalks. The Configure Street/Interstate dialog box has four settings areas, as shown in Figure 3–32.

General Settings ⟶
Track Settings ⟶
Track Operations ⟶
Preview area ⟶

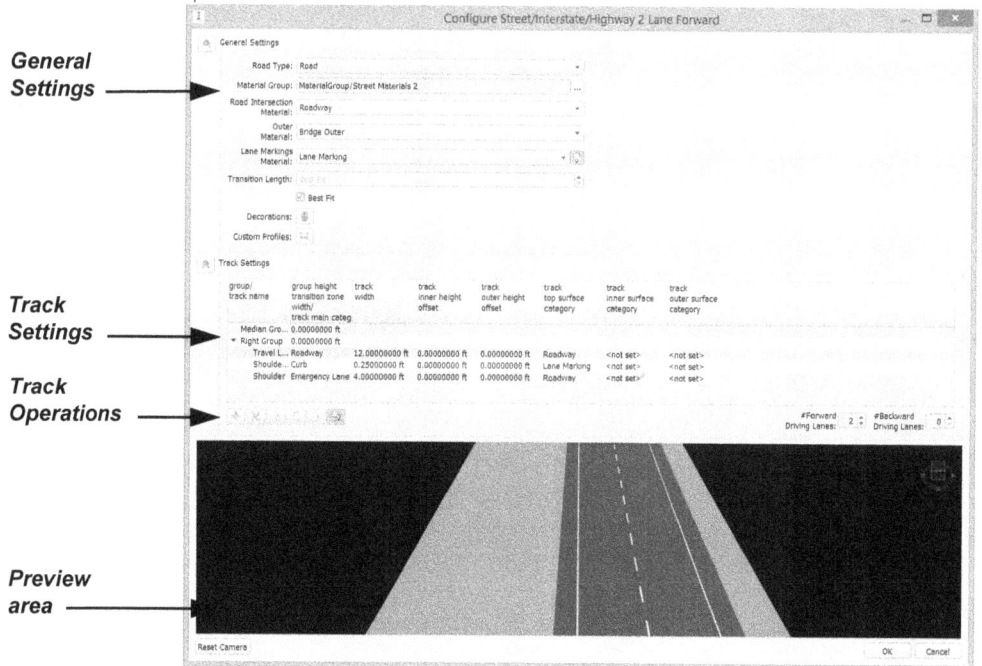

Figure 3–32

General Settings

The *General Settings* area enables you to specify the road type, road intersection material, lane marking material, and decorations.

- **Road Type:** Defines the road as a regular, above-ground road, a bridge, or a tunnel.

© 2017, ASCENT - Center for Technical Knowledge®

- **Material Group:** Maps the materials that are assigned to different parts of a road. Each component of the material groups can be defined separately in its catalog.

- **Road Intersection Material:** Specifies the category of material that is to be used for areas where road segments cross each other. If two roads with different styles share a crossing region, the road style of the road with the highest value in the *Importance* property displays. The *Importance* property is located in the Road Properties palette, as shown in Figure 3–33. You can access it by selecting the road, right-clicking and selecting **Properties**.

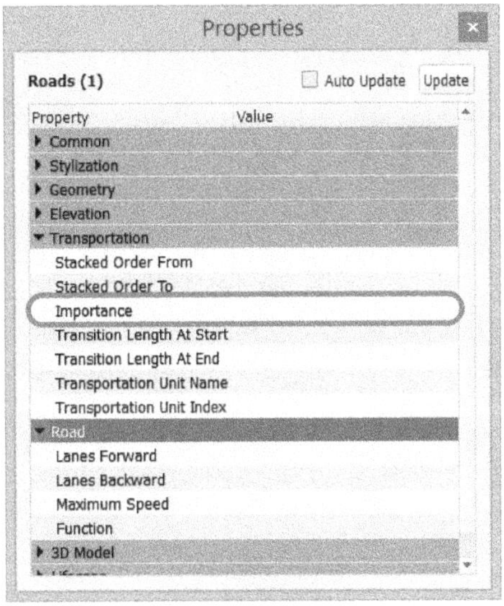

Figure 3–33

- **Outer Material:** Specifies the material applied to the terrain along the outer-most track.

- **Lane Markings Material:** Specifies the category of material to be used for lane markings. Lane markings can be toggled

  on or off using [icon] to the right of the *Lane Marking Material* field. By default, lane markings are not generated for intersecting regions.

- **Transition Length:** Specifies the default transition length for the style. Selecting the **Best Fit** option permits the software to set the transition length.

- **(Decorations):** Opens the Decoration Editor dialog box, as shown in Figure 3–34. It enables you to add 3D models to the roadway at specified intervals. The 3D models can include barriers, signs, light poles, and other city furniture. In the *Decoration Target* field, select the location that you want the 3D model to display. Click to select a 3D model in the Select Style dialog box. Finally, set the spacing and rotation for the 3D model in the *Decoration Settings* area in the Decoration Editor dialog box.

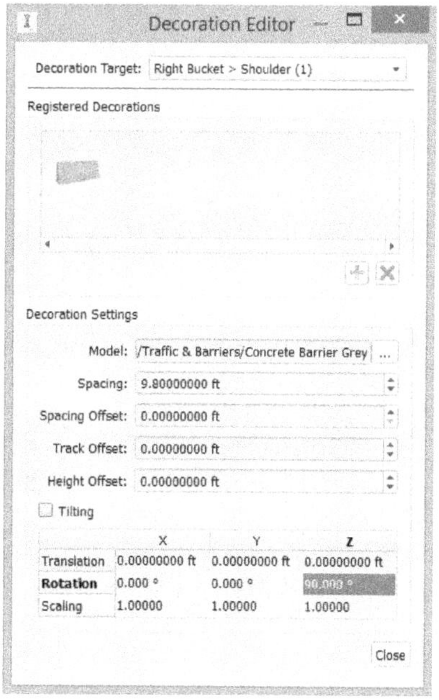

Figure 3–34

- **(Custom Profiles):** Specifies a 2D cross section (.SDF or SQLite file format) to create or display decorations that follow the path along curved roads. This is most useful for customizing the profile of medians, bike-ways, curbs, green space, sidewalks, etc.

Track Settings

The *Track Settings* area defines the road elements. Each row of the table sets the width, height, and surface categories for one element or track for the road. There is usually only one row dedicated for lane elements because the number of lanes is defined by the *#Forward/#Backward Driving Lanes* fields, as shown in Figure 3–35.

© 2017, ASCENT - Center for Technical Knowledge®

The order of the tracks in the Track Settings area determines the order in which they display in the model.

Figure 3–35

By default, only the right side of the road displays in the *Preview* area because the software mirrors the right side of the road to create the left side in the model. To create an asymmetric road

and display the left side, click (Create Asymmetric Road) below the table. You can create additional rows/tracks by clicking

(Add New Element) below the table. The columns in the *Track Settings* area are described as follows:

Column	Description
Group/Track Name	The track name identifies the track use. The group name identifies where the track falls: either in the median or on the left/right side of the road.
Group Height Transition Zone Width/Track Main Category	The *Track Main* category is the basic material type for the road element. Options in this column depend on the Material Group selected in the *General Settings* area. The *Group Height Transition Zone Width* category applies to the group.
Track Width	Sets the width for the corresponding road element.
Track Inner Height Offset	Sets the starting height of the corresponding road element relative to the previous track. Note: The initial height is based on the center line of the road.
Track Outer Height Offset	Sets the finishing height of the corresponding road element relative to the next track.
Track Top Surface Category	Sets the material to be used for the top surface of the road. Options in this column depend on the Material Group selected in the *General Settings* area.
Track Inner Surface Category	Sets the material to be used for the vertical geometry that is created if the inner offset height value is not equal to zero.
Track Outer Surface Category	Sets the material to be used for the vertical geometry that is created if the outer offset height value is not equal to zero.

Track Operations

The *Track Operations* area (shown in Figure 3–36) is where you set the number of lanes for the road, both forward and backward. It is also used to modify the Track Settings table.

Track Settings

group/ track name	group height transition zon width/ track main ca	track width	track inner height offset	track outer height offset	track top surface category	track inner surface category	track outer catego
Travel Lane	Roadway	12.0000000...	0.00000000 ft	0.00000000 ft	Roadway	<not set>	<not s
Shoulder Stripe	Curb	0.25000000 ft	0.00000000 ft	0.00000000 ft	Lane Marking	<not set>	<not s
Shoulder	Emergency ..	4.00000000 ft	0.00000000 ft	0.00000000 ft	Roadway	<not set>	<not s

#Forward Driving Lanes: 4   #Backward Driving Lanes: 0

Figure 3–36

The available icons and their uses are described as follows:

Icon	Description
(Add New Element)	Creates a new road element in the *Track Settings* area.
(Delete Selected Element)	Removes the selected road element or group from the *Track Settings* area.
(Copy Selected Element)	Makes a copy of the selected road element in the *Track Settings* area.
(Move Element Up)	Moves the selected road element up in the track list and changes its location in the *Preview* area.
(Move Element Down)	Moves the selected road element up in the track list and changes its location in the *Preview* area.
(Create Asymmetric Road)	Adds a median group and a left group to the track list, which enables you to create an asymmetric road.

Preview Area

The *Preview* area displays an image of how the road is going to display when applied to road centerlines in the model. The camera position can be moved using the ViewCube in the *Preview* area, or by using the mouse, similar to working in the model.

© 2017, ASCENT - Center for Technical Knowledge®

Practice 3b

Create Styles

Practice Objective

Estimated time for completion: 15 minutes

• Create new visual style for model features.

In this practice you will create a coverage style for a parking lot and a road style.

Task 1 - Create and use a coverage style.

A new commuter parking lot is being built next to the freeway entrance. Coverages are a great way to grade parking lots and other grading sites. Using a custom coverage style, provides the opportunity to make the graded site look however you would like. In this task, you create a material style and a coverage style that looks like a parking lot. Then, you apply the style to a coverage in the model.

1. Continue working in the same model as the last practice. If you closed it, navigate to the *C:\InfraWorks Fundamentals Practice Files\Styles* folder, select **Styles.sqlite** and click **Open**.

2. In the Utility Bar, click ▣ (Bookmark your current location) and select **ParkingLot**. Also ensure that **B_Task1** is the current proposal.

3. In the In Canvas tools, click ▣ (Build, manage, and analyze your industry model)> ▣ (Create and manage your model)> ▣ (Style Palette), select the *Material* tab, and double-click on **Roadway** to display all of the available road materials.

4. In the *Style Editing* area at the bottom of the Style Palette, click ✛ (Add new style).

---

*Click **OK** in the Added Texture File to Model Resources dialog box.*

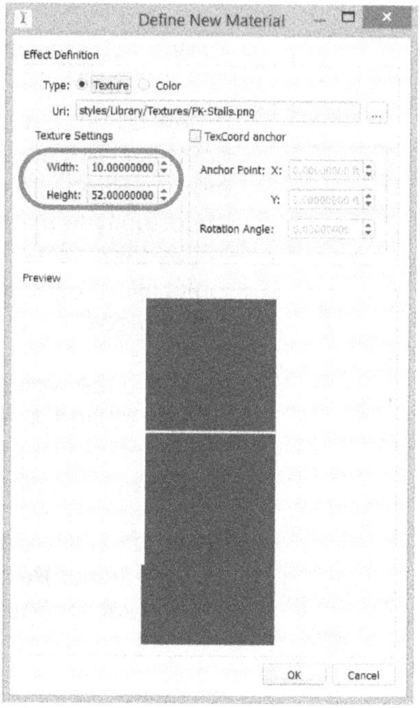

5. In the Define New Material dialog box:
   - For the *Type*, select **Texture**.
   - To the right of the *Uri* field, click ⋯ (Browse).
   - In the *C:\InfraWorks Fundamentals Practice Files\Styles* folder, select **PK-Stalls.png** and click **Open**.
   - In the *Texture Settings* area, for the *Width*, type **10** and for the *Height*, type **52**, as shown in Figure 3–37. Click **OK**.

Figure 3–37

6. For the name of the new material, type **PK-Stalls**.

7. In the Style Palette, select the *Coverage* tab.

8. In the *Style Editing* area at the bottom of the Style Palette, click ➕ (Add new style).

9. In the Define New Coverage dialog box, to the right of the *Fill Style* field, click ⋯ (Browse).

© 2017, ASCENT - Center for Technical Knowledge®

10. In the Select Style/Color dialog box:
    - Select the *Material* tab.
    - Double-click on Roadway.
    - Select **PK-Stalls**, as shown in Figure 3–38. Click **OK**.

Figure 3–38

11. In the Define New Coverage dialog box, to the right of *Outline Style*, click ⋯ (Browse).

12. In the Select Style/Color dialog box:
    - Select the *Material* tab.
    - Double-click on Roadway.
    - Select **Curb 0.1w 2h** as shown in Figure 3–39. Click **OK**.

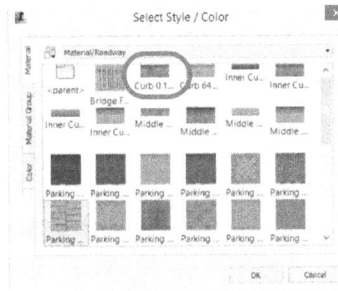

Figure 3–39

13. Leave the *Outline Width* set to **0.82** and click **OK**.

14. For the coverage style name, type **ParkingLot**.

15. Drag the new **ParkingLot** coverage style to the new commuter parking lot shown in Figure 3–40.

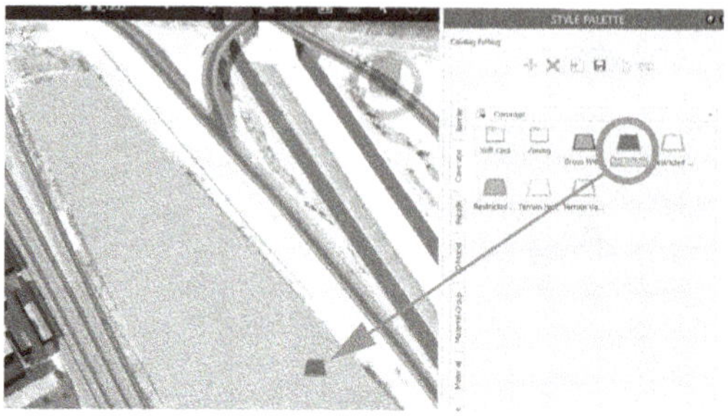

Figure 3–40

Task 2 - Create a new road style.

Stylizing the road centerlines according the road class helps create a more realistic model. However, the road style used to display the I-15 corridor does not have enough lanes and needs to have the correct barriers to protect drivers from running off the road or into oncoming traffic. In this task, you will create a new catalog and create a copy of the style that is currently used for I-15. You will make the required modifications to the style and apply it to the style rules.

If you did not complete the previous task, set the B_Task2 proposal to current in the Utility Bar.

1. In the Utility Bar, click 🔖 (Bookmark your current location) and select **Road Styles**.

2. In the Style Palette, select the *Road* tab.

3. Expand the drop-down list and select **Street/Interstate**.

4. In the *Catalog Editing Tools* area at the top, click ➕ (Add New Style Catalog).

5. For the *Catalog Name*, type **Training** and press <Enter>.

6. Expand the drop-down list and select **Street/Interstate**.

7. In the *Style Preview* area, select the **Highway 2 Lane** style.

© 2017, ASCENT - Center for Technical Knowledge®

8. In the *Style Editing* area at the bottom of the Style Palette, click 📋 (Copy Selected Style to Another Catalog).

9. In the Copy Item dialog box, select the **Street/Interstate/ Training** option, as shown in Figure 3–41. Click **OK**.

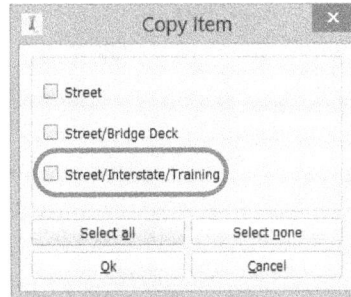

Figure 3–41

10. Expand the drop-down list and select **Street/Interstate/ Training**.

11. In the *Style Preview* area, select the **Highway 2 Lane** style.

12. In the *Style Editing* area at the bottom of the Style Palette, click 🔲 (Rename Selected Style). Type **Highway 4 Lane Forward** and press <Enter>.

13. In the *Style Editing* area at the bottom of the Style Palette, click ✏ (Edit Selected Style).

14. In the Configure Style dialog box, do the following, as shown in Figure 3–42:

- Set the #*Forward Driving Lanes* to **4**.

- Click ⬚ (Create Asymmetric Road) to make the road asymmetrical.

- Click ⬚ (Decoration).

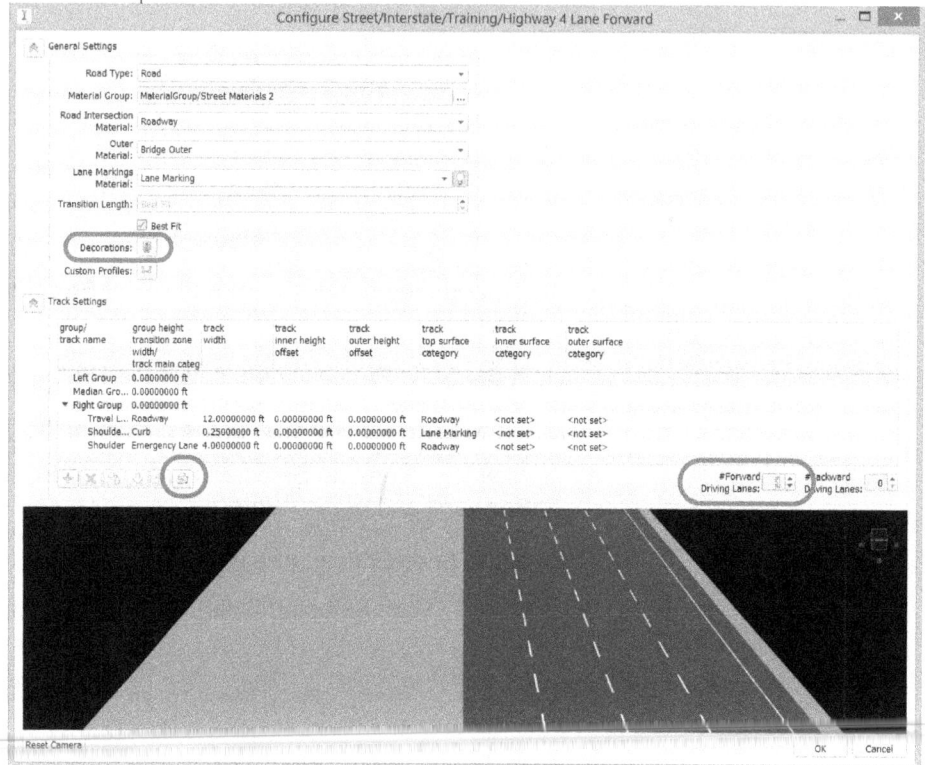

Figure 3–42

15. In the Decorations Editor dialog box:
- The Decoration Target drop-down list should be set to **Right Bucket>Travel Lane**.

16. In the Select 3D Model Style dialog box:
- Click ✛ (Add 3D Model) and double-click on **<parent>** then **Vehicles**.
- Select **BMW 7 Series**, as shown in Figure 3–43.

© 2017, ASCENT - Center for Technical Knowledge®

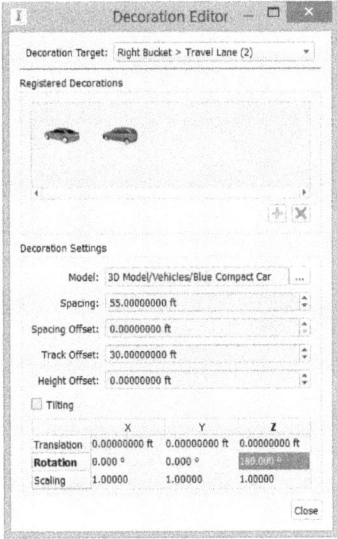

Figure 3–43

17. Click **OK**.

18. Move the Decoration Editor dialog box so that the *Preview* area in the Style Configuration dialog box displays. Continue setting the following, as shown in Figure 3–44:
    - *Track Offset* field: **6**
    - *Spacing* field: **50**.

    Note the change in the *Preview* area.

19. In the Select 3D Model Style dialog box, click ✛ (Add 3D Model) and then select **Blue Compact Car**. Continue setting the following, as shown in Figure 3–45:
    - *Track Offset* field: **30**
    - *Spacing* field: **55**

If you live in the United States (or another country that drives on the right side of the road), in the Z column, change the Rotation to 180.

Figure 3–44   **Figure 3–45**

20. Expand the Decoration Target drop-down list and select **Right Bucket>Shoulder**.

21. In the Select 3D Model Style dialog box, click ✛ (Add 3D Model) and double-click on **Concrete Barrier Grey**.

22. Move the Decoration Editor dialog box so that the *Preview* area in the Style Configuration dialog box displays clearly. Continue setting the following, as shown in Figure 3–46:
    - *Z Rotation* field: **90**
    - *Track Offset* field: **-50**

    Note the change in the *Preview* area.

23. To the right of *Spacing*, click the down-arrow until the barriers abut each other in the *Preview* area in the Style Configuration dialog box (the *Spacing* should be close to 9.8'), as shown in Figure 3–46.

24. Click **Close**.

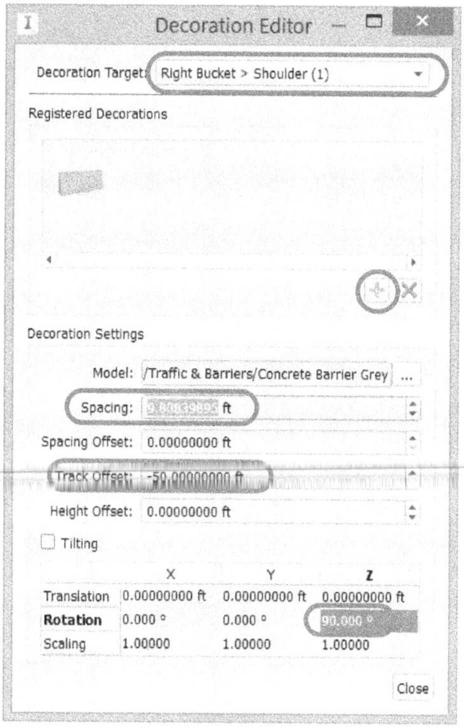

Figure 3–46

© 2017, ASCENT - Center for Technical Knowledge®

25. In the Style Configuration dialog box, click **OK** to accept the changes.

26. Open the Style Rules palette and change the **Freeway** style rule to make it use the **Highway 4 Lane Forward** style that you just created, as shown in Figure 3–47.

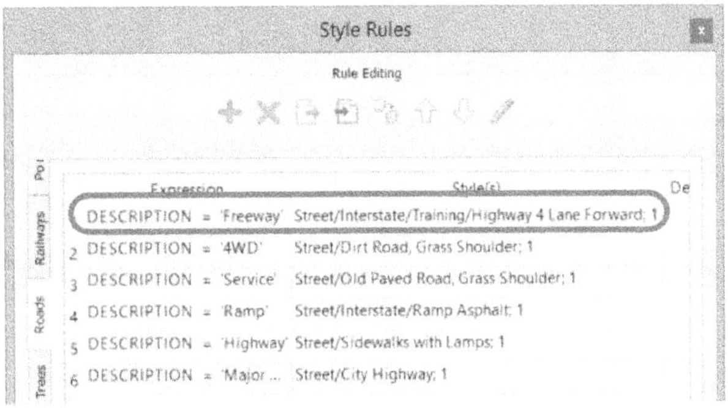

Figure 3–47

27. Click ⓘ (Run Rules) to display the changes in the model.

28. Close the model.

Chapter Review Questions

1. Which programming language is used to change the appearance of data sources on import?

   a. HTML

   b. C++

   c. .Net

   d. JavaScript

2. When working with expressions, which of the following operators can be used for text fields?

   a. Like

   b. Not Like

   c. = (Equal To)

   d. All of the above.

3. When changing a model feature's style automatically, two filter types are available: Location and Property.

   a. True

   b. False

4. When creating new styles, which of the following cannot be set for a barrier style?

   a. Length

   b. 3D Model

   c. Height

   d. Spacing

5. When creating new styles, in which of the following areas would you set the number of lanes for a road style?

   a. *General Settings area*

   b. *Track Settings* area

   c. *Track Operations* area

   d. *Preview* area

© 2017, ASCENT - Center for Technical Knowledge®

Command Summary

Button	Command	Location
	Style Palette	• **In Canvas Tools:** Build, manage, and analyze your industry model>Create and manage your model
	Style Rules	• **In Canvas Tools:** Build, manage, and analyze your industry model>Create and manage your model

© 2017, ASCENT - Center for Technical Knowledge®

Create Model Elements

Using conceptual design tools, you can add roads, railway lines, bodies of water, and coverage areas to a model. In this chapter you learn how to add many of these model elements and how to edit the elements once they have been created.

Learning Objectives in this Chapter

- Review the basic commands that are available to make changes to model elements.
- Create conceptual designs of roads, bridges, and tunnels.
- Create coverages and land areas to shape and stylize the terrain surface.
- Add pipelines and pipeline connectors to a model to indicate where utilities are to be located.
- Create railways in a model to indicate the locations of the mass transit lines or freight lines.
- Create water features in a model to represent lakes, ponds, rivers, or streams.

4.1 Basic Commands

To work with features in the model, you must be able to select them. The same selection tools are used to select features from imported source data and features that you have created. Knowing which selection tools are available and how to use them helps you to be more efficient.

Selecting Features

Before you can edit an item, you must be able to select it. By default, you can click on any entity in the model to select it. In the

In Canvas Tools, click ▮ (Build, manage, and analyze your

industry model)> ◣ (Select Model Features) to see additional options. The following selection options are available:

Icon	Description
(Zoom to Selected)	Zooms in and center on the selected feature(s).
(Clear Selected)	Clears the current selection. You can also use the keyboard shortcut by pressing <Esc>
(Window Select)	Enables you to select an area based on two opposite corners of a rectangle by dragging the cursor over a region of the model. Any features that are within or touching the edge of the window are selected.
(Rectangular Select)	Enables you to define a box with three points (*Min/Max* for X, Y, and Z). Any features that are completely inside the box are selected. Note: You must double click on the last point to complete the command.
(Polygon Select)	Enables you to define any shape based on three or more points. Any feature(s) that are inside or touching the edge of the polygon are selected. Note: You must double-click on the last point to complete the command.
(Radius Select)	Enables you to define a circular region by selecting the center point. Any features that are completely inside the defined circle are selected. Note: You must double-click to set the distance from the center and complete the command.
(Filter Select)	Enables you to define an expression to select features according to specific attributes. When clicked, the Create an attribute filter dialog box opens, which enables you to create filter expressions to use with this selection option.

© 2017, ASCENT - Center for Technical Knowledge®

- Multiple selections can be made by holding down <Ctrl> when selecting features in the model.

- To select a feature, the feature class or layer must be unlocked in the Model Explorer, and *Edit mode* must be toggled on in the View Settings asset card.

How To: Toggle Edit Mode On/Off

1. In the Utility Bar, expand the View Style drop-down and click ⚙ (Configure current view).

2. In the View Settings asset card, click 🔍 (Change navigation and application feedback settings) to open the *Interaction* stack.

3. Under *Feedback*, click the **Edit mode** slider to toggle it on or off, as shown in Figure 4–1.

This only toggles the Edit mode for the current view style.

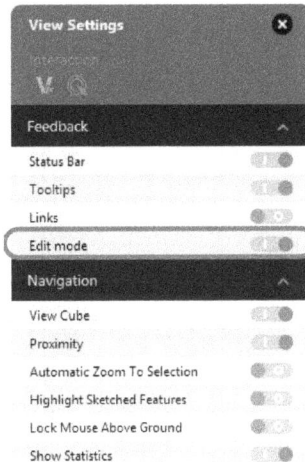

Figure 4–1

Shortcut Commands

Many Windows programs use common shortcut keys. Many of these keys can also be used in the Autodesk® InfraWorks® software. Shortcut keys can be used in conjunction with the clipboard to share features between different proposals or models.

Some of the shortcut keys are described as follows:

Command /Icon	Keyboard Shortcut	Description
Select All	\<Ctrl>+\<A>	Selects all of the contents (i.e., created features and data sources) in the current model.
Invert Selection	\<Alt>+\<I>	Inverts the currently selected contents. These are cleared, while previously unselected objects become selected.
Deselect	\<Esc>	Clears the selection of any objects that were selected in the model.
Zoom Selected	\<F>	Zooms in on the currently selected objects in the model.
Copy	\<Ctrl>+\<C>	Copies features to a clipboard for use later. You can copy an individual feature, an entire feature class, or multiple feature classes using the **Copy** command.
Duplicate	\<Ctrl>+\<D>	Copies features without copying to the clipboard. You can duplicate an individual feature, an entire feature class, or multiple feature classes using the **Duplicate** command. Note: You can press \<Shift>+\<Ctrl> while dragging selected features to duplicate them without using the clipboard.
Paste	\<Ctrl>+\<V>	Pastes items from the clipboard into the model. Hold \<Ctrl>+\<V> and double-click in the model where you want the copied feature to be placed.
Paste in Place	\<Shift>+\<Ctrl>+\<V>	Pastes items at their original locations.
Delete	\<Delete>	Removes selected features from the model.
Cut	\<Ctrl>+\<X>	Removes selected features from the model and places them on the clipboard for use later. You can cut an individual feature, an entire feature class, or multiple feature classes using the **Cut** command.
(Undo)	\<Ctrl>+\<Z>	Undoes the last command used in the model. Repeating the **Undo** command undoes commands in the order in which they were executed. The Icon is found on the Utility Bar.

© 2017, ASCENT - Center for Technical Knowledge®

Create Model Elements

(Redo)	<Ctrl>+<Y>	Reverses an **Undo** command, reissuing the last command that was undone in the model.
		Repeating the **Redo** command reissues commands in the order in which they were undone. Note: **Redo** only reissues commands that were successive. For example, if you undo five commands, redo three of those commands, and then issue a new command, the **Redo** command is disabled when you execute the new command. The Icon is found on the Utility Bar.

Gizmos

Gizmos enable you to quickly modify model features, similar to the way grips are used in AutoCAD®-based programs. In the model, click the entity you wish to edit to cause gizmos to display when objects are selected. Different gizmos display depending on the type of feature that is selected when you access the Edit Features mode.

A few of the available gizmos are described as follows:

Gizmos	Transformation	Description
	Elevation	Used with linear features (i.e., roads, railways, and coverages). In a 3D View, it stretches features vertically by changing the elevation of a linear feature vertex.
	Height	Only used with buildings, city furniture, and trees. Changes the height of a building while leaving the footprint unchanged. Changes the scale of trees and city furniture proportionally.
	Rotate	Rotates a feature around the Z-axis.
	Control Point	Displays at each corner, point of intersection, or base of features. Stretches linear features (i.e., roads, rails, coverages, and building outlines) by moving the selected vertex of the feature. Moves the location of point features (i.e., trees or city furniture). Note: Additional control points can be added by holding down <Alt> and selecting the new control point location.
	Move	Moves the selected feature or vertex.

© 2017, ASCENT - Center for Technical Knowledge®   4–5

The Move gizmo has four handle options for moving model elements. These handles can be selected to move features in specific planes. The available handles are as follows.

Handle	Transformation	Description
	Move in XY Plane	Select the square between the X- and Y-axes to move a feature to a new location in the XY plane.
	Move in X Axis	Select the red arrow to constrain the movement of a feature to a new location along the X-axis.
	Move in Y Axis	Select the green arrow to constrain the movement of a feature to a new location along the Y-axis.
	Move in Z Axis	Select the blue arrow to constrain the movement of a feature to a new location along the Z-axis.

© 2017, ASCENT - Center for Technical Knowledge®

4.2 Create Conceptual Roads in a Model

Every design project needs to be accessed in some way, and this is easily done by creating a new road or simple driveway into the site. Using the **Create Roads** command you can add roads, bridges, and tunnels to a model. Which of these three features you create depends on the style of road that you select in the Select Draw Style Asset Card when starting the **Roads** command, as shown in Figure 4–2. To find a required style faster, you can filter the available styles by typing in the filter field.

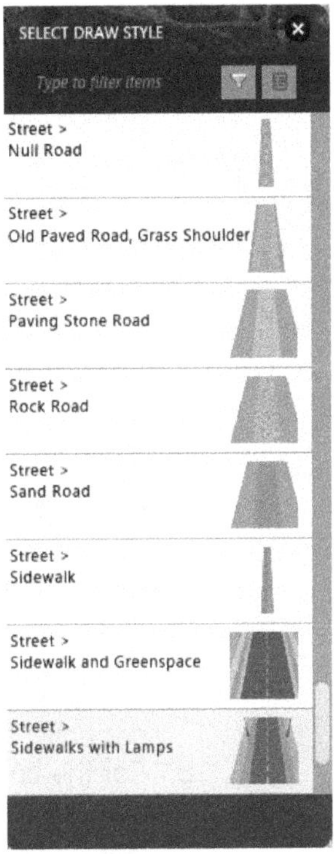

Figure 4–2

How To: Create a Road

1. In the In Canvas tools, click ⬛ (Build, manage, and analyze your infrastructure model)> ✏️ (Create conceptual design features)> 🔧 (Roads).

Once you have selected the first road style in the model, that style becomes the active style. To change the active style, click

![Roads icon] *(Roads) and select a different style from the Select Draw Style asset card.*

2. The Select Draw Style asset card opens, as shown in Figure 4–3. In the Select Draw Style asset card, select the required style.

Figure 4–3

3. Click in the model where you want to start the road, bridge, or tunnel.
4. Move the cursor in the direction the road needs to follow. Type a distance to the first point of intersection (PI). Click the model at the locations of each additional required point of intersection (PI).
5. If crossing existing roads, ensure that you place a PI at the intersection to ensure that the intersection is created correctly.
6. For the final PI, double-click on the location at which you want to end the road, bridge, or tunnel. Doing so ends the **Road** command.
7. Press <Esc> to clear the selection of the newly created road, bridge, or tunnel.

Edit Roads

Once a road, bridge, or tunnel has been created, you can change the design options. For example, you might need to add more curves to the road or change the elevation at specific locations. To edit a road, select the road and use the gizmos to make changes. You can also right-click on the road to access the following options.

© 2017, ASCENT - Center for Technical Knowledge®

Icon	Command	Description
⌖	**Add Vertex**	Adds a point of intersection (PI) at the point at which you right-clicked.
⌖	**Remove Vertex**	Removes the PI on which you right-clicked.
⟋	**Split Feature**	Breaks the road, bridge, or tunnel into multiple features at the point at which you right-clicked.
⬳ 2D	**Drape Feature**	Drapes the roadway on the surface terrain, reducing the need to add PVIs along the road.
N/A	**Convert to Design Road**	Converts a conceptual road to a design road enabling you to add more design parameters (curve radius, daylight slope, etc).
N/A	**Properties**	Opens the Properties palette in which you can change the style, number of lanes, elevation offset, etc.

When working with roads created using the conceptual **Roads** tool, you must add a vertex where you need to add a horizontal or vertical curve to the road. This helps reduce the amount of cut and fill required to build the road, as shown in Figure 4–4.

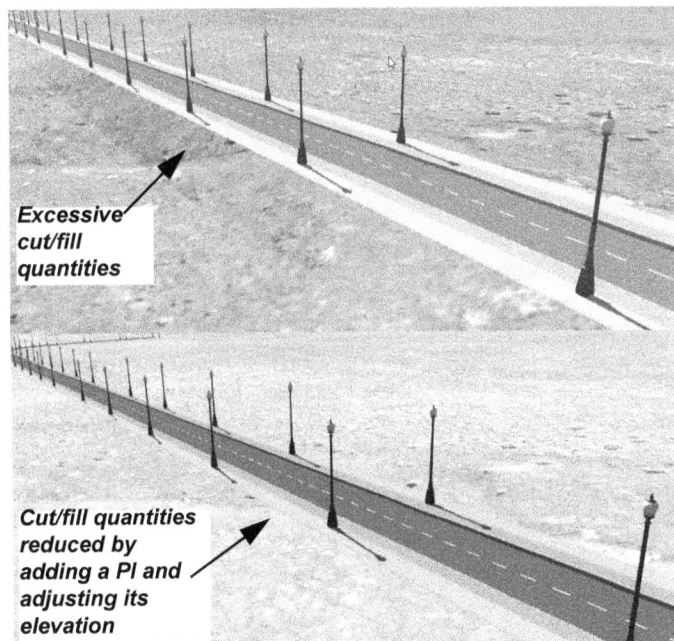

Figure 4–4

If you only need to change the style of road for part of the roadway, use the **Split Feature** command. Then use the Road asset card or Properties to change the style for the segment of road that needs to be changed. In the Properties palette, select an option in the *Manual Style* field and click **Update**, as shown in Figure 4–5.

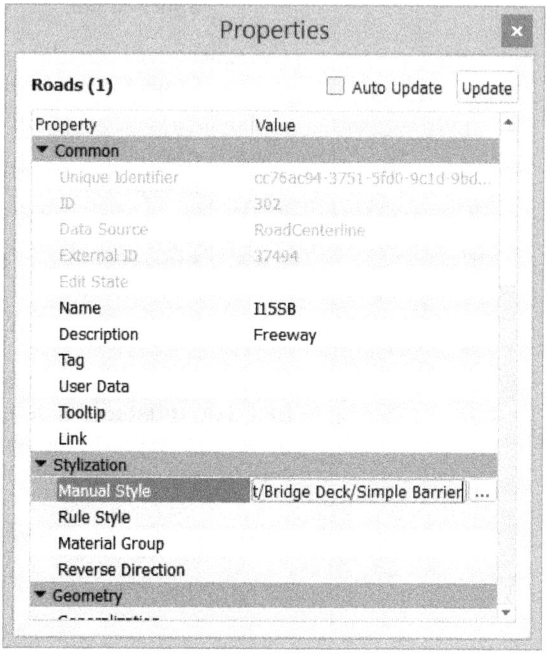

Figure 4–5

Practice 4a

Estimated time for completion: 25 minutes

Create Roads in the Model

Practice Objective

• Create multiple roads in the model to display the design concept.

In this practice you will create a road that ends at a pier. You will use a bridge style to create the pier. You will then create additional roads for a new subdivision that will connect to an existing subdivision.

Task 1 - Create roads.

1. In the Home Screen, click **Open**.

2. In the *C:\InfraWorks Fundamentals Practice Files\Create* folder, select **CreateFeatures.sqlite** and click **Open**.

3. In the Utility Bar, click ▣ (Bookmark your current location) and select **Bridge**.

4. In the Utility Bar, expand *Switch Active Proposal* and select **A_Task1**.

5. In the In Canvas tools, click ▣ (Build, manage, and analyze your infrastructure model)> ✎ (Create conceptual design features)> ▣ (Roads).

6. In the Select Draw Style asset card, type **Sidewalk** in the filter field, and then select **Street>Sidewalk with Lamps**, as shown in Figure 4–6.

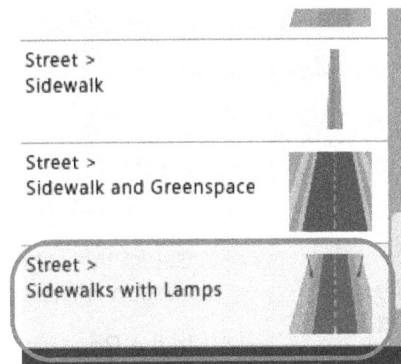

Figure 4–6

If the distance field does not display initially, move the cursor further away from the starting point until it displays.

Note that going off the terrain created by the .DEM file can cause the model to crash.

7. To start the road in the model, click near the center line of Redwood Rd just south of the dirt road, as shown in Figure 4–7. Type **125**, press <Enter>, and then click north-east of that point to make the road perpendicular to Redwood Rd.

8. Move the cursor due east and double-click to end the road inside the water, as shown in Figure 4–7.

Figure 4–7

9. Press <Esc> twice to end the command and release the roadway selection.

Task 2 - Edit the roads.

1. Continue working in the same model. If you did not complete the last task, in the Utility Bar, expand *Switch Active Proposal* and select the **A_Task2** proposal.

2. In the model, select the new road. Right-click near the center of the road to the west of the barn in the fields and select **Split Feature**, as shown in Figure 4–8.

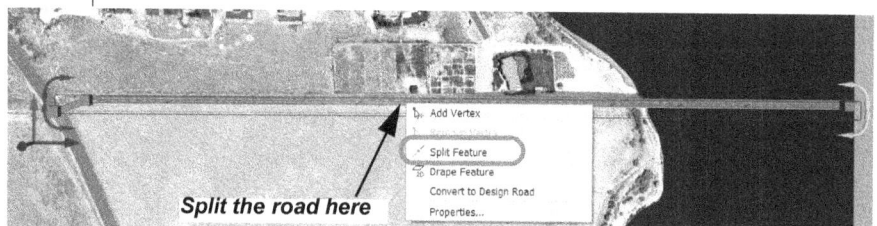

Figure 4–8

You might need to select close to the split point to select the correct portion of the road.

3. Select the segment of road to the right of the split. This section will become the new pier.

4. In the Road asset card, click the *Manual Style* thumbnail and select **More Styles**.

© 2017, ASCENT - Center for Technical Knowledge®

5. In the Select Style dialog box, select the **Street** catalog, then the **Bridge** style, as shown in Figure 4–9. Click **OK**.

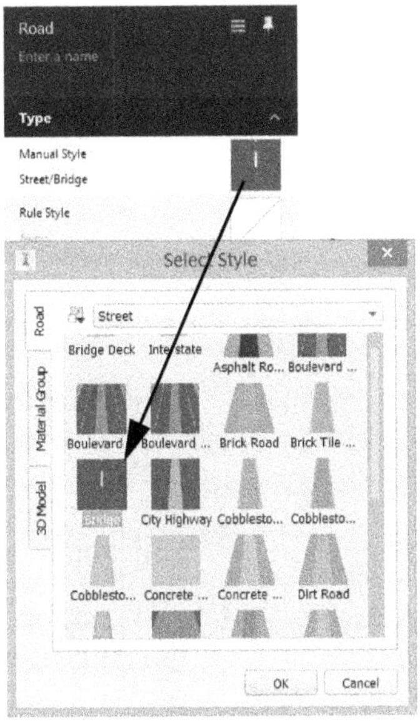

Figure 4–9

6. In the Utility Bar, click ▯ (Bookmark your current location) and select **Bridge Elevation**. The view displays as shown in Figure 4–10.

Figure 4–10

7. The bridge goes down into the water. Select the bridge and use ▯ (Elevation Gizmo) to raise the right side of the bridge so that it is parallel with the water line, as shown in Figure 4–11.

Figure 4–11

Task 3 - Create subdivision roads.

1. Continue working in the same model. If you did not complete the last task, in the Utility Bar, expand *Switch Active Proposal* and select the **A_Task3** proposal.

2. In the Utility Bar, click ▣ (Bookmark your current location), and select **New Neighborhood**.

3. In the In Canvas tools, click 🔲 (Build, manage, and analyze your infrastructure model)> ✏️ (Create conceptual design features)> 🛣️ (Roads). The **Sidewalk with Lamps** road style is automatically selected because it was the last style that was used. Continue using this style.

Note that placing the west PIs causes the road to form one large curve. This is corrected in the next step.

4. In the model, create the road shown in Figure 4–12 by typing the distances and pressing <Enter> before clicking to place each PI. Double-click the last PI to end the command.

270 ft
2400 ft
2875 ft
335 ft

Figure 4–12

5. Press <Esc> to end the command and show the road's gizmos.

6. Orbit the model more than 45 degrees past the plan view orientation to display the vertical gizmos. Orient the view so that you are looking east, similar to the view shown in Figure 4–13.

© 2017, ASCENT - Center for Technical Knowledge®

This vertex reduces the curve radii of the horizontal curves at the north and south ends of the road.

7. Add a new vertex at the approximate mid-point of the north-south segment of the new road, as shown in Figure 4–13. To add a vertex, right-click where you want to place the vertex, and select **Add Vertex**. Adjust the elevation of the new vertex using 🔺 (Elevation Gizmo).

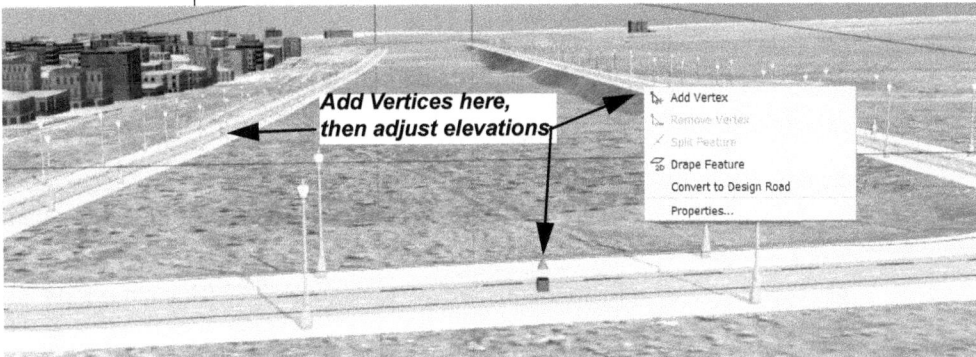

Figure 4–13

8. Add additional vertices as required to reduce the cut and fill volumes for the new road.

9. In the Utility Bar, click 🔲 (Bookmark your current location), and select **New Neighborhood**.

10. Add additional neighborhood roads, as shown in Figure 4–14. Place a point of intersection (PI) at locations where one road intersects another by clicking on the midpoint of the roads where they will intersect. Doing so results in clean intersections, rather than overpasses or underpasses.

Figure 4–14

11. Press <Esc> to clear the selection of all of the roads.

4.3 Create Coverages in a Model

Coverages are used to shape the terrain and change the way the ground displays. Coverages can be used to add ground cover in a landscape design, set the elevation of a building pad, or create a parking lot for a site design. Additionally, Terrain Hole material can be used on a coverage to create openings in a surface with a clean edge. This enables you to display what is going on underground. If you just need to reshape the terrain surface without changing how it displays, a transparent material style can be used.

How To: Shape and Style the Terrain Surface

1. In the In Canvas tools, click ▨ (Build, manage, and analyze your infrastructure model)>▨ (Create conceptual design features)>▨ (Coverages).
2. Select the style for the surface you are creating from the Select Draw Style asset card that displays, as shown in Figure 4–15.

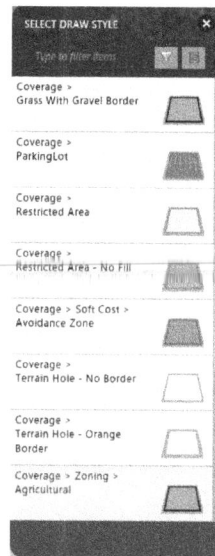

Figure 4–15

3. In the model, click to place the corners of the coverage footprint. After the first corner has been placed, move the cursor in the direction in which you want the next corner to be placed. Note the dimensions that display, as shown in Figure 4–16.

© 2017, ASCENT - Center for Technical Knowledge®

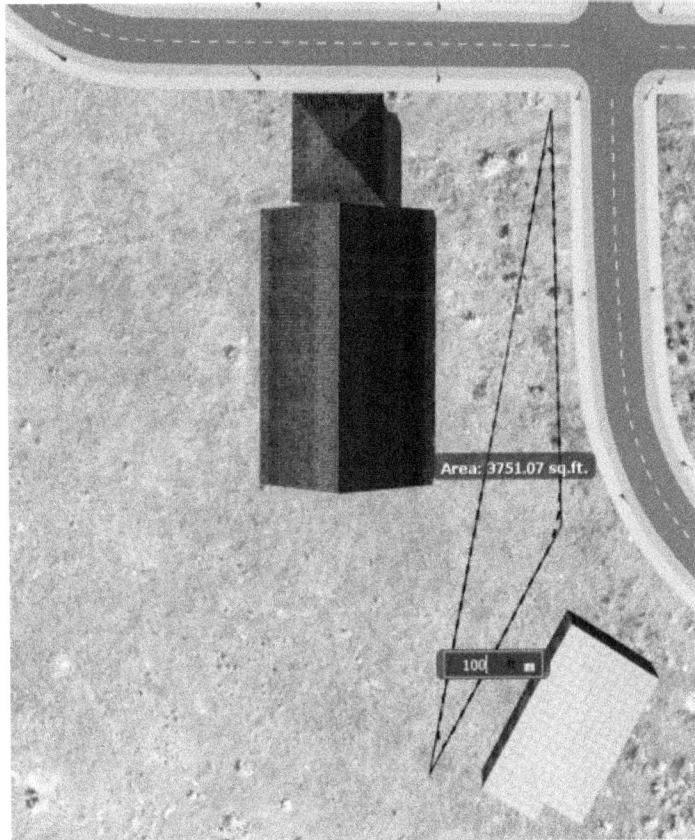

Figure 4–16

Locking a length means that even if you drag the cursor, the dimension value does not change.

4. Type the required length for that side of the coverage and press <Enter> to lock the length. Move the cursor as required to set the correct angle and click to place the vertex.
5. Continue clicking in the model until all but the last vertices have been set.
6. Double-click on the location at which you want to place the final vertex. Doing so ends the command.
7. Press <Esc> to clear the selection of the newly created coverage.

Edit Coverages

Once a coverage has been created, it can be re-shaped using

 (Control Point Gizmo). The gizmos display at each vertex when the coverage is selected in the model and Edit mode is toggled on in the View Settings Interaction stack. If you orbit the

model more than 45 degrees, (Elevation Gizmo) displays and can be used to adjust the elevation of each corner.

As you adjust the elevation of a coverage, the surrounding terrain updates to gradually slope toward the new elevation, as shown in Figure 4–17.

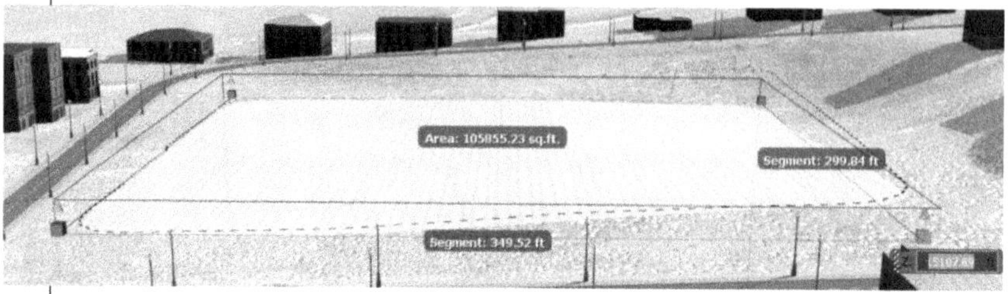

Figure 4–17

How gradual the slope is depends upon the *Smooth Radius* value for the coverage, as shown in Figure 4–18. This value is changed by selecting the coverage and changing the *Smooth Radius* value in the asset card or the Properties palette.

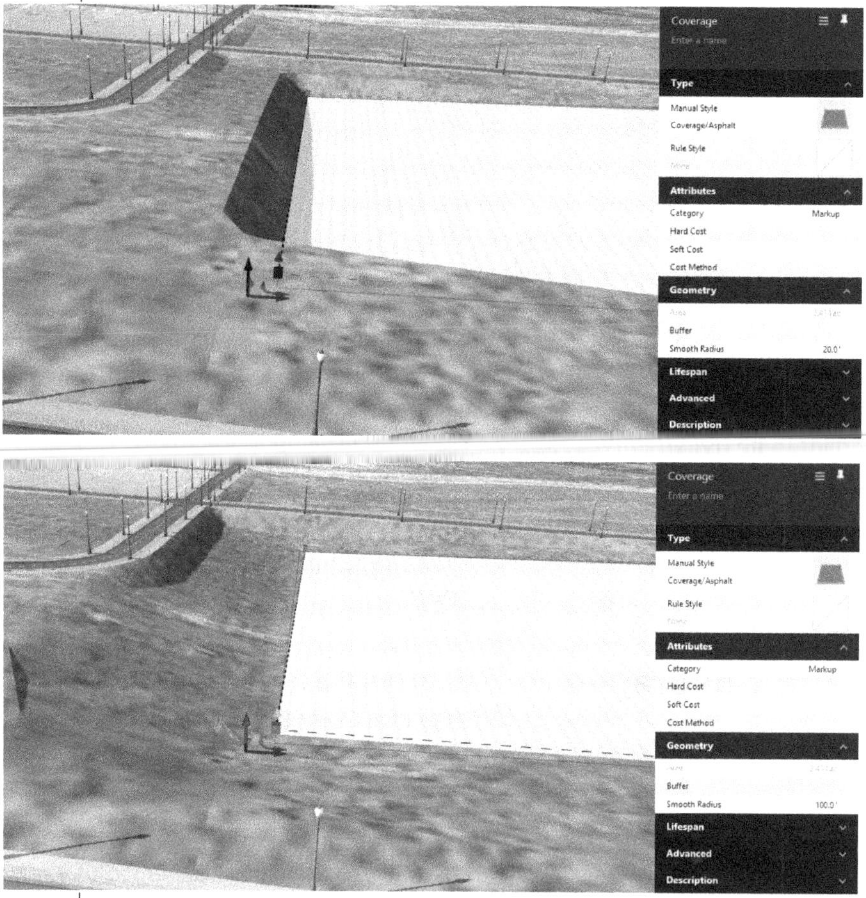

Figure 4–18

© 2017, ASCENT - Center for Technical Knowledge®

If a flat coverage is desired (i.e., with all vertices having the same elevation), right-click on the selected coverage and select **Shape Terrain**. Then use the ↑ (Elevation Gizmo) at the center of the coverage to adjust the elevation of all vertices at once, as shown in Figure 4–19.

Figure 4–19

Vertices can be added anywhere along a side to add additional control and elevation points. To add a vertex, select the coverage, right-click on the side at which you want to have additional control, and select **Add Vertex**, as shown in Figure 4–20.

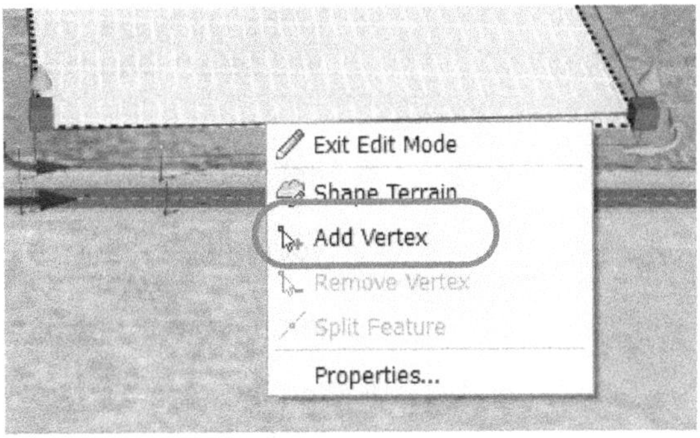

Figure 4–20

Practice 4b

Create Coverages in the Model

Practice Objectives

- Change the look of the terrain surface using coverages to display parking lots and other surface materials.
- Shape the terrain surface using coverages to change the elevations.

Estimated time for completion: 25 minutes

In this practice you will create coverages to change the display settings and elevations associated with a terrain surface.

Task 1 - Create a parking lot.

1. In the Home Screen, click **Open**.

2. In the *C:\InfraWorks Fundamentals Practice Files\Create* folder, select **CreateFeatures.sqlite** and click **Open**.

3. In the Utility Bar, expand *Switch Active Proposal* and select **B_Task1**.

4. In the Utility Bar, click ▣ (Bookmark your current location) and select **Church**.

5. In the In Canvas tools, click ▣ (Build, manage, and analyze your infrastructure model)> ▨ (Create conceptual design features)> ▨ (Coverages).

6. In the Select Draw Style asset card, select the **ParkingLot** style that was created in an earlier practice, as shown in Figure 4–21.

Figure 4–21

© 2017, ASCENT - Center for Technical Knowledge®

7. Click in the model to place the vertices of the parking lot similar to that shown in Figure 4–22. Ensure that you double-click on the last corner to place it and end the command.

A building will be added later which sits in the middle of the parking lot.

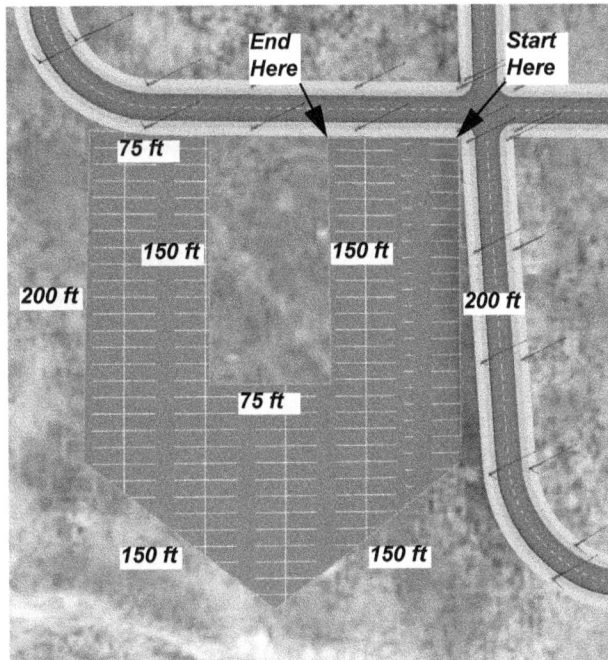

Figure 4–22

8. Press <Esc> twice to clear the selection of the newly created parking lot.

Task 2 - Shape the terrain using a coverage.

In this task you will shape the ground surface in preparation for a school. You will create another coverage and adjust its elevations.

1. In the Utility Bar, click ⬚ (Bookmark your current location) and select **School**. Expand *Switch Active Proposal* and then select **B_Task2**.

2. In the In Canvas tools, click ▮ (Build, manage, and analyze your infrastructure model)> ✎ (Create conceptual design features)> ▦ (Coverages).

3. In the Select Draw Style asset card, select **Asphalt**.

4. In the model, click to place the corners of the asphalt slab in the field reserved for the school, as shown in Figure 4–23. Make the measurement **350' x 300'** with the long side running east to west. Double-click on the last corner to place it and end the command.

Figure 4–23

5. Press <Esc> to show the coverage's gizmos.

6. With the new asphalt coverage selected, orbit the view so that the elevation of the south side displays, as shown in Figure 4–24.

A box displays indicating orthogonal directions otherwise known as level lines. The level line in the view can help you to level the pad if you are shaping it manually.

Figure 4–24

© 2017, ASCENT - Center for Technical Knowledge®

7. Right-click and select **Shape Terrain**.

8. With the new asphalt coverage selected, click ↑ (Elevation Gizmo), type **4612** in the elevation field (as shown in Figure 4–25), and then press <Enter>.

Elevation: 4612   ft ▾

Figure 4–25

The surrounding ground gradually slopes into the school pad based on the change in elevation and Smooth Radius value in the Coverage asset card.

9. With the coverage still selected, in the asset card, change the *Smooth Radius* value to **20**.

10. Change the *Smooth Radius* value to **100** and press <Enter>. Note the change in the surrounding grade.

11. Press <Esc> to clear the selection of the newly created school pad.

4.4 Create Pipe Networks in a Model

Utilities are a very important part of a project. They provide electricity, gas, water, etc., to a project site. They also provide a way to divert excess storm water.

Creating conceptual utilities in the Autodesk InfraWorks software is a two step process, as both pipelines and pipeline connectors must be created separately. Once created, they can be imported into the AutoCAD® Civil 3D® software where they become a pipe network. Pipelines become AutoCAD Civil 3D pipes, while Pipeline Connectors become AutoCAD Civil 3D structures. If you enter a name for the Pipeline in the *Network Name* field in the Properties palette (as shown in Figure 4–26), the name can be used in the AutoCAD Civil 3D software to identify the pipe network.

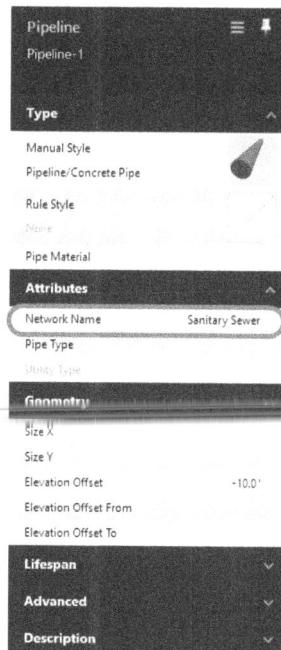

Figure 4–26

Hint: Order of Operations

It is easier to create the pipeline connectors first. Pipelines snap to existing pipeline connectors and stay connected. This enables you to control the location of any pipeline by moving the pipeline connectors to which it is connected.

© 2017, ASCENT - Center for Technical Knowledge®

Pipeline Connectors

Pipeline connectors are nodes that connect to pipe ends. They can represent pipeline structures (such as manholes and catch-basins) along a pipeline.

How To: Create Pipeline Connectors

1. In the In Canvas tools, click ![icon] (Build, manage, and analyze your infrastructure model)> ![icon] (Create conceptual design features)> ![icon] (Pipeline Connectors). The Select Draw Style asset card displays.
2. In the Select Draw Style asset card, select a pipeline connector style, as shown in Figure 4–27.

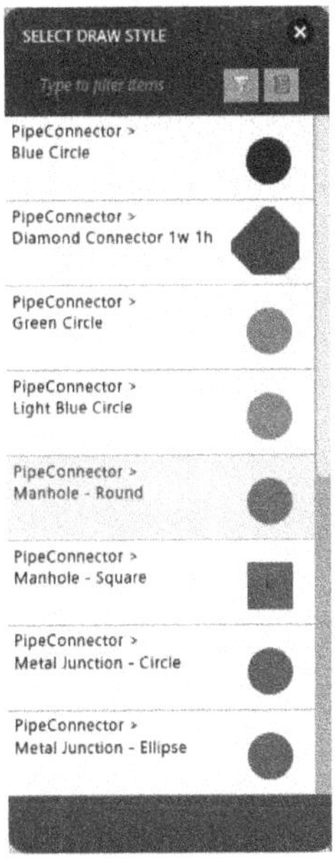

Figure 4–27

3. Double-click in the model to place the Pipeline Connector. Each pipeline connector is added separately as required.

Create Pipelines

Pipelines represent various utility lines (e.g., gas, water, sanitary sewer, storm sewer, etc.). Pipelines can connect to pipeline connectors or other pipe ends.

How To: Create Pipelines

1. In the In Canvas tools, click ![icon] (Build, manage, and analyze your infrastructure model)> ![icon] (Create conceptual design features)> ![icon] (Pipelines).
2. In the Select Draw Style asset card, select the required pipeline style, as shown in Figure 4–28.

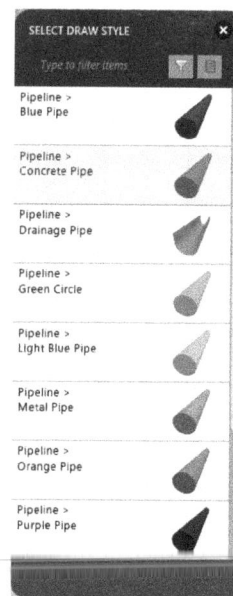

Figure 4–28

If you click in the model near a pipeline connector, the pipeline automatically snaps to the connector

3. Click in the model to place the first pipe end.
4. Move the cursor in the direction in which you want the pipeline to run. Type a distance for the pipe length and press <Enter> to set the distance. Click in the model to place a pipe bend.
5. Continue clicking in the model to place pipe bends until all of the lengths of pipe have been created for the Pipeline.
6. Double-click to place the last pipe segment and end the command.

© 2017, ASCENT - Center for Technical Knowledge®

Edit Pipelines

Pipelines are created as 2D features that drape on the terrain surface. However, in the real world, most pipes are buried below the ground. Therefore, once you lay out the horizontal location of pipelines, you must adjust the vertical layout by adding a negative value in the *Elevation Offset* field in the Pipeline asset card (as shown in Figure 4–29) or by using 🔺 (Elevation Gizmo) in the model.

Figure 4–29

Note: After a pipeline elevation has been adjusted below a surface, the pipeline gizmos continue to drape on the terrain surface, as shown in Figure 4–30.

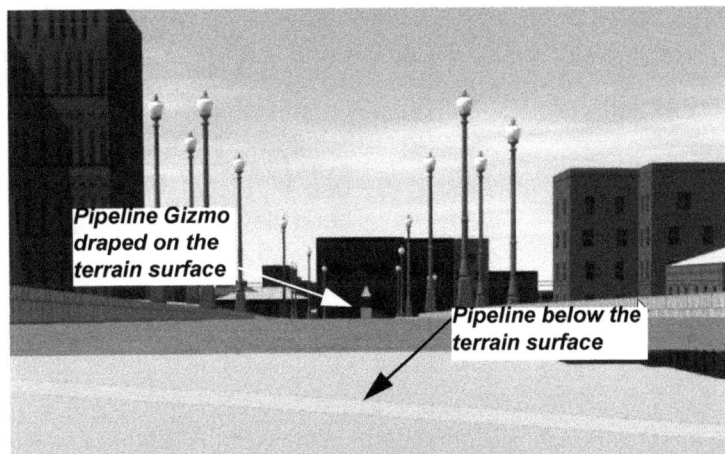

Figure 4–30

How To: Adjust the Pipeline Elevations

1. Select the Pipeline in the model and orbit the view to a side view. The pipes lie on the road surface, and a box displays indicating the orthogonal directions (also known as level lines), as shown in Figure 4–31.

Level Line

Figure 4–31

2. In the asset card, type a negative value in the *Elevation Offset* field (as shown in Figure 4–32) to place the pipes below ground.

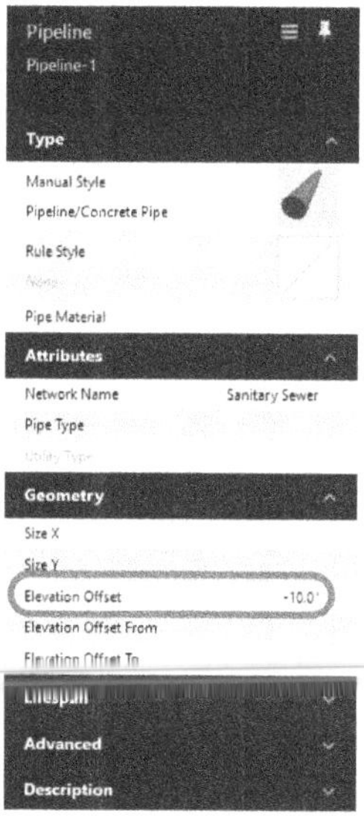

Figure 4–32

3. Use 🔴 (Elevation Gizmo) to make changes to individual pipe bend elevations.

© 2017, ASCENT - Center for Technical Knowledge®

Practice 4c

Estimated time for completion: 20 minutes

Create Utilities in the Model

Practice Objective

- Create a sanitary sewer in the model to illustrate the design concept.

In this practice you will create manholes and connect them with a pipeline that will act as a sanitary sewer for the project.

Task 1 - Create manholes.

1. In the Home Screen, click **Open**.

2. In the *C:\InfraWorks Fundamentals Practice Files\Create* folder, select **CreateFeatures.sqlite** and click **Open**.

3. In the Utility Bar, expand *Switch Active Proposal* and select **C_Task1**.

4. In the Utility Bar, click ⬛ (Bookmark your current location) and select **Church**.

5. In the In Canvas tools, click 🔨 (Build, manage, and analyze your infrastructure model)> ✏️ (Create conceptual design features)> 🔧 (Pipeline Connectors).

6. In the Select Draw Style asset card, select the **Manhole-Round** style, as shown in Figure 4–33.

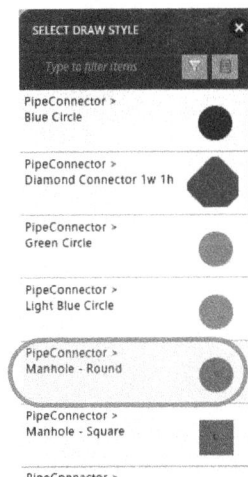

Figure 4–33

7. Double-click near the centerline of the road in line with the edge of the parking lot (as shown in Figure 4–34) to place the first Pipeline Connector (Point 1).

Figure 4–34

8. Pan the model and double-click to place a pipeline connector at each intersection, as shown in Figure 4–35. You will place seven pipeline connectors in total.

Figure 4–35

Task 2 - Create the pipeline to connect the manholes.

1. In the Utility Bar, click ▣ (Bookmark your current location) and select **Church**. Expand *Switch Active Proposal* and then select **C_Task2**.

© 2017, ASCENT - Center for Technical Knowledge®

2. In the In Canvas tools, click ▮ (Build, manage, and analyze your infrastructure model)> ✎ (Create conceptual design features)> ⬯ (Pipelines). The Select Draw Style asset card displays.

3. In the Select Draw Style asset card, select the **Concrete Pipe** pipeline style, as shown in Figure 4–36.

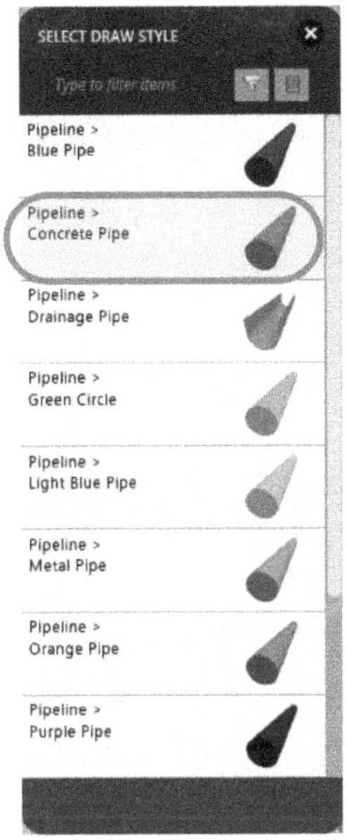

Figure 4–36

4. Click near the Point 1 Pipeline Connector to connect the Pipe.

5. Pan the model to the right and click in each intersection to connect the pipe to the pipeline connector located at each intersection, as shown in Figure 4–37. Double-click when you connect the pipeline to Point 7 to end the command.

Figure 4–37

6. Press <Esc> to show the pipe gizmos, and then orbit the view to a side view. The pipes lie on the road surface, and a box displays indicating the orthogonal directions (also known as level lines), as shown in Figure 4–38.

Figure 4–38

7. In the Pipeline asset card, for the *Network Name,* type **Storm**. In the *Elevation Offset* field, type **-10** (as shown in Figure 4–39) to place the pipes below ground.

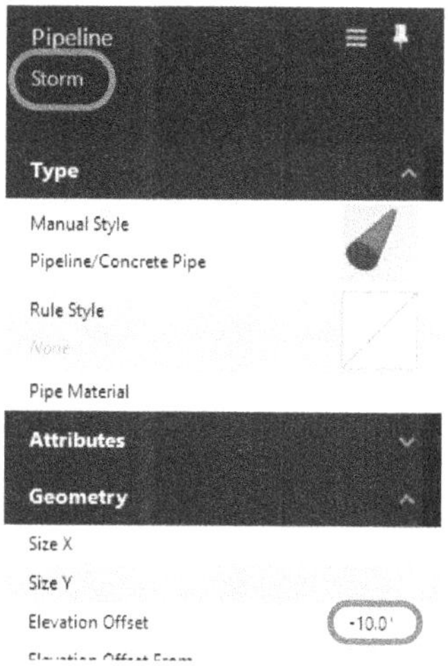

Figure 4-39

8. In the Utility Bar, expand the View Style drop-down and click ⚙ (Configure current view).

9. In the View Settings asset card, click 🔧 (Change navigation and application feedback settings) to open the *Interaction* stack.

10. Under *Navigation*, click the **Lock Mouse Above Ground** slider to the left to toggle it off.

11. Orbit the model to display the pipes below ground.

12. Press <Esc> to clear the selection of the Pipeline.

Although the pipes are below the ground, the gizmos remain draped on the terrain surface.

© 2017, ASCENT - Center for Technical Knowledge®

4.5 Create Railways in a Model

Many cities are searching for cost-effective, environmentally sensitive, and socially responsible ways to provide public transportation systems. At the same time, freight trains are still used for transporting goods from one location to another. Both freight and commuter rail projects can be modeled in the Autodesk InfraWorks software.

Create Railways

It does not matter if you are creating a freight railway line or a commuter railway line. Both use the same command. The style for a railway determines how the railway tracks and the ground below and adjacent to the tracks display in the model. By default a dirt and grass look is provided, as shown in Figure 4–40. Additional styles can be created using the Railway material group provided with the software.

Figure 4–40

Regardless of the style that is used, the railway and road are automatically cleaned up where they intersect. This ensures that the rails display flush with the road surface, as they would in the real world. An example is shown in Figure 4–41.

Figure 4–41

How To: Create Railways

1. In the In Canvas tools, click (Build, manage, and analyze your infrastructure model)> (Create conceptual design features)> (Railways).

2. In the Select Draw Style asset card, select the railway style, as shown in Figure 4–42.

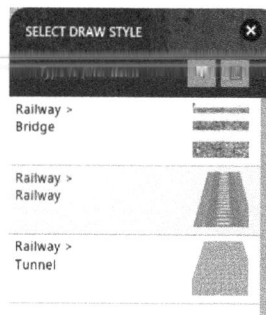

Figure 4–42

3. Click in the location at which you want the railway to start.
4. Move the cursor in the direction in which you want the railway to run. Type a distance for the length to the next point of intersection and press <Enter> to set the distance. Click in the model to place the point of intersection.

© 2017, ASCENT - Center for Technical Knowledge®

5. Continue clicking in the model to place points of intersection until all of the lengths of rail have been created for the railway.

6. Double-click to place the last railway point and end the command.

Edit Railways

Once a railway has been created, it can be re-shaped using

🟦 (Control Point Gizmo), which displays at each Point of Intersection (PI) when the railway is selected in the model. If you

orbit the model more than 45 degrees, 🔶 (Elevation Gizmo) displays and can be used to adjust the elevation of each PI.

Additional vertices can be added anywhere along the railway to add additional control and elevation points. To add a vertex, select the railway, right-click in the location to which you want the additional control, and select **Add Vertex**, as shown in Figure 4–43.

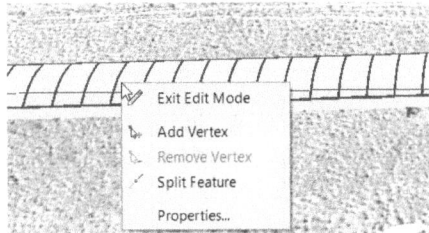

Figure 4–43

Similar to conceptual roads, conceptual railways must be split where bridges are required, and then the style must be changed where a section of the railway goes over a bridge. This can be accomplished by dragging the Railway>Bridge style from the Style palette, or by using the manual style field in the Railway asset card, as shown in Figure 4–44.

Figure 4–44

Practice 4d

Create a Passenger Railway in the Model

Practice Objective

- Create a passenger railway in the model.

Estimated time for completion: 15 minutes

In this practice you will create a light rail system for commuter passengers that provides transportation options for the new community.

Task 1 - Create a railway.

1. In the Home Screen, click ⌷ (Open).

2. In the *C:\InfraWorks Fundamentals Practice Files\Create* folder, select **CreateFeatures.sqlite** and click **Open**.

3. In the Utility Bar, expand the *Switch Active Proposal* and select **D_Task1**.

4. In the Utility Bar, click ⌷ (Bookmark your current location) and select **Railway**.

5. In the In Canvas tools, click ⌷ (Build, manage, and analyze your infrastructure model)> ⌷ (Create conceptual design features)> ⌷ (Railways).

6. In the Select Draw Style asset card, select the **Railway** style, as shown in Figure 4–45.

Figure 4–45

© 2017, ASCENT - Center for Technical Knowledge®

7. In the model, click points on the west side of Redwood Road to place the railway, similar to that shown in Figure 4–46.

Figure 4–46

8. Double-click north of the road that runs into the new neighborhood to place the last point and end the command.

9. In the Utility Bar, click ▥ (Bookmark your current location) and select **RailCrossing**.

    Note that the intersection at the road automatically adjusted where the railway crosses the road (the road elevation was modified).

4.6 Create Water Features in a Model

When designing a new community, water features are often required. Water features have a number of purposes. They can act as a water retention area that is used by local residents for drinking water, such as a reservoir. They can also be used to divert excess water away from homes and businesses to avoid flooding. This is often required when new hard surfaces prevent water from being absorbed into the ground, as it did before the land was developed. Finally, water areas can be used to provide recreation and make an area more visually appealing.

Water areas are a surface layer in the Model Explorer. You can create the following two types of water features:

- **Water Areas:** Enables you to create bodies of water, such as ponds, lakes, and wetlands. To create a body of water, you click points that act as a boundary for the water area. Figure 4–47 shows a small pond water area.

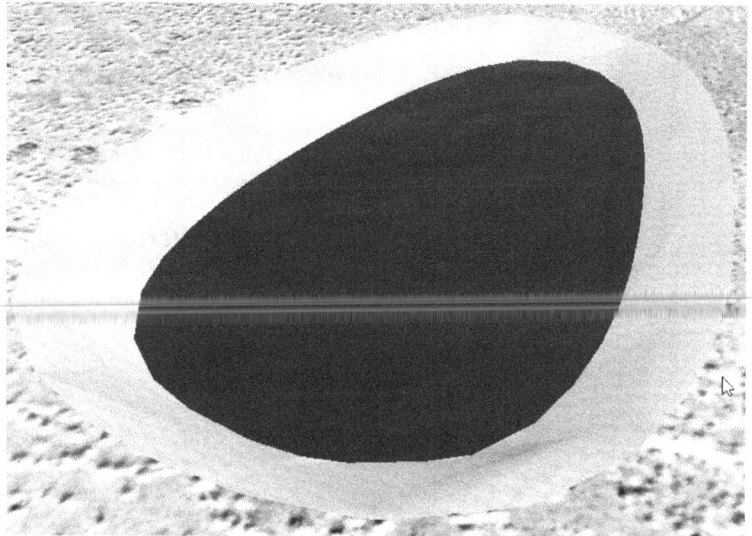

Figure 4–47

- **Rivers:** Enables you to create linear water features, such as canals, rivers, and streams. To create a river, you click points along a linear path. A buffer surrounds the water on either side. The buffer width is set in the Water asset card, as shown in Figure 4–48.

© 2017, ASCENT - Center for Technical Knowledge®

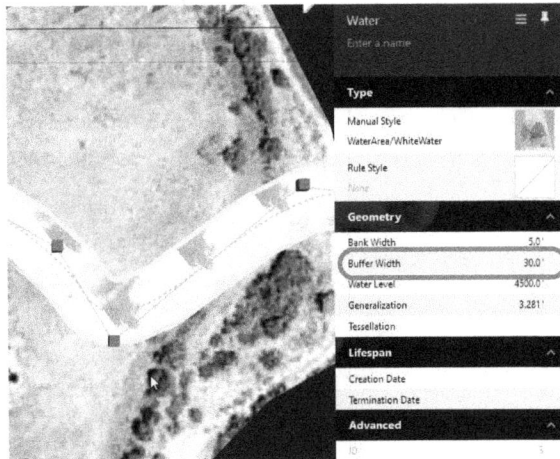

Figure 4–48

How To: Create Rivers or Streams

1. In the In Canvas tools, click (Build, manage, and analyze your infrastructure model)> (Create conceptual design features)> (Rivers).

2. In the Select Draw Style asset card, select the required water style, as shown in Figure 4–49.

Figure 4–49

3. Click in the model to define the start location of the linear path for the water area.

4. Move the cursor in the direction in which you want the river or steam to run. Type a distance for the length to the next point of intersection (PI) and press <Enter> to set the distance. Click in the model to place the PI.

5. Continue clicking PIs until all of the lengths of the river or stream have been created for the water area.

6. Double-click to place the last point and end the command.

7. With the water area selected, in the Water asset card, do the following, as shown in Figure 4–50:
   - Set the required *Bank Width*.
   - Set the required *Buffer Width*.
   - Set the required *Water Level*.

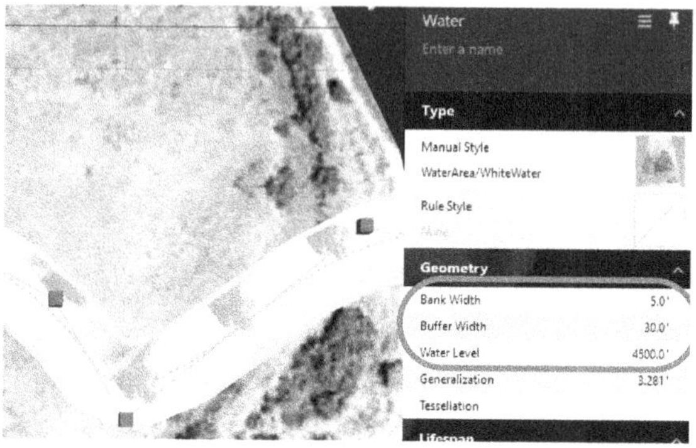

Figure 4–50

How To: Create Lakes or Ponds

1. In the In Canvas tools, click (Build, manage, and analyze your infrastructure model)> (Create conceptual design features)> (Water Areas).
2. In the Select Draw Style asset card, select the required water style, as shown in Figure 4–51.

Figure 4–51

3. Click in the model to start the creation of the water boundary.
4. Move the cursor in the direction that you want the water boundary to follow. Type a distance for the length to the next point on the boundary and press <Enter> to set the distance. Click in the model to place the boundary point.
5. Continue clicking in the model until all of the boundary points have been created for the water area.
6. Double-click to place the last boundary point and end the command.

© 2017, ASCENT - Center for Technical Knowledge®

Practice 4e

Estimated time for completion: 20 minutes

Create Water Features in the Model

Practice Objective

- Create water features in the model to represent a retention pond.

In this practice you will create a water area that represents a water retention pond for the new subdivision and a new white water park.

Task 1 - Create water areas.

1. In the Home Screen, click **Open**.

2. In the *C:\InfraWorks Fundamentals Practice Files\Create* folder, select **CreateFeatures.sqlite** and click **Open**.

3. In the Utility Bar, expand *Switch Active Proposal* and select **E_Task1**.

4. In Utility Bar, click (Bookmark your current location) and select **Pond**.

5. In the In Canvas tools, click (Build, manage, and analyze your infrastructure model)> (Create conceptual design features)> (Water Areas).

6. In the Select Draw Style asset card, select **Splined Water**, as shown in Figure 4–52.

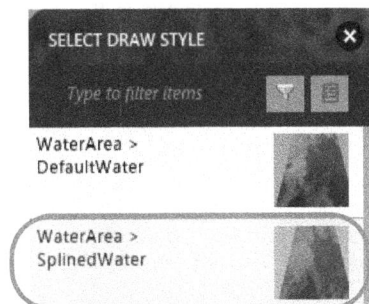

Figure 4–52

7. Click near the entrance to the new neighborhood to start the boundary, as shown in Figure 4–53. Ensure that you leave room for the new railway to be expanded in the future.

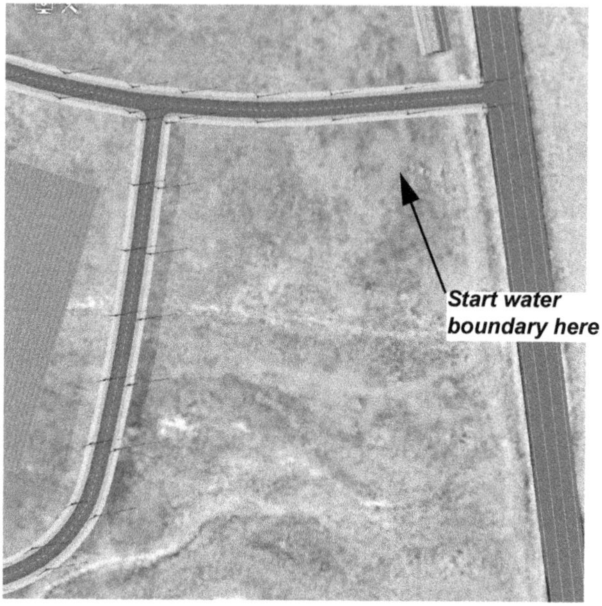

Start water boundary here

Figure 4–53

8. In the model, move the cursor to the west. Type **50** for the length to the next point on the boundary and press <Enter> to set the distance. Click in the model to place the boundary point.

9. Move the cursor to the south parallel to the road. Type **150** for the length to the next point on the boundary and press <Enter> to set the distance. Click in the model to place the boundary point.

10. Move the cursor to the east. Type **100** for the length to the next point on the boundary and press <Enter> to set the distance. Double-click to place the last boundary point and end the command, as shown in Figure 4–54.

© 2017, ASCENT - Center for Technical Knowledge®

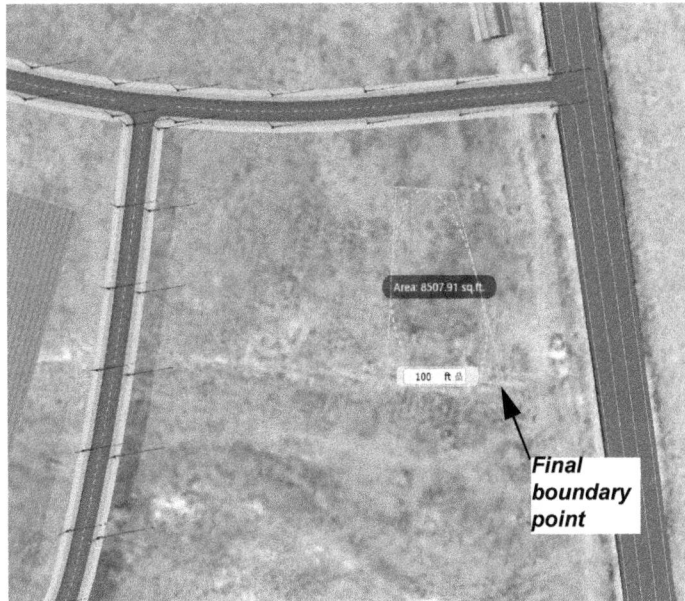

Figure 4–54

11. Press <Esc> twice to clear the selection of the new water area.

Task 2 - Create a river.

The developer on the project is proposing that a white water park be created to attract active people to the community. For practice, you will create a new material style, and then add it to a new water style. You will then use the new water style to create a river to the east of Redwood Rd and south of the new bridge, as shown in Figure 4–55.

Figure 4–55

1. Continue working in the same model as the previous task.

2. In Utility Bar, click ⬚ (Bookmark your current location) and select **River**. Expand *Switch Active Proposal* and then select **E_Task2**.

3. Open the Style palette and select the *Material* tab.

4. At the bottom of the *Material* tab, click ✛ (Add new style to current catalog above).

5. Use the following parameters to create the new material style, as shown in Figure 4–56:

   • Set the *Type* to **Texture**.
   • Browse for the **WhiteWater.png** (found in *C:\InfraWorks Fundamentals Practice Files\Create*) to use as the texture.
   • Set the sizes to be **100** ft by **100** ft.
   • Click **OK**.
   • Name it **WhiteWater**.

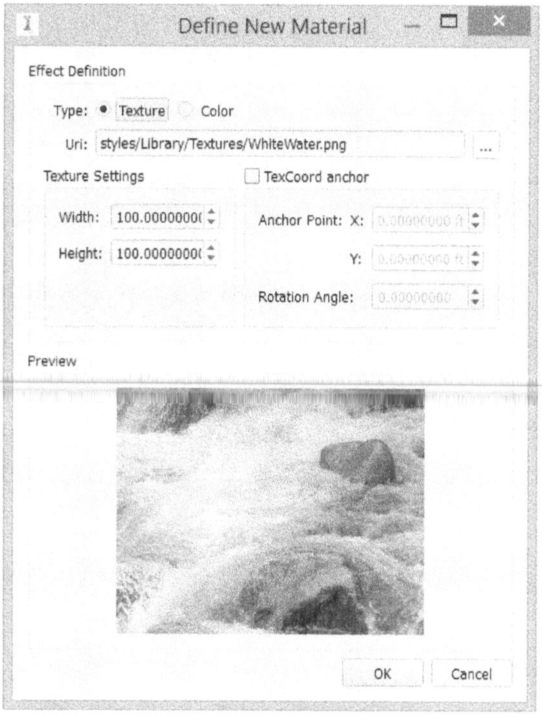

Figure 4–56

6. In the Style palette, select the *Water* tab.

© 2017, ASCENT - Center for Technical Knowledge®

7. Select the **SplinedWater** style, then at the bottom of the *Water* tab, click 🗐 (Make a local copy of the selected style to the current catalog).

8. Name the copied style **WhiteWater**.

9. Double-click on the WhiteWater style. Modify the new style as follows so that it matches Figure 4–57:

   - Set the Bank width to **30 ft**.
   - Set the water level offset to **-5 ft**.
   - Set the Water surface material to **WhiteWater**.
   - Click **OK**.

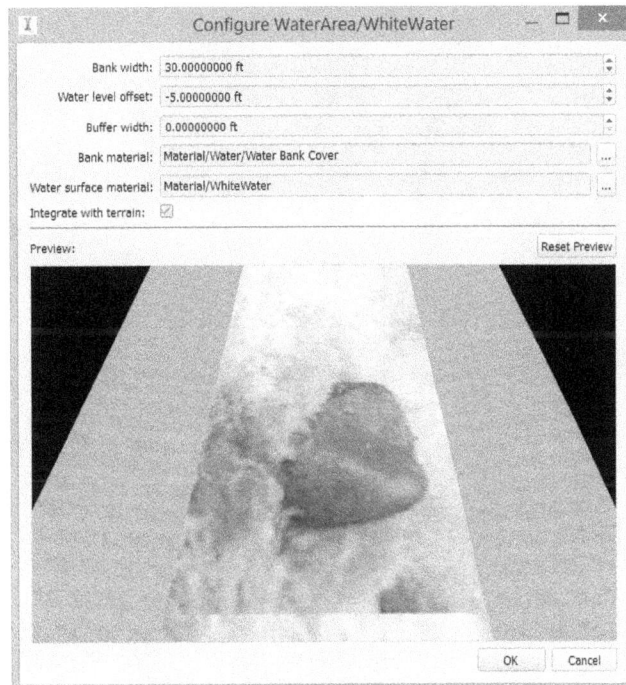

Figure 4–57

10. In the In Canvas tools, click ▮ (Build, manage, and analyze your infrastructure model)> 🖉 (Create conceptual design features)> 🜄 (Rivers).

11. In the Select Draw Style asset card, select **WhiteWater**.

12. Create a river similar to that shown in Figure 4–58.

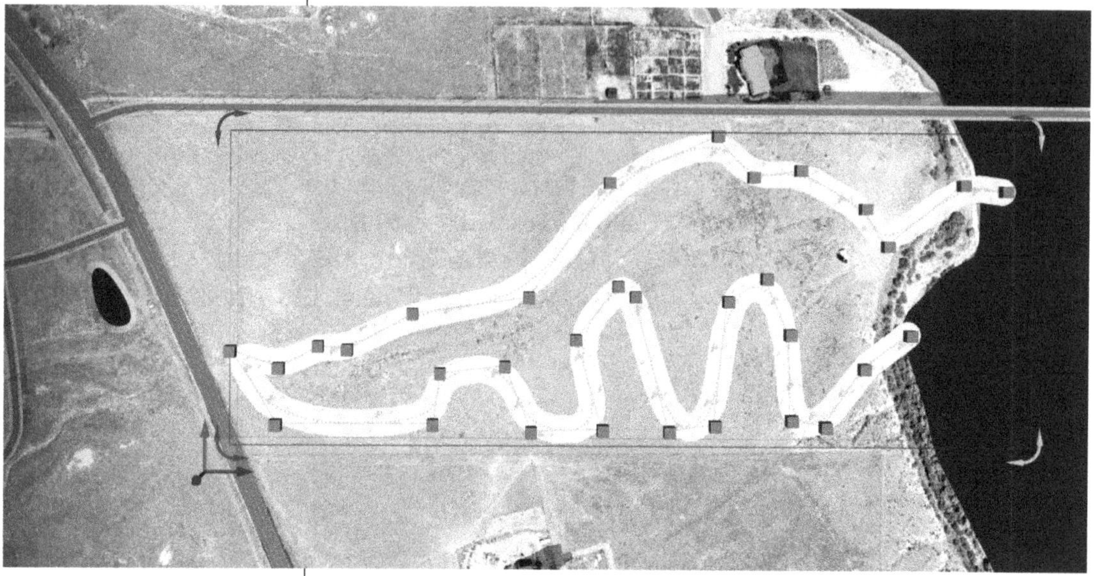

Figure 4–58

13. Press <Esc> to show the river gizmos.

14. In the Water asset card, set the following:
    - *Bank Width* to **5 ft**
    - *Buffer Width* to **30 ft**
    - *Water Level* to **4500 ft**

15. Press <Esc> to release the river selection.

© 2017, ASCENT - Center for Technical Knowledge®

4.7 Create Land Areas (Preview)

Similar to coverages, land areas provide a way for you to grade areas and change how the terrain displays. There are two key differences that land areas provide over coverages:

* The top surface of a land area is automatically flattened, as shown in Figure 4–59. A coverage drapes on the surface until the terrain is manually shaped.

* Land areas enable you to control the display of cut and fill areas separately. Figure 4–59 shows a land area with a 3:1 grass material for the fill and a 1:1 stone wall material for the cut.

Figure 4–59

How To: Create a Land Area

1. In the In Canvas tools, click ![icon] (Build, manage and analyze your infrastructure model) > ![icon] (Create conceptual design features) > ![icon] (Land Areas).

To use this feature, access to the Internet is required.

AUTODESK
INFRAWORKS 360

This style is used for the land area top surface only, not the cut and fill slopes. The cut and fill styles are set later.

2. Select the material style for the top surface you are creating from the Select Draw Style asset card that displays, as shown in Figure 4–60.

Figure 4–60

3. In the model, click to place the vertices of the land area footprint. After the first vertex has been placed, move the cursor in the direction in which you want the next vertex to be placed.

Locking a length means that even if you move the cursor, the dimension value does not change.

4. Type the required length for the side of the land area and press <Enter> to lock the length. Move the cursor as required to set the correct angle and click to place the vertex.
5. Continue adding vertexes in the model until all but the last vertex has been set.
6. Double-click on the location at which you want to place the final vertex. Doing so ends the command.
7. Press <Esc> to clear the selection of the newly created land area.

Hint: Accessing the Land Areas Tool

If the (Land Areas) tool is not available in the In Canvas Tools, toggle on the **Land Areas & Grading Behaviors** option on the Home Screen, as shown in Figure 4–61.

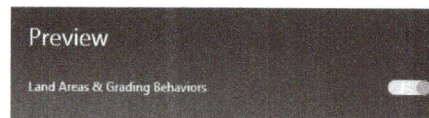

Figure 4–61

© 2017, ASCENT - Center for Technical Knowledge®

Grading Styles

Grading styles control how the cut and fill slopes display. Several grading styles are provided in the Autodesk InfraWorks software (as shown in Figure 4–62) and additional styles can be created as required. The thumbnails in the Style palette display a preview of the materials and slopes that are used in each style. If the cut and fill slopes use the same material, only one material is shown in the thumbnail. If the cut and fill slopes use different materials, both materials display in the thumbnail with their slope values, as shown in Figure 4–63.

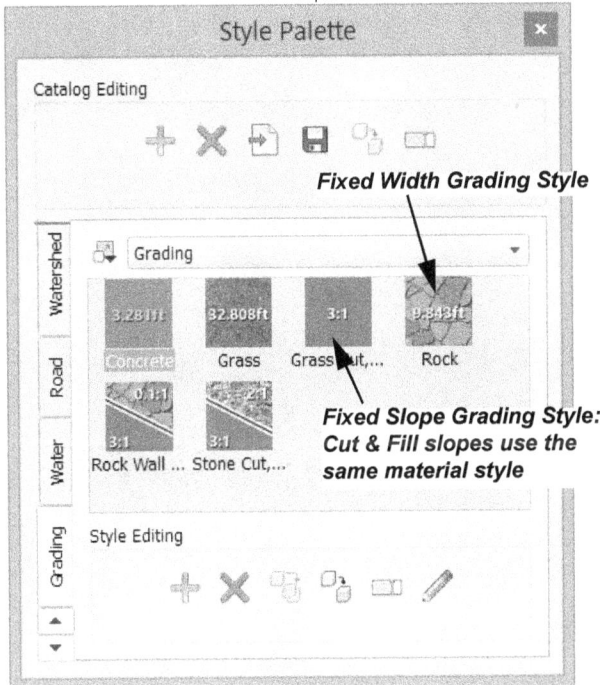

Figure 4–62

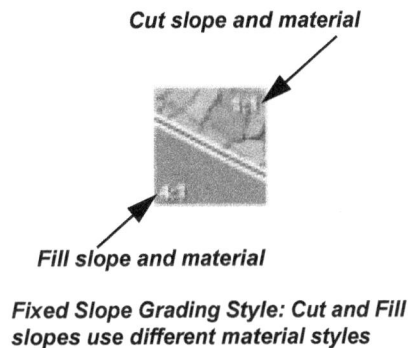

Cut slope and material

Fill slope and material

Fixed Slope Grading Style: Cut and Fill slopes use different material styles

Figure 4–63

How To: Create a New Grading Style

1. Open the Style palette and select the *Grading* tab.
2. In the *Style Editing* area at the bottom of the Style palette,

   click ✛ (Add new style to the current catalog above).
3. In the Define New Grading dialog box, set the *Grading Method* to either **Fixed Width** or **Fixed Slope**.

4. If **Fixed Slope** is selected, set the following options and then click **OK**, as shown in Figure 4–64. Otherwise, continue to the next step.

- Set the *Cut Slope* (Run:Rise)
- Set the *Fill Slope* (Run:Rise)
- If the Cut/Fill Materials use different styles, clear the **Cut and Fill Material use the same Style** checkbox.
- Select the appropriate Cut and Fill Material styles.
- Set the *Grading Limit*, if required. Otherwise, clear the **Set Limit for Grading** checkbox.

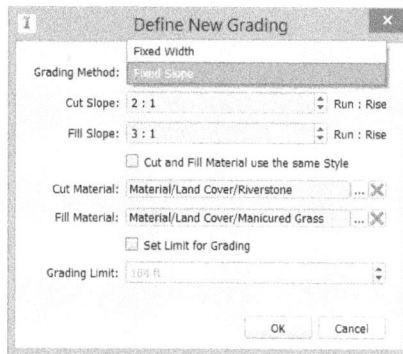

Figure 4–64

5. If **Fixed Width** is selected, set the following options, as shown in Figure 4–65.

- Set the *Grading Width*.
- Select a *Grading Material*.

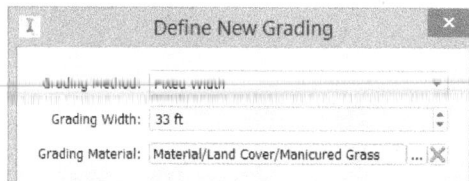

Figure 4–65

6. Click **OK**.

Edit Land Areas

Once a land area has been created, it can be re-shaped using

(Control Point Gizmo). The gizmos display at each vertex when the land area is selected in the model. By default, land area top surfaces are flat with all of the footprint vertices sharing the same elevation. If the model is orbited more than 45

degrees, (Elevation Gizmos) display and can be used to adjust the elevation of each vertex independently.

© 2017, ASCENT - Center for Technical Knowledge®

Vertices can be added anywhere along a side to add additional control and elevation points. To add a vertex, select the land area, right-click on the point at which you want to have additional control, and select **Add Vertex**, as shown in Figure 4–66.

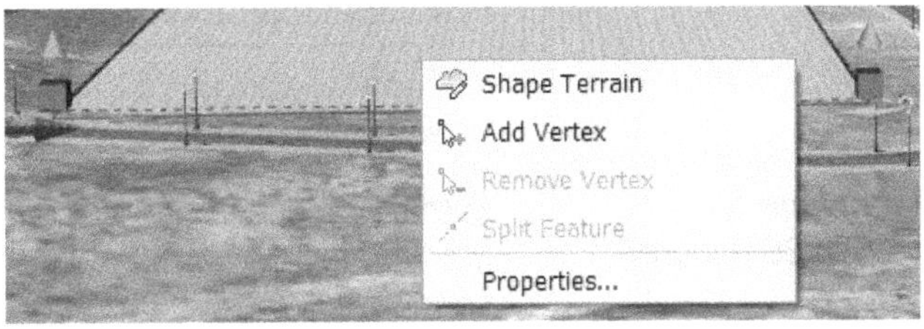

Figure 4–66

Set Cut/Fill Slopes

The graduation of a slope that extends from a land area footprint depends upon the grading style selected for the land area. This value is changed by setting the *Rule Grading* value for the land area.

How To: Apply a Cut/Fill Slopes to a Land Area

1. Create a land area.

2. On the Utility Bar, click ▣ (Edit).

3. With the land area still selected, in the Land Areas asset card, change the *Rule Grading* style, as shown in Figure 4–67.

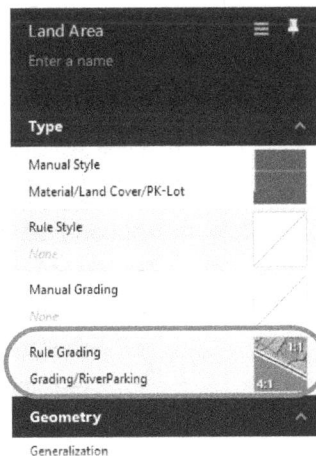

Figure 4–67

Practice 4f

Estimated time for completion: 20 minutes

Grade a Parking Lot Using a Land Area (Preview)

Practice Objective

- Create land areas in the model to represent a parking lot and surrounding grass.

In this practice you will use land areas to create a parking lot for the white water park, setting the cut and fill slope displays separately. You will then add another land area with a gradual slope covered in grass for the patrons to access the river.

Task 1 - Create a new grading style.

In this task, you will create a new grading style which uses river stone for the cut and grass for the fill of the proposed parking lot.

1. In the Home Screen, click **Open**.

2. In the *C:\InfraWorks Fundamentals Practice Files\Create* folder, select **CreateFeatures.sqlite** and then click **Open**.

3. In the Utility Bar, expand *Switch Active Proposal* and select **F_Task1**.

4. In Utility Bar, click ▣ (Bookmark your current location) and select **River**.

5. Open the Style palette and select the *Grading* tab.

6. In the *Style Editing* area at the bottom of the Style palette, click ➕ (Add new style to the current catalog above).

7. In the Define New Grading dialog box, set the following options, as shown in Figure 4–68:
   - *Grading Method:* **Fixed Slope**.
   - *Cut Slope:* **1:1**
   - *Fill Slope:* **4:1**
   - Clear the **Cut and Fill Material use the same Style** checkbox.
   - *Cut Material:* Select **Material>Land Cover>Riverstone**.
   - Fill Material: Select **Material>Land Cover>Manicured Grass**.
   - Clear the **Set Grading Limit** checkbox.
   - Click **OK**.

© 2017, ASCENT - Center for Technical Knowledge®

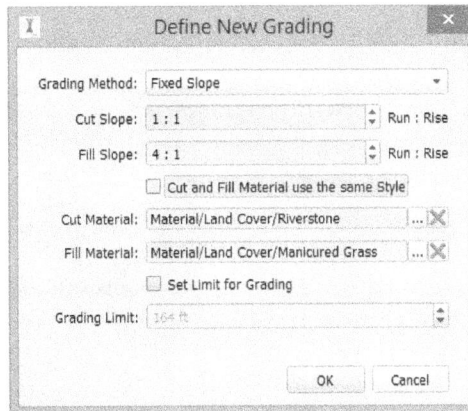

Figure 4–68

8. Type **RiverParking** for the name.

Task 2 - Create a parking lot and grass area for park patrons.

In this task, you will create a parking lot for the white water park patrons and a grass area which provides a more gradual slope to the river on the south side.

1. Continue working in the same model as the last task. If you did not complete the last task, in the Utility Bar, expand *Switch Active Proposal* and select **F_Task2**.

If the Land Areas tool is unavailable, you might need to toggle on the Preview of Land Areas & Grading Behaviors in the Home Screen.

2. In the In Canvas tools, click (Build, manage and analyze your infrastructure model) > (Create conceptual design features) > (Land Areas).

3. In the Select Draw Style asset card that displays, type PK and select **PK-Lot**, as shown in Figure 4–69.

This style is used for the land area top surface only, not the cut and fill slopes. The cut and fill styles are set later.

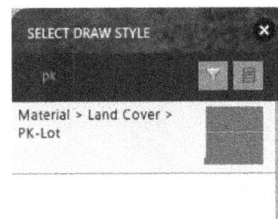

Figure 4–69

4. In the model, click to place the first vertex of the land area footprint, as shown in Figure 4–70.

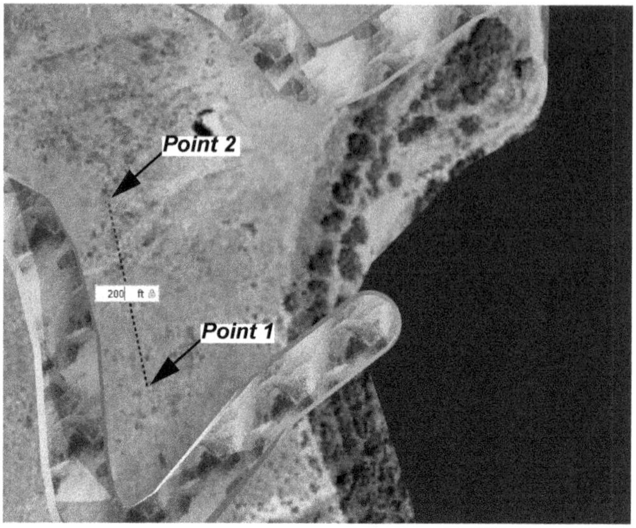

Figure 4–70

5. Move the cursor in the Northwest direction, type **200**, and then press <Enter> to lock in the distance. Click to place the second vertex, as shown in Figure 4–70.

6. Move the cursor in the Northeast direction, type **100**, and then press <Enter> to lock in the distance. Click to place the third vertex, as shown in Figure 4–71.

7. Move the cursor in the Southeast direction, type **200**, and then press <Enter> to lock in the distance. Double-click to place the final vertex and end the command, as shown in Figure 4–71.

Figure 4–71

© 2017, ASCENT - Center for Technical Knowledge®

8. Restart the **Land Area** command.

9. Select **ManacuredGrass** for the style.

10. Set the points for the vertices, as shown in Figure 4–72.

Ensure that you double-click the last point to end the command.

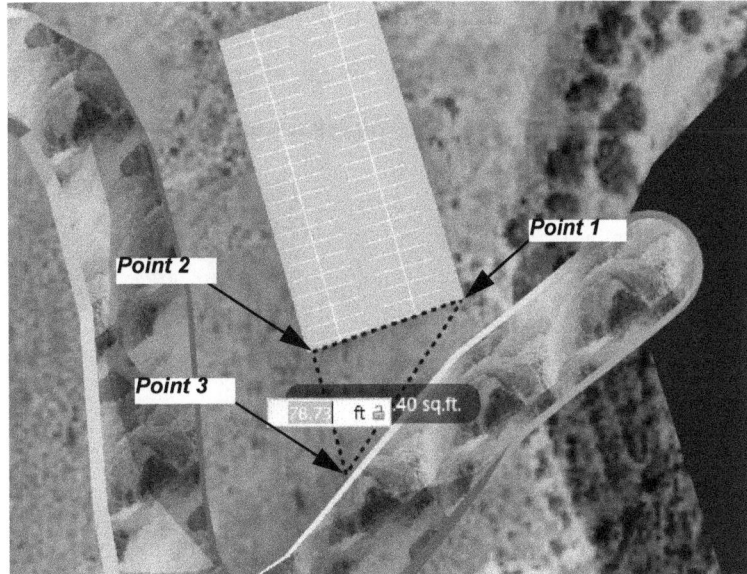

Figure 4–72

11. Press <Esc> twice to end the command.

12. Select the Parking lot land area.

13. In the Land Area asset card, change the *Rule Grading* style to the new **RiverParking** grading style, as shown in Figure 4–73.

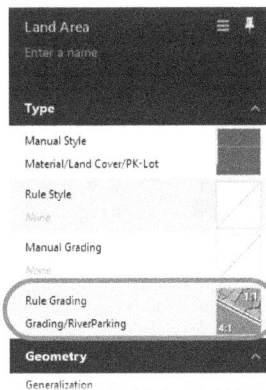

Figure 4–73

14. Press <Esc> to clear the selection of the parking lot land area.

15. Select the grass land area to the south of the parking lot.

16. In the Land Areas asset card, change the **Rule Grading** style to the **GrassCut, Fill** grading style.

17. Press <Esc> to clear the selection of the grass land area.

The results are shown in Figure 4–74.

Figure 4–74

© 2017, ASCENT - Center for Technical Knowledge®

Chapter Review Questions

1. Which selection tool would you use to select multiple model elements completely inside a specified area?

   a. (Window Select)

   b. (Rectangle Select)

   c. (Polygon Select)

2. Which of the following gizmos would not change the height or elevation of a model element?

   a. (Elevation Gizmo)

   b. (Height Gizmo)

   c. (Control Gizmo)

   d. (Move Gizmo)

3. How do you change the elevation of a road at a point at which a point of intersection does not exist?

   a. Select the road, right-click and select **Add Vertex**. Use (Elevation Gizmo) to adjust the elevation.

   b. Select the road, right-click and select **Add Vertex**. Use (Control Gizmo) to adjust the elevation.

   c. Select the road, right-click and select **Split Feature**. Use (Elevation Gizmo) to adjust the elevation.

   d. You cannot adjust the elevation of roads.

4. How do you change the appearance or elevation of a terrain surface?

   a. Apply a different terrain style to it to change the appearance and right-click to add elevation points.

   b. Create a coverage or land area and adjust the elevations at each vertex along the boundary of the coverage.

   c. You cannot change the appearance or elevation of surfaces.

   d. Import a new surface from external data sources.

5. Where are pipeline gizmos located?

   a. At the end of each pipe length, draped on the terrain surface.

   b. At the end of each pipe length and at the elevation of the pipe ends.

   c. Only at the beginning and end of the entire pipe network, draped on the terrain surface.

   d. Only at the beginning and end of the entire pipe network and at the elevation of the pipe ends.

6. To make a railway flush with a road (as shown in Figure 4–75) you must split the railway into multiple segments and apply different styles at the road intersection.

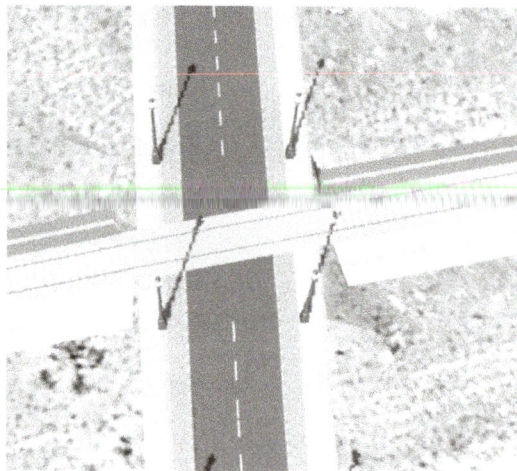

Figure 4–75

   a. True

   b. False

© 2017, ASCENT - Center for Technical Knowledge®

7. How do you set the width of a river?

    a. Create a polyline area manually that sets where each bank ends.

    b. Select the river and change the buffer width in the Water Area asset card.

    c. After creating the centerline of the river, click a point to set the width.

    d. The width cannot be changed.

8. How are Land Areas different than Coverages? (Select all that apply.)

    a. Land Area top surfaces start out flat while coverages drape on the terrain surface.

    b. Land Areas are used to create piles of rock and dirt.

    c. Land Areas enable you to control the cut slope separate from the fill slope.

    d. There are no differences between land areas and coverages.

Command Summary

Button	Command	Location
N/A	Copy	• **Shortcut Key:** <Ctrl>+<C>
	Coverages	• **In Canvas Tools:** Build, manage, and analyze your industry model > Create conceptual design features
N/A	Cut	• **Shortcut Key:** <Ctrl>+<X>
N/A	De-select	• **Shortcut Key:** <Esc>
N/A	Delete	• **Shortcut Key:** <Delete>
N/A	Invert Selection	• **Shortcut Key**: <Alt>+<I>
	Land Areas	• **In Canvas Tools:** Build, manage, and analyze your industry model > Create conceptual design features
N/A	Paste	• **Shortcut Key:** <Ctrl>+<V>
N/A	Paste In Place	• **Shortcut Key:** <Shift>+<Ctrl>+<V>
	Pipeline Connectors	• **In Canvas Tools:** Build, manage, and analyze your industry model > Create conceptual design features
	Pipelines	• **In Canvas Tools:** Build, manage, and analyze your industry model > Create conceptual design features
	Railways	• **In Canvas Tools:** Build, manage, and analyze your industry model > Create conceptual design features
	Redo	• **Utility Bar** • **Shortcut Key:** <Ctrl>+<Y>
	Rivers	• **In Canvas Tools:** Build, manage, and analyze your industry model > Create conceptual design features
	Roads	• **In Canvas Tools:** Build, manage, and analyze your industry model > Create conceptual design features
N/A	Select All	• **Shortcut Key:** <Ctrl>+<A>
	Undo	• **Utility Bar** • **Shortcut Key:** <Ctrl>+<Z>
	Water Areas	• **In Canvas Tools:** Build, manage, and analyze your industry model > Create conceptual design features
N/A	Zoom Selected	• **Shortcut Key:** <Alt>+<Z>

© 2017, ASCENT - Center for Technical Knowledge®

Add Model Details

Using conceptual design tools, you can add additional details to a model, including buildings, landscaping, city furniture, and points of interest. In this chapter you learn how to add many of these model elements and how to edit the elements once they have been created.

Learning Objectives in this Chapter

- Create buildings in a model using the draw tools.
- Add predefined 3D buildings to a model.
- Create city furniture to add bike racks and other 3D models to a model.
- Add landscaping details to a model using trees and other vegetation.
- Create barriers to add fences and traffic control to a model.
- Draw attention to specific points in a model using points of interest markers.

5.1 Create Buildings in a Model

Custom buildings can be added to a model to add additional detail to the design. When creating a custom building, the look of the outside of the building is defined using a Facade style in the Select Draw Style asset card, as shown in Figure 5–1.

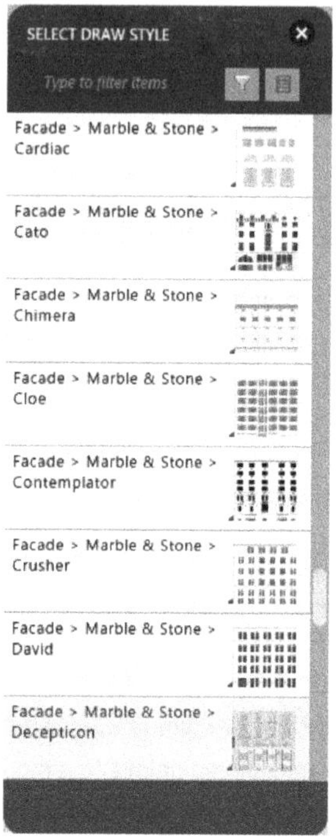

Figure 5–1

How To: Create Custom Buildings

1. In the In Canvas tools, click ![icon] (Build, manage, and analyze your infrastructure model)> ![icon] (Create conceptual design features)> ![icon] (Buildings).
2. The Select Draw Style asset card opens, as shown in Figure 5–2. Select the style for the exterior of the building.

© 2017, ASCENT - Center for Technical Knowledge®

Note that the asset card
has the option to filter by
building material types,
such as bricks, marble,
concrete, etc.

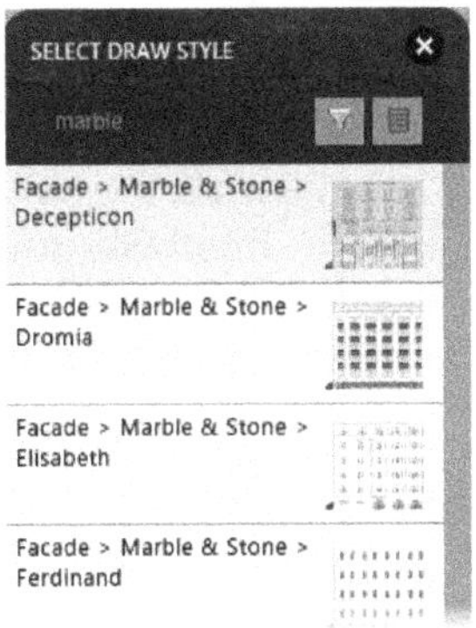

Figure 5–2

3. In the model, click to place the first corner of the building footprint.

4. After the first corner has been placed, move the cursor to where you want the next corner to be placed. The dimensions for that side of the building display as shown in Figure 5–3.

Figure 5–3

5. Type the required length for that side of the building and press <Enter> to lock the length. Move the cursor as required to set the correct angle and click to place the corner.
6. Repeat Steps 4 to 5 until all but the last corner have been set.
7. Double-click on the location at which you want to place the final corner to end the command.
8. Press <Esc> to clear the selection of the newly created building.

If you start drawing a
building and enter a
distance for the first side
(for example 100') and
then hold <Shift> you
can snap to a right
angle.

Edit Buildings

Once a building has been created, the height should be adjusted by using the Building asset card, or by using 🏛 (Height Gizmo) while the building is selected. Clicking and dragging 📛 (Control Point Gizmo) enables you to reshape the building footprint.

Hint: Changing Building Attributes

The roof material, slope, height, and other attributes can be set in the Building asset card, as shown in Figure 5–4.

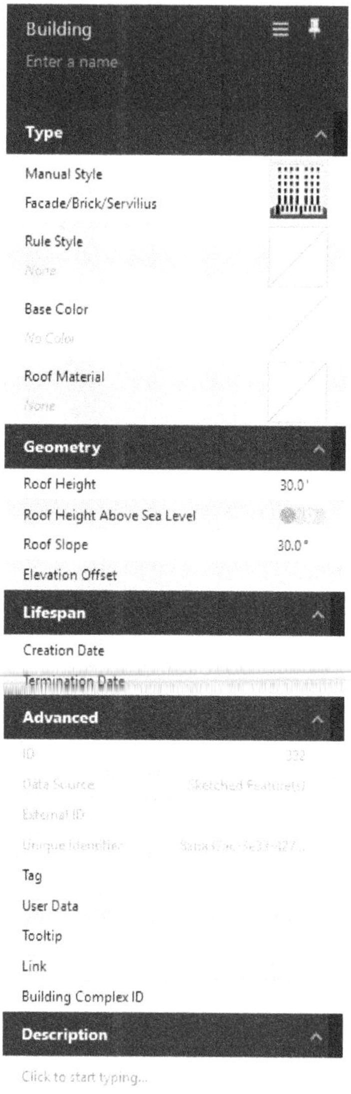

Figure 5–4

© 2017, ASCENT - Center for Technical Knowledge®

Practice 5a

Create Buildings in the Model

Practice Objective

- Create buildings in the model.

Estimated time for completion: 15 minutes

In this practice you will create buildings using exact measurements to populate the new subdivision.

Task 1 - Create a building using specific measurements.

1. In the Home Screen, click **Open**.

2. In the *C:\InfraWorks Fundamentals Practice Files\AddDetails* folder, select **CreateDetails.sqlite** and click **Open**.

3. Set the proposal to **A_Task1** in the Utility Bar.

4. In the Utility Bar, click ▣ (Bookmark your current location) and select **AddHomes**.

5. In the In Canvas tools, click ▣ (Build, manage, and analyze your infrastructure model)> ✎ (Create conceptual design features)> ▣ (Buildings)

6. In the Select Draw Style asset card, type **Brick** in the filter field. Then select **Servillius**.

7. In the model, click to place the first corner of the building footprint, as shown in Figure 5–5.

First point of building

Figure 5–5

8. After the first corner has been placed, move the cursor due east and type **40** for the length of the first side, as shown in Figure 5–6. Click to place the second corner.

Figure 5–6

9. In the model, move the cursor due south, type **40** for the length of the second side, and then press <Enter>. Hold <Shift> to snap to a right angle and click to place the third corner.

10. Move the cursor due west, type **30** for the length, and then press <Enter>. Hold <Shift> to snap to a right angle and click to place the fourth corner.

11. Move the cursor due north, type **15** for the length, and then press <Enter>. Hold <Shift> to snap to a right angle and click to place the fifth corner.

12. Move the cursor due west, type **10** for the length, and then press <Enter>. Hold <Shift> to snap to a right angle and double-click to place the sixth corner and end the command.

© 2017, ASCENT - Center for Technical Knowledge®

13. Press <Esc> twice to clear the selection of the newly created building. The last corner lines up with the first corner, as shown in Figure 5–7.

Figure 5–7

14. Create a similar building to the south of the one you just created. Use measurements that are close to those shown in Figure 5–8.

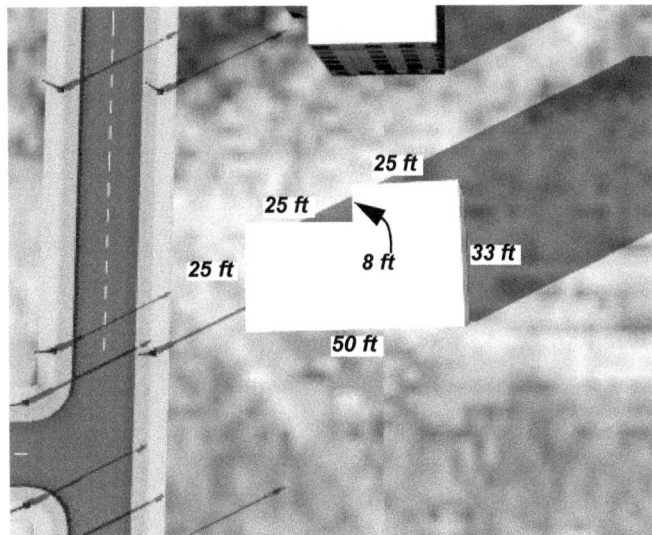

Figure 5–8

15. Press <Esc> to show the second building's gizmos. Hold <Ctrl> and click on the first build to select it as well.

16. In the Building asset card, set the *Roof Height* and *Roof Slope* to **30**, as shown in Figure 5–9. Both buildings should update.

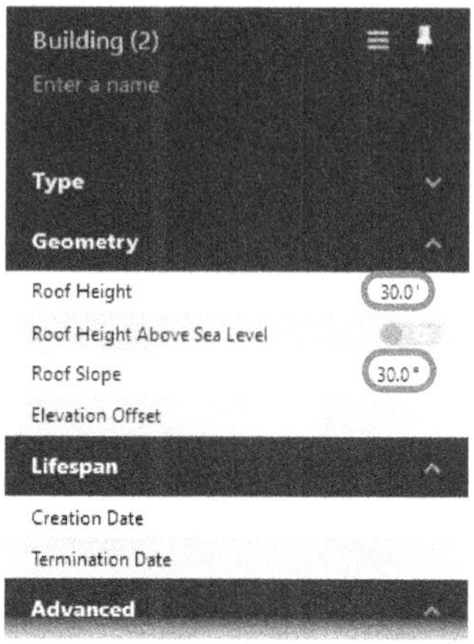

Figure 5–9

17. Press <Esc> to clear the selection.

© 2017, ASCENT - Center for Technical Knowledge®

5.2 Create City Furniture in a Model

If you need to create multiple predefined 3D buildings or other 3D models in your model, it is recommended that you use

(City Furniture). This command enables you to create multiple 3D models spaced along a path or a single feature at the location specified. Any type of 3D model style can be selected as city furniture, including trees and railway models. However, these models display in the *Furniture* category in the Model Explorer and are furniture features in the database.

The following 3D models can be added as city furniture to a model:

- **Bridge Components:** There several 3d models of various barriers and other components you would find on a bridge. Figure 5–10 shows a list of what is available in the software out of the box. Others can be added as required.

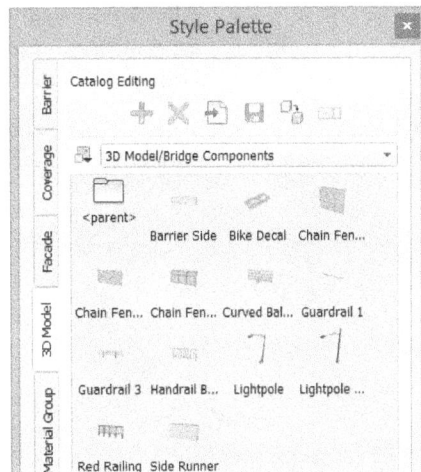

Figure 5–10

- **Buildings:** There are a number of predefined 3D building models. They fall into three categories of from which you can select:
  - **Furniture:** 3D models of roof-top items, such as solar panels and HVAC units.
  - **Neighborhood:** A few common building types that are found in a typical city, such as gas stations, churches, and post offices.
  - **Residential:** Multiple single-family home models.

These 3D model options are located in the *3D Model* tab of the Style Palette. The **Neighborhood** and **Residential** style options are shown in Figure 5–11.

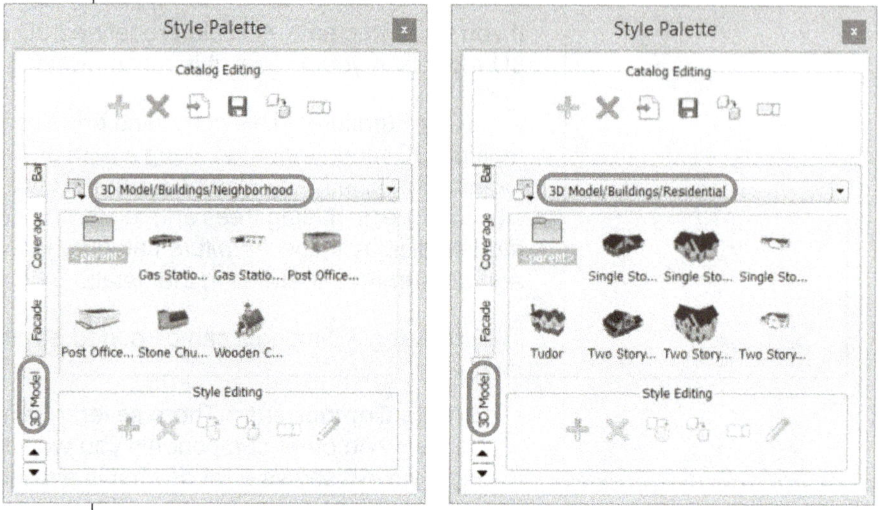

Figure 5–11

- **City Furniture:** Objects found in a city, including signs, fences, bike stands, parking meters, dumpsters, etc., as shown in Figure 5–12.

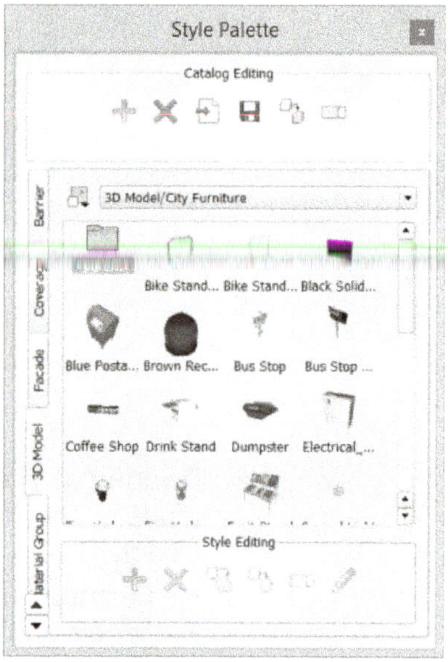

Figure 5–12

© 2017, ASCENT - Center for Technical Knowledge®

- **Construction:** Objects found on a construction site, including piles of dirt or sand, various pieces of equipment, Port-a-Potties, etc., as shown in Figure 5–13.

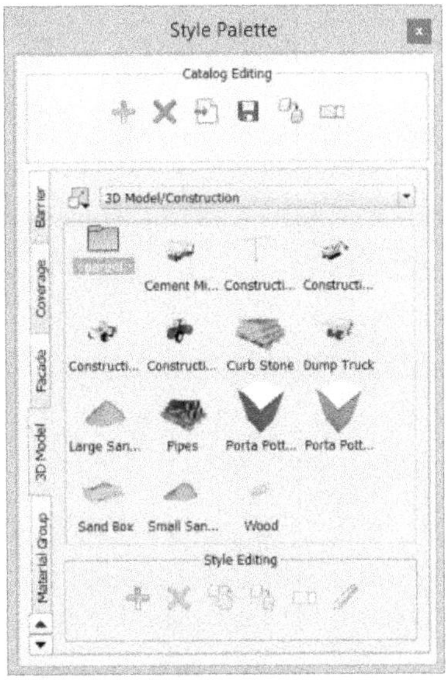

Figure 5–13

- **Energy:** Objects used to deliver energy to specific areas, including distribution pylons, solar panels, oil pumps, oil rigs, transmission poles, and wind turbines, as shown in Figure 5–14.

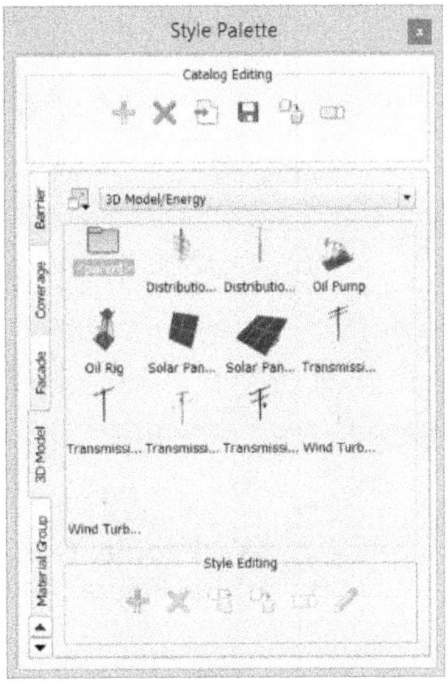

Figure 5–14

- **Highway:** Safety features used in road design, including guard rails and noise barriers, as shown in Figure 5–15.

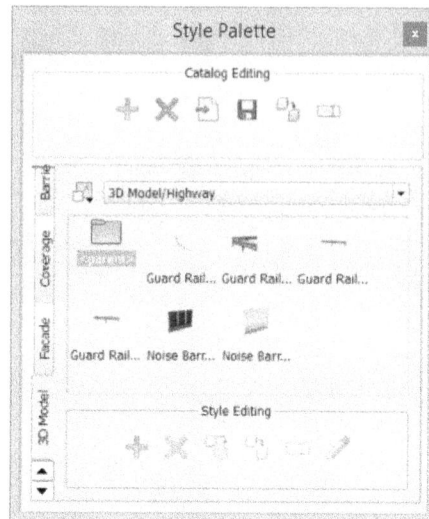

Figure 5–15

- **POI (Points of Interest):** Markers and flag pins used to draw attention to specific areas of the model, as shown in Figure 5–16.

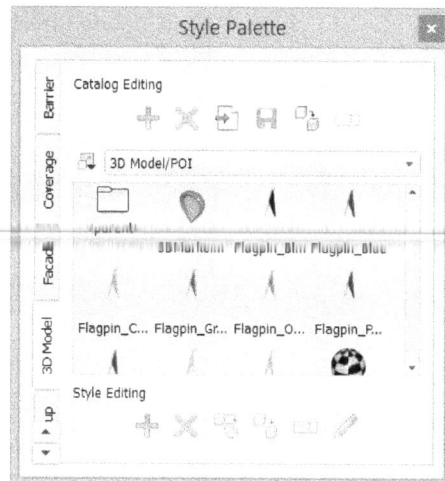

Figure 5–16

- **People:** One or more people walking or standing, as shown in Figure 5–17.

© 2017, ASCENT - Center for Technical Knowledge®

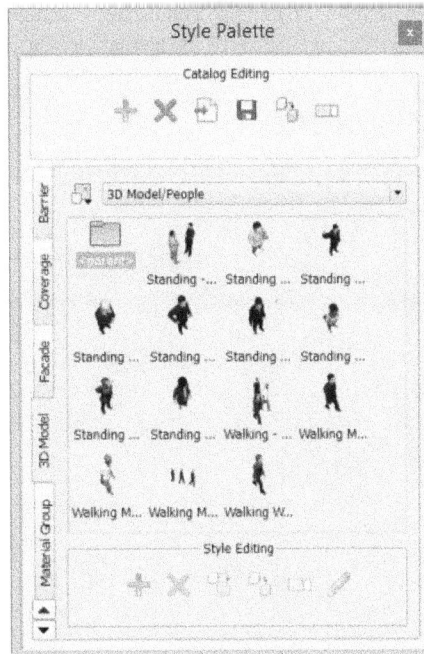

Figure 5–17

- **Planes & Ships:** Planes, helicopters, and water vessels, as shown in Figure 5–18.

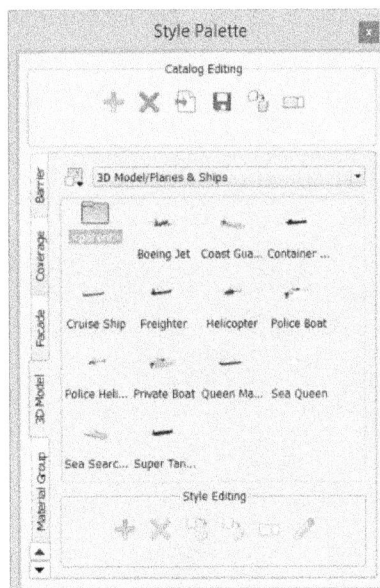

Figure 5–18

- **Railway:** Passenger cars, freight cars, and railway furniture, as shown in Figure 5–19.

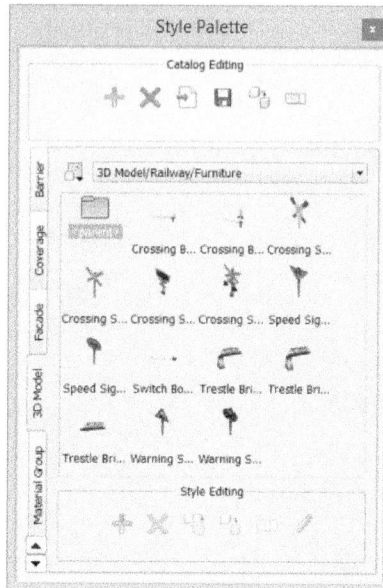

Figure 5–19

- **Shapes:** Shapes in multiple colors can be used to draw attention to specific areas of the model, as shown in Figure 5–20.

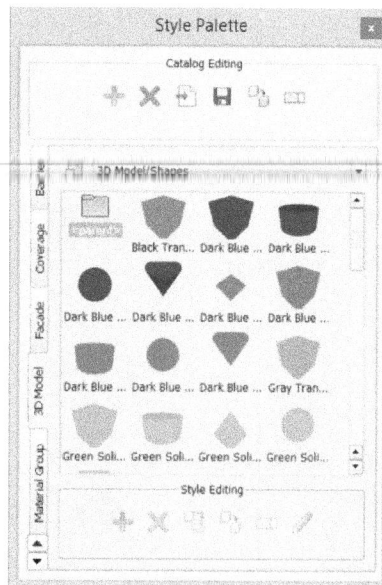

Figure 5–20

© 2017, ASCENT - Center for Technical Knowledge®

- **Traffic & Barriers:** Objects used to control traffic, including traffic lights, construction cones, metal fences, barriers, etc., as shown in Figure 5–21.

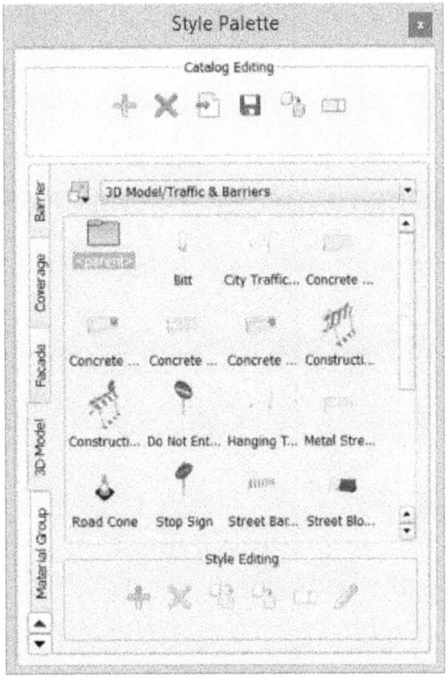

Figure 5–21

- **Vegetation:** Objects used in landscaping, including trees and bushes, as shown in Figure 5–22.

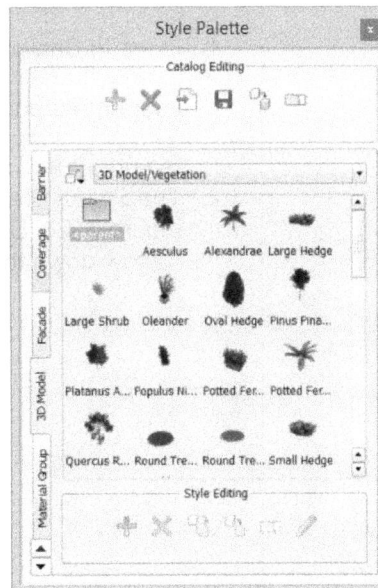

Figure 5–22

- **Vehicles:** Cars, trucks, vans, buses, and bicycles, as shown in Figure 5–23.

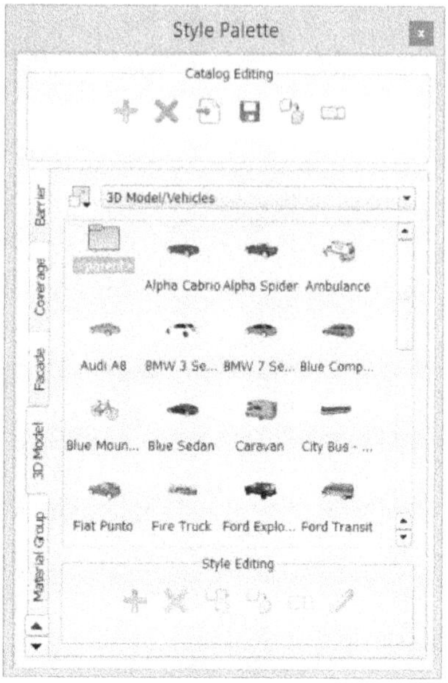

Figure 5–23

How To: Add One Predefined 3D Building or Another Single Piece of City Furniture

1. In the In Canvas tools, click (Build, manage, and analyze your infrastructure model)> (Create conceptual design features)> (City Furniture)

2. The Select Draw Style asset card displays, as shown in Figure 5–24. Select the 3D Model or type in the filter area to narrow down the selection options.

© 2017, ASCENT - Center for Technical Knowledge®

Figure 5–24

3. In the model, double-click to place the model and end the command. The size is not important because the 3D Model size and shape are predetermined as part of the 3D model.

4. Press <Esc> to clear the selection of the newly created building.

Hint: Model Size/Shape

You cannot reshape or change the height of a building created from a 3D Model. The height and shape are predetermined by the model style. However, you can change the scale of the building using the 🔼 (Height Gizmo) or the Properties palette. Using the Height Gizmo causes the building to change scale while keeping the same ratio in the X,Y, and Z planes. However, changing the scale in the properties palette enables the model to be stretched in one or more directions, as shown in Figure 5–25.

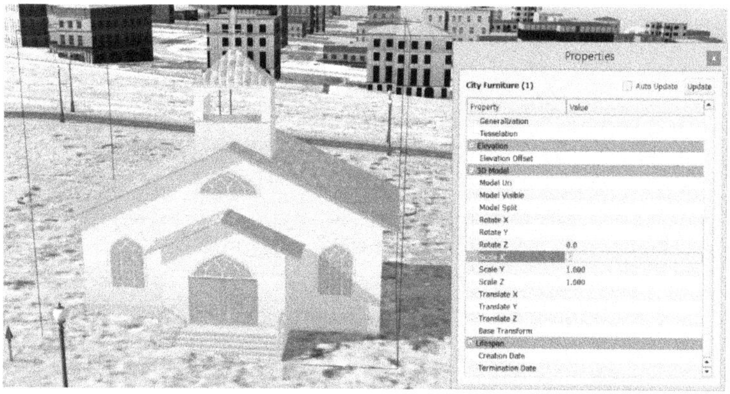

Figure 5–25

How To: Add Multiple Predefined 3D Buildings or Other City Furniture

1. In the In Canvas tools, click 📊 (Build, manage, and analyze your infrastructure model)> 🔧 (Create conceptual design features)> 🏙 (City Furniture).
2. The Select Draw Style asset card displays, as shown in Figure 5–26. Select the 3D Model (or type in the filter area) to narrow down the selection options.

Figure 5–26

© 2017, ASCENT - Center for Technical Knowledge®

3. In the model, single-click to start the path to be followed by the 3D models.
4. In the model, move the cursor in the direction in which you want the 3D model path to follow. Type a distance for the length to the next point of intersection and press <Enter> to set the distance. Click in the model to place the point of intersection.
5. Continue clicking in the model until the full path has been created.
6. Double-click to place the last point and end the command.
7. To change the number of items that display along the path, slide the *Density* Slider (shown in Figure 5–27) until the model density is set as required.

Figure 5–27

8. Press <Esc> to clear the selection of the newly created 3D models.
9. Move and rotate each 3D model by selecting it and using

 (Rotate Gizmo), (Height Gizmo), and (Move Gizmo) as required. If you need to change which 3D model displays at specific locations, you can drag and drop another 3D model in its place from the Style Palette, as shown in Figure 5–28.

Figure 5–28

Practice 5b

Add Buildings and City Furniture to the Model

Practice Objective

- Add buildings and other 3D models to the model.

Estimated time for completion: 45 minutes

In this practice you will create buildings to populate the new subdivision. First, you will use a predefined 3D model to place a church and a row of houses. Next, you will create copies of existing buildings to make populating the subdivision more efficient. Finally, you will add vehicles and a traffic light to roads and a passenger car and a crossing barrier to the railway.

Task 1 - Add predefined buildings.

1. In the Home Screen, click **Open**.

2. In the *C:\InfraWorks Fundamentals Practice Files\AddDetails* folder, select **CreateDetails.sqlite**, and then click **Open**.

3. In the Utility Bar, expand *Switch Active Proposal* and select **B_Task1**.

4. In the Utility Bar, click ▣ (Bookmark your current location) and select **Church**.

5. In the In Canvas tools, click ▤ (Build, manage, and analyze your infrastructure model)> ✎ (Create conceptual design features)> ▦ (City Furniture).

6. In the Select Draw Style asset card that displays, type **church** in the search field. Select the **Wooden Church**, as shown in Figure 5–29.

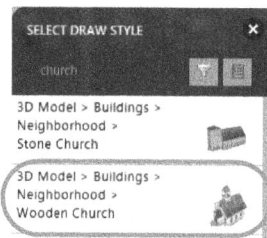

Figure 5–29

© 2017, ASCENT - Center for Technical Knowledge®

7. In the model, double-click in the open area at the center of the parking lot to place the church and end the command, as shown in Figure 5–30.

Figure 5–30

8. Press <Esc> to display the building gizmos.

9. With the church still selected, use ⟋‾‾⟍ (Rotate Gizmo), ⬆ (Height Gizmo), and ⬌ (Move Gizmo) as required to relocate it, as shown in Figure 5–31.

Figure 5–31

10. Press <Esc> to clear the selection of the church.

11. In the Utility Bar, click ▯ (Bookmark your current location) and select **New Neighborhood**.

12. In the In Canvas tools, click ▯ (Build, manage, and analyze your infrastructure model)> ▯ (Create conceptual design features)> ▯ (City Furniture).

13. In the Select Draw Style asset card, type **stucco** in the search field. Select the **Two Story Stucco**, as shown in Figure 5–32.

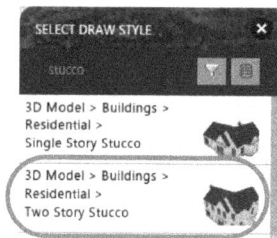

Figure 5–32

14. In the model, click to start a path, and then continue clicking PIs for the path the buildings should follow, as shown in Figure 5–33. Double-click to place the last point of the path and end the command.

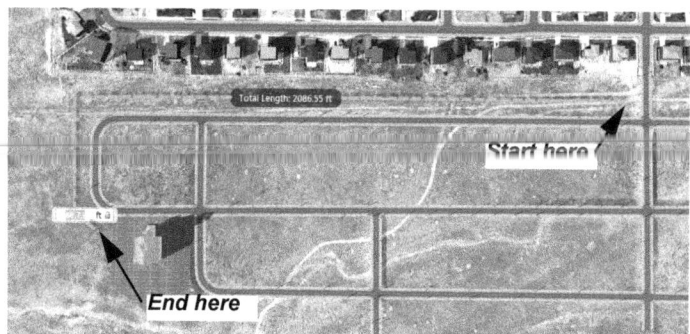

Figure 5–33

15. Press <Esc> to display the gizmos and Feature Density slider.

© 2017, ASCENT - Center for Technical Knowledge®

16. Slide the Feature Density slider to the left to thin out the homes (set to approximately 40%), as shown in Figure 5–34.

Figure 5–34

17. With the homes still selected as a group, right-click and select **Properties.**

18. In the Properties palette, change *Scale X*, *Scale Y*, and *Scale Z* to **1.5**, as shown in Figure 5–35. Click **Update**.

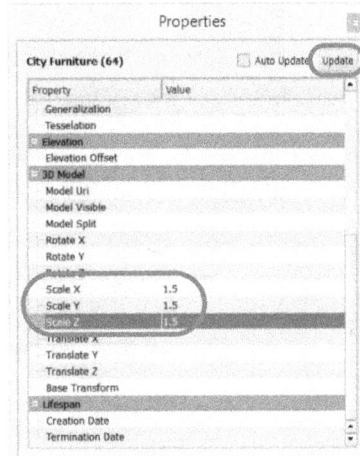

Figure 5–35

19. Press <Esc> to clear the selection. Close the Properties palette.

20. In the Utility Bar, click 🔲 (Bookmark your current location) and select **SingleStoryHome.**

21. In the In Canvas tools, click 🔲 (Build, manage, and analyze your infrastructure model)> 🔲 (Create conceptual design features)> 🔲 (Style Palette).

22. In the Style palette, select the *3D Model* tab and double-click **Buildings>Residential**. Select the **Single Story Brick** style and drag it to the house closest to the church, as shown in Figure 5–36.

Figure 5–36

23. In the model, select the single story home and use gizmos to move and rotate it appropriately. then adjust the height to **30 ft**, as shown in Figure 5–37.

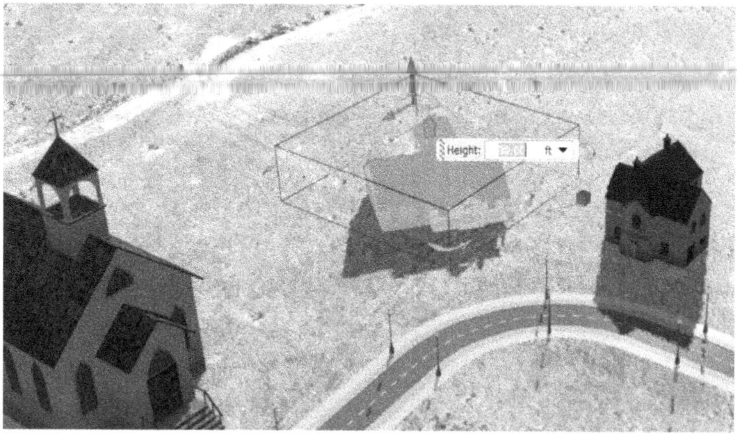

Figure 5–37

24. Press <Esc> to clear the selection.

© 2017, ASCENT - Center for Technical Knowledge®

Task 2 - Create copies of existing buildings.

1. Continue working in the same model. If you did not complete the last task, set the proposal to **B_Task2** in the Utility Bar.

2. In the Utility Bar, click ▣ (Bookmark your current location) and select **New Neighborhood**. Pan the model to the north to display the yellow highlighted homes shown in Figure 5–38.

Figure 5–38

3. In the In Canvas tools, click ▆ (Build, manage, and analyze your industry model)> ◣ (Select model features)> ▣ (Rectangular Select).

4. In the model, create the selection rectangle as shown in Figure 5–39. Remember to double-click on the third point to end the selection.

Second point of rectangle ──→   ←── *Third point of rectangle*

1535212.5, 7273627.5

First point of rectangle ──→

Figure 5–39

5. Press <Ctrl>+<C> to copy the selected homes to the clipboard.

6. Press <Ctrl>+<V> and double-click in the model to place the homes as shown in Figure 5–40.

Figure 5–40

7. Continue to create or copy homes to fill in the new neighborhood using any of the tools discussed so far. Ensure that you leave an area open for the proposed commuter station, shown in white in Figure 5–41.

Proposed Commuter Station

Figure 5–41

© 2017, ASCENT - Center for Technical Knowledge®

Task 3 - Create city furniture.

In this task, you will place a traffic light at the three-way intersection for the new neighborhood. You will then place cars on the roads to indicate how traffic should look as it enters the new neighborhood.

1. Continue working in the same model. If you did not complete the last task, set the proposal to **B_Task3** in the Utility Bar.

2. In the Utility Bar, click ▣ (Bookmark your current location) and select **Neighborhood Entrance**.

3. In the In Canvas tools, click 🔧 (Build, manage, and analyze your infrastructure model)> ✏️ (Create conceptual design features)> 🏙️ (City Furniture).

4. The Select Draw Style asset card displays. Type **Traffic** in the filter field and select the **City Traffic Light**, as shown in Figure 5–42.

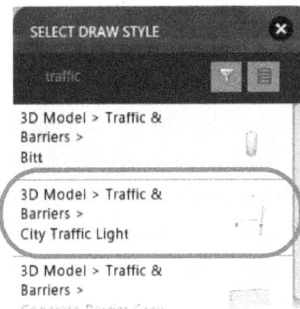

Figure 5–42

5. Double-click in the model to place a traffic light on the east side of the intersection, as shown in Figure 5–43.

Figure 5–43

6. Press <Esc> to display the gizmos. Then move and rotate it using [Rotate Gizmo] and [Move Gizmo] as required to line it up as shown in Figure 5–44.

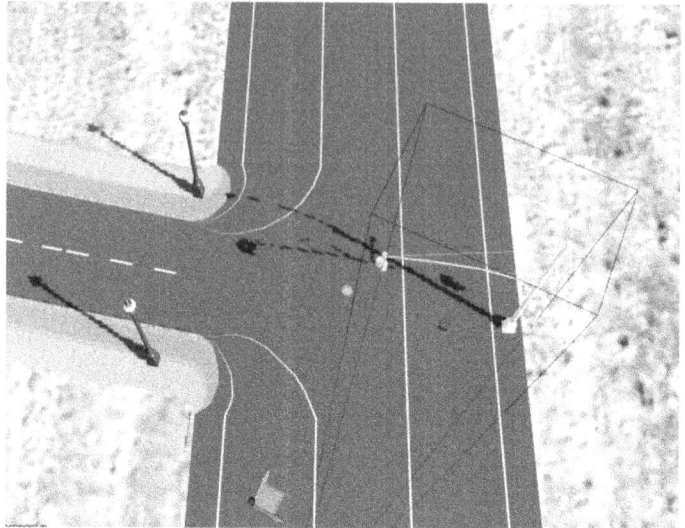

Figure 5–44

7. Press <Esc> to clear the selection of the traffic light.

8. In the Utility Bar, click (Bookmark your current location) and select **Pond**.

9. In the In Canvas tools, click (Build, manage, and analyze your infrastructure model)> (Create conceptual design features)> (City Furniture).

© 2017, ASCENT - Center for Technical Knowledge®

10. The Select Draw Style asset card displays. Type **Vehicle** in the filter field and select the **Alpha Spider**, as shown in Figure 5–45.

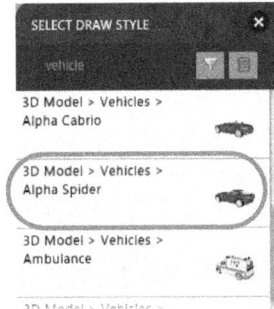

Figure 5–45

11. Create a path as shown in Figure 5–46. Remember to double-click to place the last point along the path.

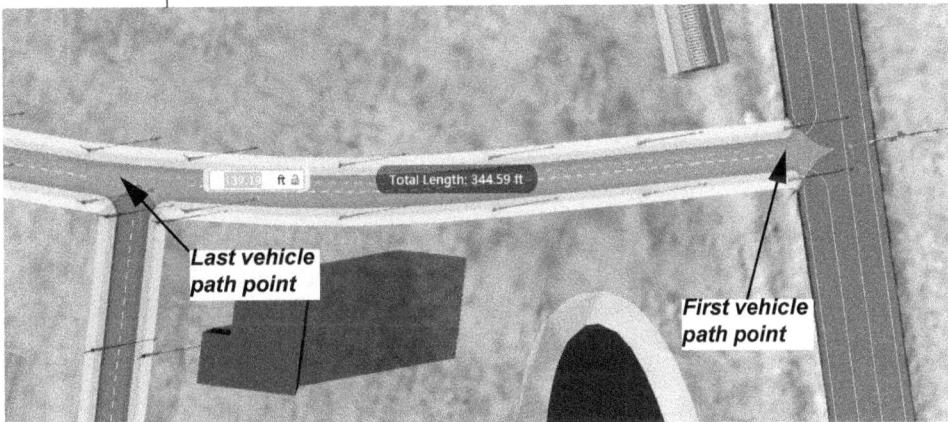

Figure 5–46

12. Press <Esc> to display the gizmos and the Density Slider. Slide the Density Slider (as shown in Figure 5–47) until the density is set close to **50%** so that there are 5 cars.

Figure 5–47

13. Press <Esc> to clear the selection of the newly created vehicles.

14. Move and rotate each vehicle using ⟨Rotate Gizmo⟩ and ↥ (Move Gizmos) as required to make them parallel to the road, as shown in Figure 5–48.

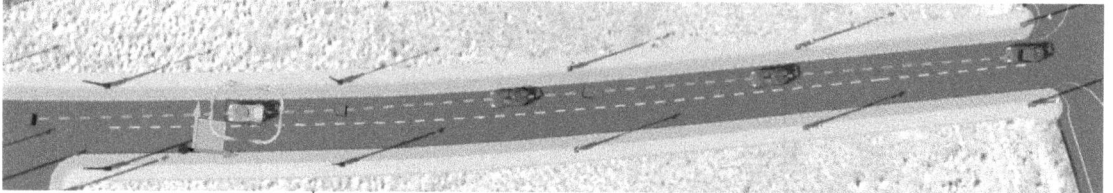

Figure 5–48

15. In the In Canvas tools, click ⬛ (Build, manage, and analyze your infrastructure model)> ✐ (Create conceptual design features)> ▦ (Style palette).

16. In the Style palette, in the *3D Model* tab, double-click on Vehicles.

17. Drag and drop various vehicle styles or colors onto the existing vehicles in the model. Figure 5–49 shows that different vehicle styles have been applied.

Figure 5–49

18. Press <Esc> to clear the selection of all of the features.

© 2017, ASCENT - Center for Technical Knowledge®

Hint: Add City Furniture to Styles

Multiple styles can incorporate city furniture to make populating the model much easier. In chapter 3, we learned how to add vehicles to a road style to quickly populate the roadway. Other items that you might want to incorporate include fire hydrants, light poles, etc. Just keep in mind that adding 3D models to a style does cause the model size to increase. Therefore, it is recommended that you only add a few vehicles to the road styles that will be used for the proposed roads. Then add vehicles sparsely to an existing roadway only where required for visualization purposes.

Task 4 - Add railway 3D models.

1. Continue working in the same model. If you did not complete the previous task, set the proposal to **B_Task4** in the Utility Bar.

2. In the Utility Bar, click ⬛ (Bookmark your current location) and select **RailCrossing**.

3. In the In Canvas tools, click 🔧 (Build, manage, and analyze your infrastructure model)> ✏️ (Create conceptual design features)> 🏙️ (City Furniture).

4. In the Select Draw Style asset card, type **Railway** and scroll down to select the **Crossing Barrier - US** style, as shown in Figure 5–50.

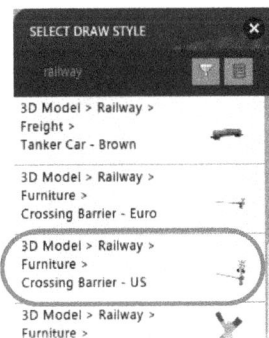

Figure 5–50

5. Double-click in the model to place the 3D model, as shown in Figure 5–51.

Figure 5–51

6. Press <Esc> to display the gizmos.

7. Use ⌒ (Rotate Gizmo) to rotate the crossing barrier arm to make it parallel to the tracks. Use ↥ (Move Gizmo) to move the model to the park strip on the right side of the road, as shown in Figure 5–52.

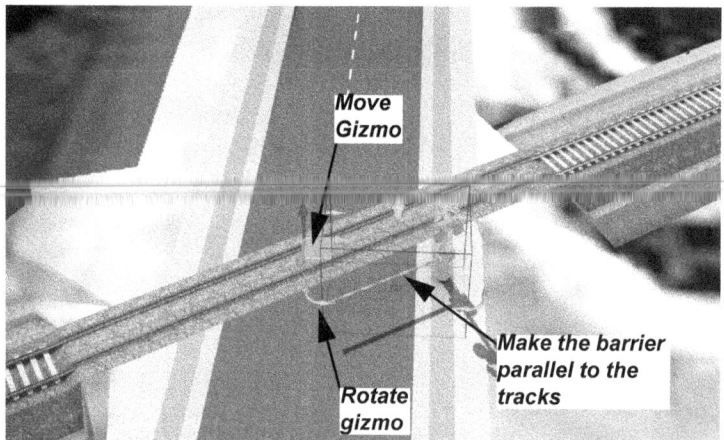

Figure 5–52

8. With the Crossing Barrier still selected, press <Ctrl>+<C> to copy the model to the clipboard.

9. Press <Ctrl>+<V> to paste a second Crossing Barrier in the model. Double-click in the model to place it across the tracks from the first one.

© 2017, ASCENT - Center for Technical Knowledge®

10. With the second Crossing Barrier still selected, use

    ⌒ (Rotate Gizmo) and ⬆ (Move Gizmo) to place and orient the 3D model similar to that shown in Figure 5–53.

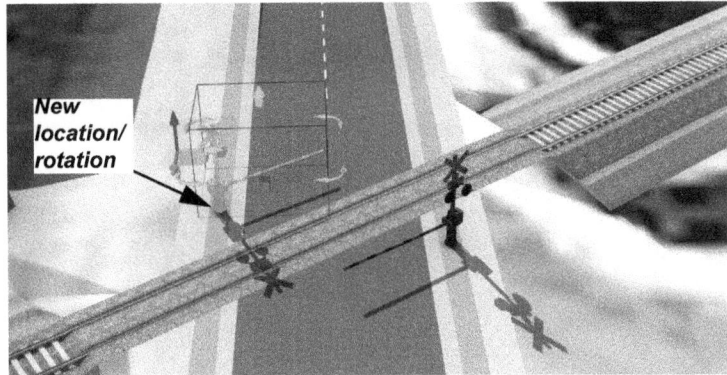

New location/rotation

Figure 5–53

11. Press <Esc> to clear the selection of the crossing barrier.

12. In the Utility Bar, click ▣ (Bookmark your current location) and select **RailCrossing**.

13. In the In Canvas tools, click ▦ (Build, manage, and analyze your infrastructure model)> ✏ (Create conceptual design features)> ▦ (City Furniture).

14. In the Select Draw Style asset card, type **Passenger** in the filter field. Select the **Light Rail - US Midwest** style, as shown in Figure 5–54.

Figure 5–54

15. Double-click to place the 3D model just north of the road crossing, as shown in Figure 5–55.

Figure 5–55

16. Press <Esc> and use ⌒ (Rotate Gizmo) to rotate the model and make it parallel to the tracks, as shown in Figure 5–56.

Figure 5–56

17. Press <Esc> to clear the selection of the railway car.

© 2017, ASCENT - Center for Technical Knowledge®

5.3 Add Vegetation to a Model

Adding vegetation can add privacy, shade, noise barriers, and landscape appeal to a project. Trees and other vegetation can also help stakeholders to better understand how the project could look when completed. You can add vegetation in three different ways:

- **Single Plant:** A single plant is placed in the model when you double-click on an insertion point, no matter which vegetation tool is used. Figure 5–57 shows a single tree.

Figure 5–57

- **Row of Trees:** A group of plants are placed in the model along a line, as shown in Figure 5–58.

Figure 5–58

- **Stand of Trees:** A group of randomly spaced plants are placed in the model inside a polygon, as shown in Figure 5–59.

Figure 5–59

If you create vegetation along a line or in a polygon, you can set the number of plants that display using the Density Slider, as shown in Figure 5–60. The higher the density (slider moved to the right), the more plants that display.

Figure 5–60

How To: Create Vegetation in a Group

1. In the In Canvas tools, click (Build, manage, and analyze your infrastructure model)> (Create conceptual design features)> (Stand of Trees).
2. In the Select Draw Style asset card, type select the type of plant required, as shown in Figure 5–61.

Figure 5–61

© 2017, ASCENT - Center for Technical Knowledge®

3. In the model, click the corners of a polygon for the vegetation group area, as shown in Figure 5–62. Remember to double-click on the final corner to finish the polygon.

Figure 5–62

4. Press <Esc> to make the Feature Density bar display. Slide the Density Slider (as shown in Figure 5–63) until the required number of plants display in the model.

Figure 5–63

5. Press <Esc> to clear the selection of the newly created trees.

How To: Create Vegetation Along a Line

1. In the In Canvas tools, click ![icon] (Build, manage, and analyze your infrastructure model)> ![icon] (Create conceptual design features)> ![icon] (Row of Trees).

2. In the Select Draw Style asset card, type vegetation in the filter field. Select the type of plant required, as shown in Figure 5–64.

Figure 5–64

3. In the model, click the vertices of a polyline for the vegetation to follow, as shown in Figure 5–65. Remember to double-click on the final vertex to finish the polyline.

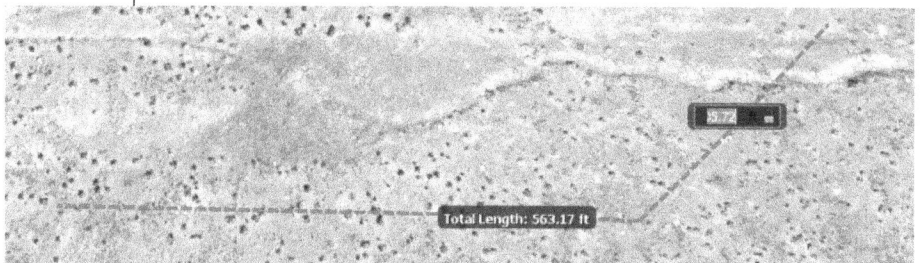

Figure 5–65

© 2017, ASCENT - Center for Technical Knowledge®

4. Press <Esc> to make the Feature Density bar display. Slide the Density Slider (shown in Figure 5–66) until the required number of plants display in the model.

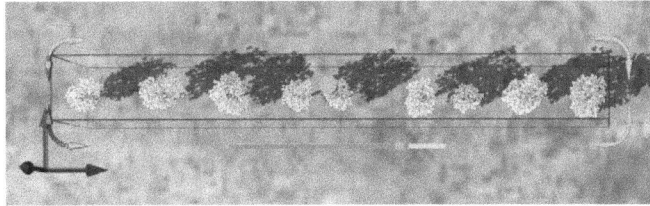

Figure 5–66

5. Press <Esc> to clear the selection of the newly created trees.

Edit Vegetation

When you select vegetation, gizmos display to enable you to modify the plants. ● (Elevation Gizmo) enables you to adjust the height of the plants, while ▯ (Height Gizmo) enables you to change the size and scale of the plants.

If you select a vegetation group (row or stand of trees), the Density Slider displays, enabling you to change the number of plants that display in the group. Move the slider left or right until the required number of plants display in the model. If the Density Slider is not displayed, orbit the view to a plan view to make it display, as shown in Figure 5–67.

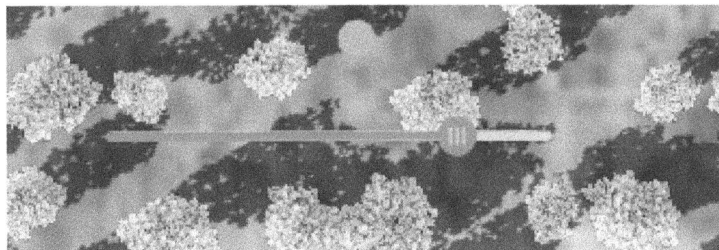

Figure 5–67

Practice 5c

Add Trees to the Model

Practice Objective

- Add trees to the model to add landscaping details.

In this practice you will create vegetation that represents a small orchard to illustrate how the final design will look in a new development.

Task 1 - Create vegetation.

The church owns a piece of land next to the parking lot, which they want to turn into a small orchard to help with fundraising. In this task, you will create trees using the **Stand of Trees** command to create an orchard in the model.

1. In the Home Screen, click **Open**.

2. In the *C:\InfraWorks Fundamentals Practice Files\AddDetails* folder, select **CreateDetails.sqlite** and click **Open**.

3. In the Utility Bar, expand *Switch Active Proposal* and select **C_Task1**.

4. In the Utility Bar, click ▢ (Bookmark your current location) and select **Church**.

5. In the In Canvas tools, click ▢ (Build, manage, and analyze your infrastructure model)> ▢ (Create conceptual design features)> ▢ (Stand of Trees).

Estimated time for completion: 15 minutes

© 2017, ASCENT - Center for Technical Knowledge®

6. In the Select Draw Style asset card, type **vegetation** in the filter field, and select **T16-V05 Dark Green**, as shown in Figure 5–68.

Figure 5–68

7. Click the corners of a polygon for the orchard area, as shown in Figure 5–69. Note: Double-click on the final corner to finish the polygon.

Figure 5–69

8. Press <Esc> to display the Feature Density bar. Use the Density Slider to set the density close to **90%**, as shown in Figure 5–70.

Figure 5–70

9. Press <Esc> to clear the selection of the newly created trees.

© 2017, ASCENT - Center for Technical Knowledge®

5.4 Add Miscellaneous Details to a Model

You can enhance the overall visualization of the final design by indicating to stakeholders where sound barriers, signs, bike stands, etc. can be placed in the project.

Barriers

Barriers are useful items to add to any project. Sound barriers are placed along transportation corridors to muffle the sound of traffic experienced by neighboring residents. To control how traffic is to be handled during construction, barriers can be used to temporarily or permanently block off an area. You might need to create a construction proposal and indicate any barriers, alternative routes, and temporary roads that are to be used during the construction process. All of these uses and more can be added to an Autodesk InfraWorks project to communicate design concepts.

Barriers can be linear features that are added using the Barrier command or 3D Models that are added using the City Furniture command. Multiple 3D Model style catalogs are available (as shown in Figure 5–71) and different barrier styles can be found in many of these catalogs.

Barriers can also be added to road or railway styles by adding Decorations.

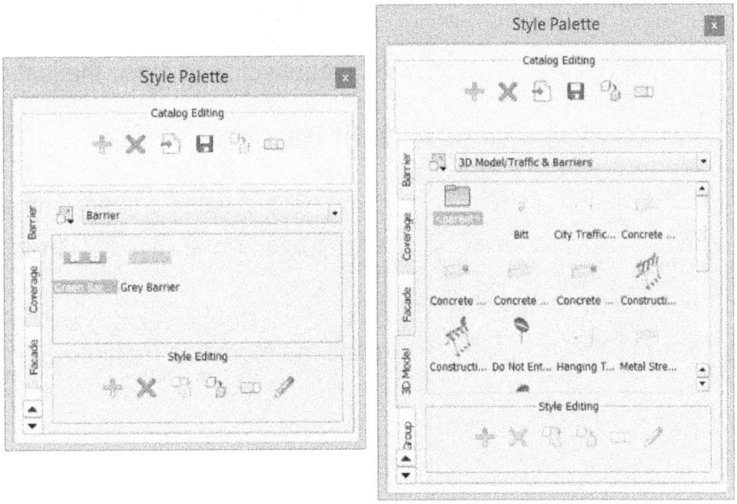

Figure 5–71

How To: Create Barriers

1. In the In Canvas tools, click ![icon] (Build, manage, and analyze your infrastructure model)> ![icon] (Create conceptual design features)> ![icon] (Barriers).
2. In the Select Draw Style asset card, in the *Barrier* tab, select the required barrier style, as shown in Figure 5–72.

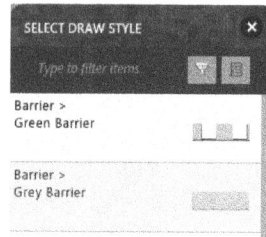

Figure 5–72

3. Click in the model to start the linear path for the barriers to follow.
4. Move the cursor in the direction in which you want the barrier to run. Type a distance for the length to the next point of intersection (PI) and press <Enter> to set the distance. Click in the model to place the next PI.
5. Continue clicking in the model to place PIs until all of the lengths of barrier have been created.
6. Double-click to place the last point and end the command.

Edit Barriers

If you have created a linear barrier, it can be modified using ![icon] (Control Point Gizmo). Once you have placed a 3D model, use ![icon] (Rotate Gizmo) and ![icon] (Move Gizmo) to move and rotate the model as required.

© 2017, ASCENT - Center for Technical Knowledge®

Points of Interest

You might need to draw attention to a specific area of your model. You can do so by adding Points of Interest (POI). In addition to drawing attention to an area, POI can be used to add text, HTML tooltips, or hyperlinks that automatically open a web page, image, or other file when you move the cursor within a specified distance of the POI. This is done using the *Proximity Distance* field in the Point of Interest asset card, as shown in Figure 5–73.

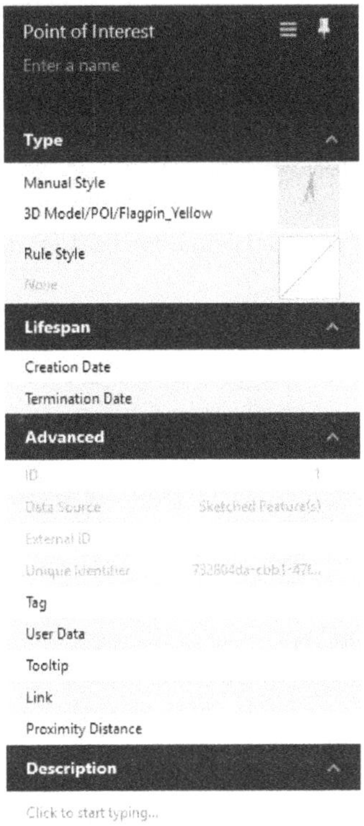

Figure 5–73

How To: Create Points of Interest

1. In the In Canvas tools, click [image] (Build, manage, and analyze your infrastructure model)> [image] (Create conceptual design features)> [image] (Points of Interest)
2. In the Select Draw Style asset card, select the required 3D model style, as shown in Figure 5–74.

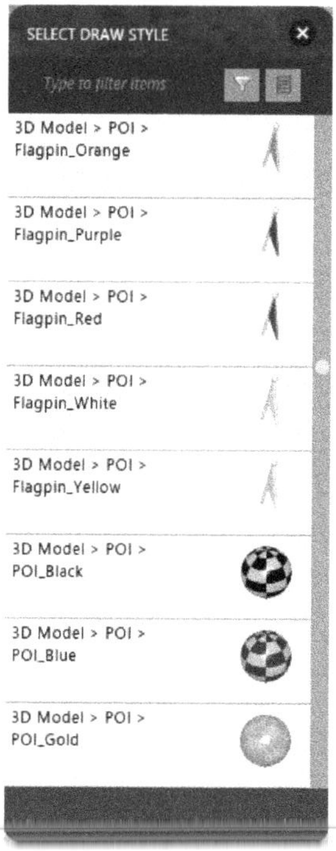

You can select any 3D Model that is listed in the City Furniture section of this chapter.

Figure 5–74

3. Depending on the model, either double-click in the model to place a single POI, or single-click in the model to start the linear path that the POIs should follow.
4. Move the cursor in the direction that you want the POIs to run. Type a distance for the length to the next point of intersection and press <Enter> to set the distance. Click in the model to place the next point of intersection.
5. Continue clicking in the model as required until all of the lengths of POI path have been created.
6. Double-click to place the last point and end the command.

© 2017, ASCENT - Center for Technical Knowledge®

How To: Create Tooltips for Points of Interest

1. In the model, select the POI.

2. In the Point of Interest asset card, expand *Advanced* and select the *Tooltips* field, and click ⊡ (Edit Tooltip).
3. In the Edit Tooltip dialog box, either enter the text you want to display in the *Visual* tab (as shown in Figure 5–75) or use HTML code to create a link in the *Html* tab. Click **OK**.

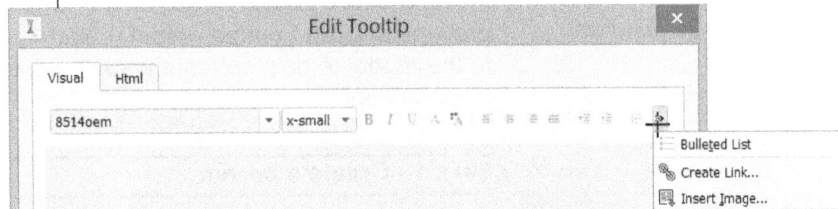

Figure 5–75

4. In the Point of Interest asset card, type a value in the *Proximity Distance* field to specify how close the cursor needs to be to the POI to activate the Tooltip, as shown in Figure 5–76.

Figure 5–76

Edit Points of Interest

If you have placed a 3D model from any category other than POI, you can select it and use ⬆ (Move Gizmo) and ⌢ (Rotate Gizmo) to move and rotate the model as required.

Practice 5d

Add Miscellaneous Details to the Model

Practice Objective

*   Add miscellaneous details to the model to better communicate the design concept.

Estimated time for completion: 25 minutes

In this practice you will create a barrier around the pond to prevent children from playing in it. You will then add city furniture to the model to help communicate the final design to stakeholders.

Task 1 - Create a barrier.

In this task, you will create a barrier around the pond.

1. In the Home Screen, click **Open**.

2. In the *C:\InfraWorks Fundamentals Practice Files\AddDetails* folder, select **CreateDetails.sqlite** and click **Open**.

3. In the Quick Access Toolbar, expand *Switch Active Proposal* and select **D_Task1**.

4. In the Utility Bar, click (Bookmark your current location) and select **Pond**.

5. In the In Canvas tools, click (Build, manage, and analyze your infrastructure model)> (Create conceptual design features)> (Barriers).

6. In the Select Draw Style asset card, select the **Grey Barrier** style, as shown in Figure 5–77.

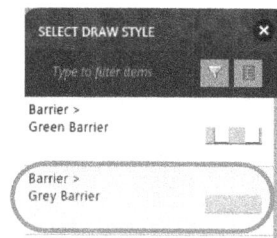

Figure 5–77

© 2017, ASCENT - Center for Technical Knowledge®

7. Click in the model to start the linear path that the barrier should follow, as shown in Figure 5–78.

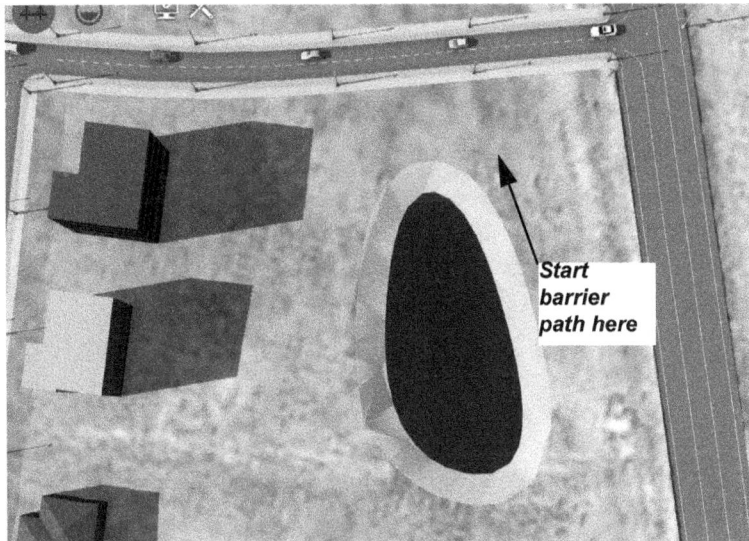

Figure 5–78

8. Move the cursor to the west. Type **100** for the length to the next point on the boundary and press <Enter> to set the distance. Click in the model to place the barrier point parallel to the road.

9. Move the cursor south by approximately the same distance to the west of the pond as the PI placed in Step 8, as shown in Figure 5–79. Type **200** for the length to the next point on the barrier path and press <Enter> to set the distance. Click in the model to place the boundary point.

10. Move the cursor to the east. Type **150** for the length to the next point on the boundary and press <Enter> to set the distance. Click to place the barrier path point near the edge of the railway.

11. Move the cursor back to the first barrier point and double-click to place the last barrier path point and end the command. Figure 5–79 shows the complete barrier path.

Figure 5–79

12. Press <Esc> to clear the selection of the barrier.

Task 2 - Add bridge components.

In this task, you will add components to the pier so that it is only available to foot and bike traffic. **Note:** In order to challenge you to remember the steps and make them more automatic, not every step of the process is listed in this task.

1. Continue working in the same model. If you did not complete the previous task, set the proposal to **D_Task2** in the Utility Bar.

2. In the Utility Bar, click [icon] (Bookmark your current location) and select **Pier**.

3. In the In Canvas tools, click [icon] (Build, manage, and analyze your infrastructure model)> [icon] (Create conceptual design features)> [icon] (City Furniture).

© 2017, ASCENT - Center for Technical Knowledge®

4. In the Select Draw Style asset card, type **bridge** and select the **Barrier Side** style, as shown in Figure 5–80.

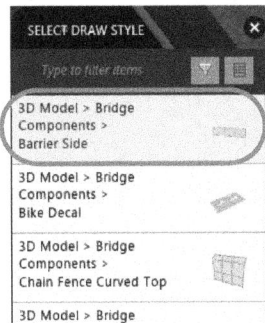

SELECT DRAW STYLE ✕

Type to filter items

3D Model > Bridge Components > Barrier Side

3D Model > Bridge Components > Bike Decal

3D Model > Bridge Components > Chain Fence Curved Top

3D Model > Bridge

Figure 5–80

The barrier likely is placed on top of the water by default. You must move it vertically and horizontally, and then rotate it as required.

5. Double-click in the model to place the barrier at the end of the pier. Add two more barriers.

6. Press <Esc> and use the ⬆ (Move gizmo) and (Rotate gizmo) as required to correctly position the barriers side-by-side so that foot and bike traffic can not go off the end of the pier, as shown in Figure 5–81.

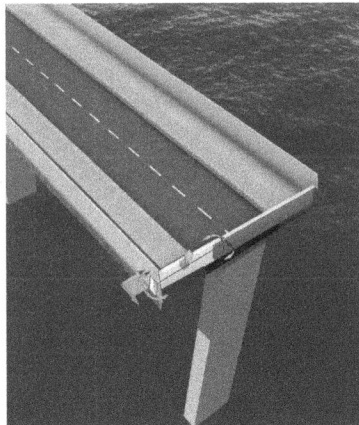

Figure 5–81

7. In the In Canvas tools, click (Build, manage, and analyze your infrastructure model)> (Create conceptual design features)> (City Furniture).

8. In the Select Draw Style asset card, type **bridge** and select the **Bike Decal** style, as shown in Figure 5–82.

Figure 5–82

The signs likely are placed on top of the water by default. You must move them vertically and horizontally, and then rotate as required.

9. Double-click in the model multiple times to place the sign on the pavement. Figure 5–83 shows suggested placements and rotations.

Figure 5–83.

10. Press <Esc> and use the ⬆ (Move gizmo) and (Rotate gizmo) as required

11. Continue adding Bike Decals to communicate where bikes can travel and the direction of travel.

12. If time permits, add additional barriers at the beginning of the bridge to block vehicular traffic to protect bikers and pedestrians. Figure 5–83 shows the suggested placement and rotation.

© 2017, ASCENT - Center for Technical Knowledge®

Chapter Review Questions

1. Which of the following is not a category for a predefined 3D building model?

    a. *Furniture*

    b. *Residential*

    c. *Neighborhood*

    d. *Commercial*

2. Once placed, you can change the shape of a building that has been created from a 3D model.

    a. True

    b. False

3. Which **Create Tree** option would you use to create a grouping of multiple trees in a specified area?

    a. (Row of Trees)

    b. (Stand of Trees)

4. Which of the following commands should you use if you want to add tooltips that are activated within a specified distance from the location of the 3D model?

    a. (City Furniture)

    b. (Barriers)

    c. (Points of Interest)

Command Summary

Button	Command	Location
	Barriers	• **In Canvas Tools:** Build, manage, and analyze your industry model > Create conceptual design features
	Buildings	• **In Canvas Tools:** Build, manage, and analyze your industry model > Create conceptual design features
	City Furniture	• **In Canvas Tools:** Build, manage, and analyze your industry model > Create conceptual design features
	Points Of Interest	• **In Canvas Tools:** Build, manage, and analyze your industry model > Create conceptual design features
	Row of Trees	• **In Canvas Tools:** Build, manage, and analyze your industry model > Create conceptual design features
	Stand of Trees	• **In Canvas Tools:** Build, manage, and analyze your industry model > Create conceptual design features

© 2017, ASCENT - Center for Technical Knowledge®

Analyzing the Model

Before progressing too far into the design process, it is important to ensure that the project area meets the project needs. You should continually analyze what is happening in the project to address issues that arise along the way. In this chapter you learn how to analyze the model using spatial and numerical analysis tools to determine the feasibility of the project.

Learning Objectives in this Chapter

- Analyze features in a model using underlying data using themes.
- Select a subset of features in a layer.
- Graphically indicate avoidance zones in the model.
- Select features that are in the line of sight from a specified view point and angle.
- Measure a model to determine the length, area, or volume of specific features.
- Analyze a model to determine whether the project receives the appropriate amount of sunlight.

6.1 Theme a Data Source

The display of a feature class can be modified by creating a theme. Themes use underlying data found in the database to highlight sets of values using various colors. Figure 6–1 shows coverages themed by the current market value, which was pulled from a parcel database.

Figure 6–1

The Themes palette is used to create new themes, modify existing themes, delete themes, and change the display settings and priority of themes. Additionally, you can share themes with other models to ensure consistency across models that use similar data sources. The icons used in the Feature Themes palette (shown in Figure 6–2) are consistent for all theme types

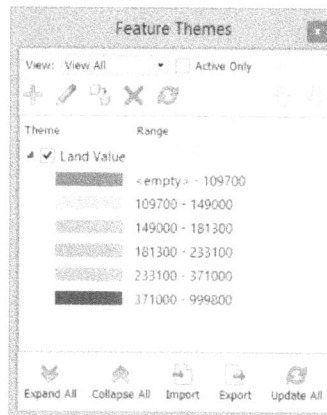

Figure 6–2

© 2017, ASCENT - Center for Technical Knowledge®

The icons in the Feature, Terrain, and Point Cloud Theme palettes are described as follows:

Icon	Purpose
(Add a New Theme)	Adds a new theme for a feature class.
(Edit Selected Theme)	Enables you to edit the properties of a selected theme.
(Duplicate Selected Theme)	Enables you to copy a selected theme.
(Delete Selected Theme(s))	Deletes any selected themes.
(Refresh Selected Themes)	Refreshes the display of selected themes.
(Move Selected Theme Up/Down)	Changes the priority of the themes by moving the selected theme up or down in the list.
(Expand/Collapse All)	Shows/hides the details of the themes in the current model.
(Import Theme(s))	Used to import one or more theme properties from an external file created in another model.
(Export Theme(s))	Used to export one or more theme properties to an external file for use in other models.
(Update All)	Refreshes the display of all themes in the current model.

Feature Themes

Creating a feature theme helps visualize specific aspects of data sources. For example, if you want to display the location of various soil types in the model, you can display each category as a different color using the individual values that are associated with a soil data source. Additionally, you can display parcels according to their market value to ensure that the project location is appropriate, and fits in the project budget.

Nearly any data source can be themed and associated with features in the model, according to data found in the database. Using a variety of distribution methods, values are divided into ranges. The distribution methods available for Feature Themes include:

- **Equal:** The difference between the high and low values is the same for every range.

- **Standard Deviation:** Ranges are based on how much the value varies from the mean value. The mean value is calculated first, and then the standard deviation is added or subtracted from the mean to calculate the ranges.

- **Quantile:** An equal number of features are included in each range.

- **Jenks:** Ranges are based on natural groupings of the data values. This is the same as a natural breaks method, because features with similar values use the same display properties.

- **Individual Values:** Ranges look at values that are most often used when the values represent categories.

- **Logarithm:** Uses a logarithmic scale to distribute values after evaluating the highest and lowest values from the source.

The Feature Themes palette is shown in Figure 6–3.

Figure 6–3

© 2017, ASCENT - Center for Technical Knowledge®

How To: Create a Feature Theme

1. In the In Canvas tools, click ![icon] (Build, manage, and analyze your infrastructure model)> ![icon] (Analyze your model)> ![icon] (Feature Themes).

2. In the Feature Themes palette, click ![icon] (Add a New Theme).

3. In the Theme Properties dialog box (shown in Figure 6–4), set the following properties and click **OK**:

   • **Name:** Enter a name for the theme.

   • **Feature Class:** Select the feature class to theme.

   • **Property:** Select the property in the database, which holds the values to be used for the theme.

   • **Distribution:** Select the distribution method to use.

   • **Number of Rules:** Set the number of rules.

   • **Color Range:** Select the color range and transparency.

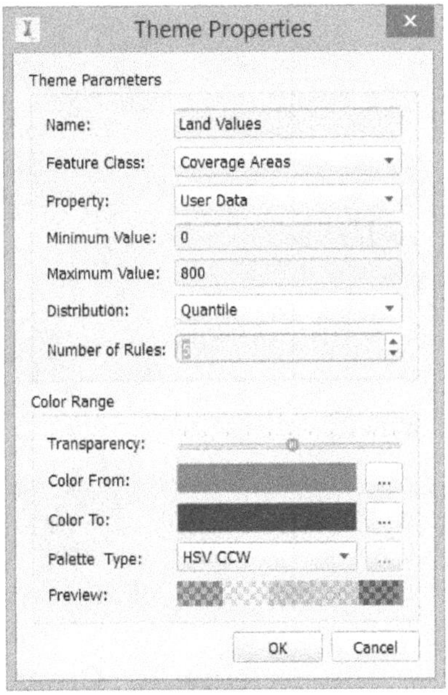

Figure 6–4

Terrain Themes

Terrain themes enable you to display surfaces according to their elevation, slope, or aspect. When creating a terrain theme, you can set the number of rules, colors, and transparency of the surface. Terrain themes only use the equal distribution method for creating ranges. There are a few predefined palettes that automatically set the number of rules and the color for each range according to the type of analysis being run. For example, the Land Cover palette sets up 13 ranges with colors starting with light cyan and ending with brown. The Slope palette sets up five ranges with colors starting with gray and ending with red, as shown in Figure 6–5.

Figure 6–5

How To: Create a Terrain Theme

1. In the In Canvas tools, click ![icon] (Build, manage, and analyze your infrastructure model)> ![icon] (Analyze your model)> ![icon] (Terrain Themes).

2. In the Terrain Themes palette, click ![icon] (Add a New Theme).

© 2017, ASCENT - Center for Technical Knowledge®

3. In the Theme Properties dialog box (shown in Figure 6–6) set the following parameters and click **OK**:

   • **Name:** Type a name for the theme.

   • **Analysis Type:** Select the analysis type.

   • **Palette Type:** Select the palette type.

   • **Number of Rules:** If the palette type was not set, set the number of rules.

   • **Color Range:** Select the color range and transparency.

Figure 6–6

Point Cloud Themes

Normal usually refers to the direction in which a surface face is pointing. For points in a point cloud, normal is derived from other points that have a planar relationship with a specific point.

Theming a point cloud enables you to view its many points using different colors. The colors are based on one of the following analysis types:

• **Normal:** Identifies points that are aligned by displaying colors assigned to the X, Y, Z values associated with the direction of the normal for the point. Colors for this type of theme cannot be specified.

• **Elevation:** Similar to the terrain theme by elevation, it colors points according to their Z value or height. The minimum and maximum values are determined automatically, but can be adjusted as required.

• **Single Color:** All points become the same color and no further options are available.

• **Classification:** This option is only available if a point cloud is classified. Points are colored by their classification ID.

Point cloud themes only use the equal distribution method for creating ranges.

How To: Create a Point Cloud Theme

1. In the In Canvas tools, click ![icon] (Build, manage, and analyze your infrastructure model)> ![icon] (Analyze your model)> ![icon] (Point Cloud Themes).

2. In the Point Cloud Themes palette, click ✛ (Add a New Theme).

3. In the Theme Properties dialog box, shown in Figure 6–7, define the following and click **OK**:

   - **Name:** Type a name for the theme.
   - **Analysis Type:** Select the Analysis Type.
   - **Palette Type:** Select the palette type.
   - **Number of Rules:** If the palette has not already been set, set the number of rules.
   - **Color Range:** Select the color range and transparency.

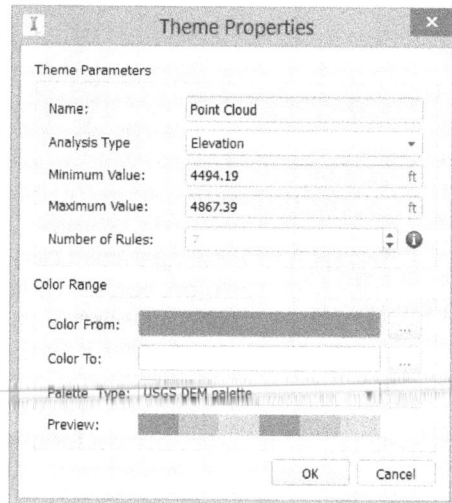

Figure 6–7

© 2017, ASCENT - Center for Technical Knowledge®

Practice 6a

Create Themes in the Model

Practice Objective

- Create themes that will be used to analyze data.

Estimated time for completion: 10 minutes

In this practice you will change the colors in the model according to underlying data to determine whether the project falls within parcels that fit the project budget. You will then perform a slope analysis to determine whether there are any unbuildable areas in the project.

Task 1 - Create a feature theme.

1. In the Home Screen, click **Open**.

2. In the *C:\InfraWorks Fundamentals Practice Files\Analyze* folder, select **Analyze.sqlite** and click **Open**.

3. In the Utility Bar, expand *Switch Active Proposal* and select **A_Task1**.

4. In the In Canvas tools, click (Build, manage, and analyze your infrastructure model)> (Analyze your model)> (Feature Themes).

5. In the Feature Themes palette, click (Add a New Theme).

6. In the Theme Properties dialog box (as shown in Figure 6–8) set the following parameters and click **OK**:

- **Name:** Land Values
- **Feature Class:** Coverage Areas
- **Property:** User Data
- **Distribution Method:** Quantile
- **Number of Rules:** 5
- **Palette Type:** HSV CCW
- **Transparency:** 50%

The current market value is already mapped to the User Data field.

Figure 6–8

Your model should look similar to that shown in Figure 6–9.

Figure 6–9

*If all of the colors do not display, open the Data Sources panel and double-click on the **TaxParcel** layer. In the Table tab, ensure that **MKT_CNTVAL** is selected for the User Data property. Click **Close & Refresh**. The theme should automatically recognize the values and update the model display.*

7. In the Feature Themes palette, clear the checkmark next to *Land Values* to toggle off the display of the theme.

© 2017, ASCENT - Center for Technical Knowledge®

Task 2 - Create a terrain theme.

1. In the In Canvas tools, click ![icon] (Build, manage, and analyze your infrastructure model)> ![icon] (Analyze your model)> ![icon] (Terrain Themes).

2. In the Terrain Themes palette, click ✚ (Add a New Theme).

3. In the Theme Properties dialog box (shown in Figure 6–10) set the following parameters and click **OK**:
   - **Name:** Slope
   - **Analysis Type:** Slope
   - **Palette Type:** Slope Palette
   - **Transparency:** 50%

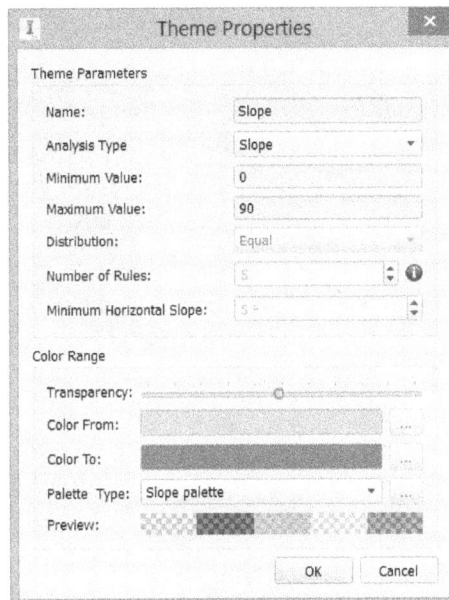

Figure 6–10

Your model should look similar to that shown in Figure 6–11. The client wants to see the slope of the site in 5% increments.

Figure 6–11

4. In the Terrain Themes palette, double-click on the *Slope* theme to open the Theme Properties dialog box. Position the box so that you can see the model as you make changes.

5. In the Theme Properties dialog box, do the following:
   - Change the Palette Type to **User Defined**.
   - Slowly click **Increase** to change the Number of Rules to **18**. Watch the model as you do so.
   - Click **OK**.

6. In the Terrain Themes palette, note that the ranges are now in 5% slope increments. Clear the checkmark next to *Slope* to toggle off the display of the theme.

© 2017, ASCENT - Center for Technical Knowledge®

6.2 Suitability Maps

AUTODESK
INFRAWORKS 360

To use this feature, access to the Internet is required.

Infrastructure projects can quickly become very expensive if the location or soil type are not suitable for the project. Suitability maps enable you to input your own data to help determine the most cost effective location for an infrastructure project. This data can come from a layer in the Model Explorer, or a subset of a layer in the Model Explorer, as shown in Figure 6–12. Layer settings enable you to set a gradient width or an offset around the feature.

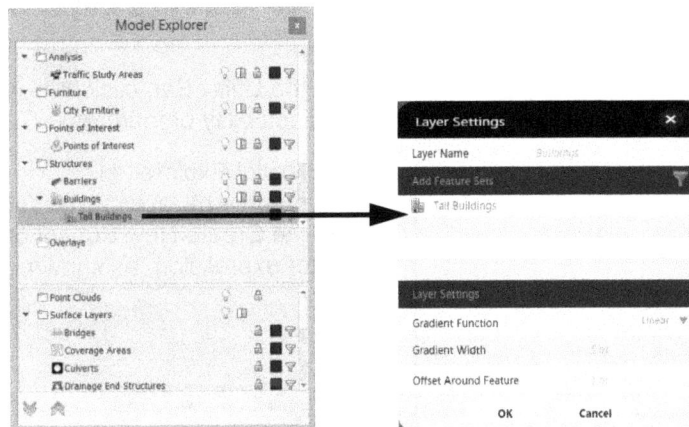

Figure 6–12

Multiple avoidance zone layers can be added to the suitability map. Weights can be adjusted to indicate that one avoidance zone has a higher or lower impact on the project cost over another, as shown in Figure 6–13.

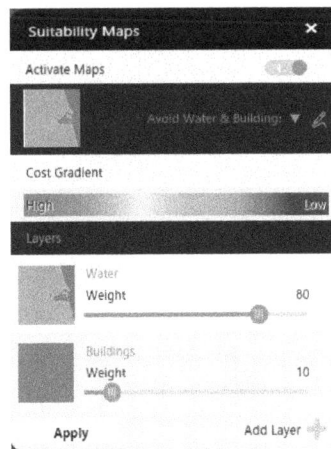

Figure 6–13

Layer Subsets

Many of the GIS layers that are used to create suitability maps require filtering to correctly create avoidance zones.

For example, it is not a good idea to place buildings or roads in liquefaction zones near fault lines. To address this, a soil map data source could be attached to the model. Then a layer subset could be created for specific soil types to indicate where liquefaction zones are expected. Finally, the layer subset(s) could be added to the suitability map with weights to indicate which soils to avoid building upon.

How To: Create a Layer Subset

1. In the Utility Bar, click (Control visibility, display, and selectability of features).
2. In Model Explorer, click (Create subset) next to the layer to create any layer subset(s) that might be required.
3. In the Create New Subset dialog box, create the necessary filter expression, as shown in Figure 6–14. Click **OK**.

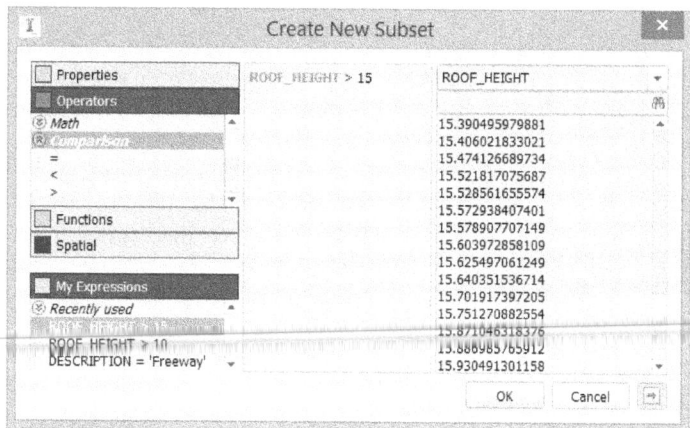

Figure 6–14

© 2017, ASCENT - Center for Technical Knowledge®

How To: Create a Suitability Map

1. In Model Explorer, create any layer subset(s) that might be required.

2. In the In Canvas tools, click (Build, manage, and analyze your infrastructure model)> (Analyze your model)> (Suitability Maps).

3. In the Suitability Maps palette, toggle on the **Activate Maps** option. Then expand **Select item** and select **Create new map...**, as shown in Figure 6–15.

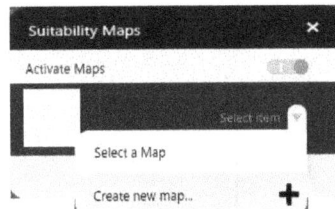

Figure 6–15

4. In the Suitability Maps palette, click (Add new suitability map layer).

5. In the Layer Settings palette, click (Select features through Model Explorer).

6. In the Feature Selection dialog box, select the layer(s) to apply a buffer to, as shown in Figure 6–16.

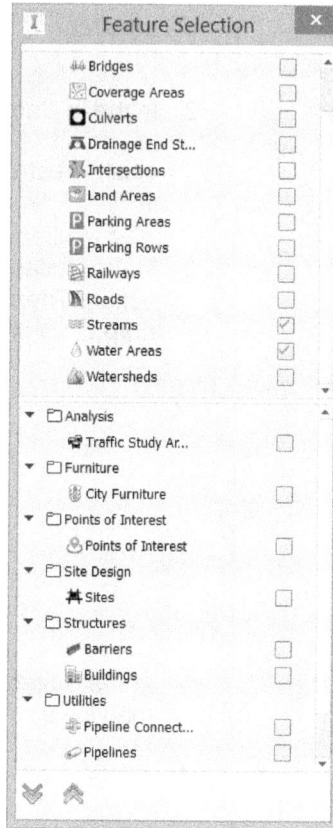

Figure 6–16

7. In the Layer Settings, type a value in the *Gradient Width* and/or *Offset Around Feature* field, as shown in Figure 6–17. Click **OK**.

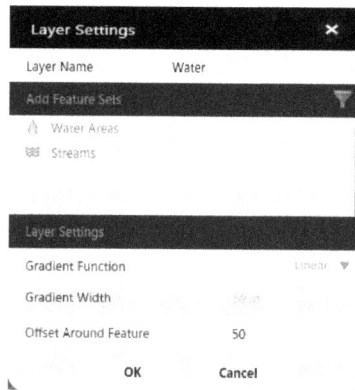

Figure 6–17

© 2017, ASCENT - Center for Technical Knowledge®

8. In the Suitability Maps palette, add any additional layers as required, and then set their weights using the sliders next to each layer, as shown in Figure 6–18.

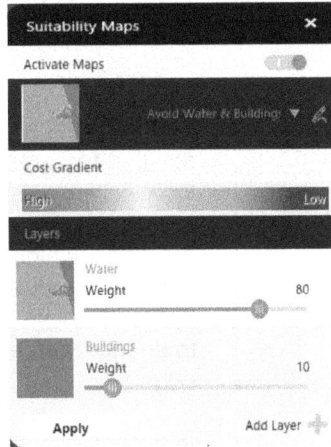

Figure 6–18

9. In the Suitability Maps palette, click **Apply** to display the results in the model.

Practice 6b

Create a Suitability Map

Practice Objective

- Determine the most cost effective location for an infrastructure project using avoidance zones.

Estimated time for completion: 15 minutes

In this practice you will create avoidance zones and analyze existing features to ensure that you have selected the best location for a new infrastructure project. First, you will create a layer subset to avoid building a road too close to the tallest buildings, which will help reduce the number of car accidents that might occur due to icy roads that are constantly in the shadows of the buildings. Next, you will use the water areas and streams to ensure that the road is not built within 50 meters of the water's edge.

Task 1 - Create a suitability map.

1. In the Home Screen, click **Open**.

2. In the *C:\InfraWorks Fundamentals Practice Files\Analyze* folder, select **Analyze.sqlite** and click **Open**.

3. In the Utility Bar, expand *Switch Active Proposal* and select **B_Task1**.

4. In the Utility Bar, click ⬚ (Control visibility, display, and selectability of features).

5. In Model Explorer, next to the **Buildings** layer, click ⬚ (Create subset).

6. In the Create New Subset dialog box, do the following, as shown in Figure 6–19:

   - Under *Properties*, expand *Building* and double-click on **ROOF_HEIGHT**.
   - Under *Operators*, expand *Comparison* and double-click on **>**.
   - Select the value in the *Expression* area and type **15**.
   - Click **OK**.
   - For the subset name, type **Tall Buildings**.

© 2017, ASCENT - Center for Technical Knowledge®

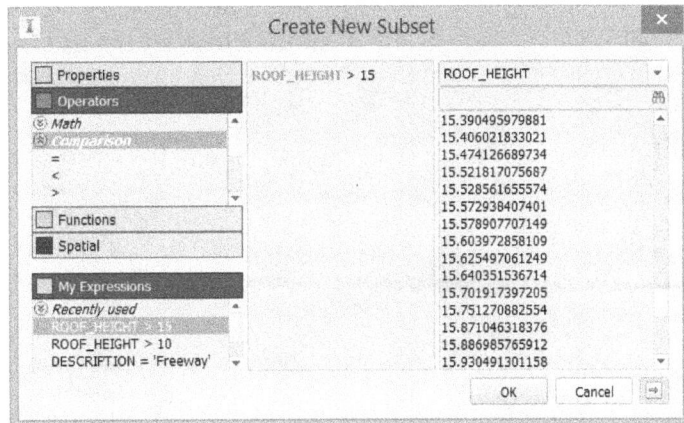

Figure 6–19

7. In the In Canvas tools, click ▆ (Build, manage, and analyze your infrastructure model)> ▆ (Analyze your model)> ▆ (Suitability Maps).

8. In the Suitability Maps palette, toggle on the **Activate Maps** option. Expand **Select a Map** and select **Create new map...**, as shown in Figure 6–20.

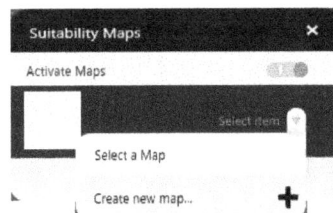

Figure 6–20

9. In the Suitability Maps palette, click ▆ to rename the map. In the *Map Name* field, type **Avoid Water & Buildings**.

10. In the Suitability Maps palette, click ✚ (Add a new suitability map layer).

11. In the Layer Settings palette, type **Water** for the name and then click ▆ (Select features through Model Explorer).

12. In the Feature Selection dialog box, select the **Streams** and **Water Areas** layers, as shown in Figure 6–21. Close the Feature Selection dialog box.

Figure 6–21

13. In the Layer Settings, in the *Gradient Width* and *Offset Around Feature* fields, type **50**, as shown in Figure 6–22. Click **OK**.

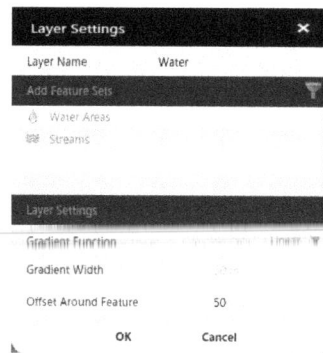

Figure 6–22

14. In the Suitability Maps palette, click **Apply** to see the results in the model.

15. In the Suitability Maps palette, click (Add new suitability map layer).

© 2017, ASCENT - Center for Technical Knowledge®

16. In the Layer Settings palette, type **Buildings** for the name and then click ▼ (Select features through Model Explorer).

17. In the Feature Selection dialog box, expand the *Buildings* layer and select the **Tall Buildings** subset. Close the Feature Selection dialog box.

18. In the Layer Settings, in the *Offset Around Feature* field, type **10**. Click **OK**.

19. In the Suitability Maps palette, click **Apply** to display the results in the model.

20. In the Suitability Maps palette, adjust the layer weights using the sliders next to each layer. Set the *Water* weight to **80** and the *Building* weight to **10**, as shown in Figure 6–23.

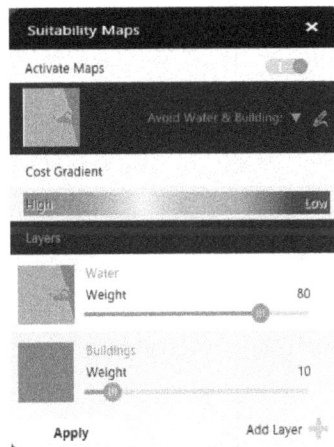

Figure 6–23

21. In the Suitability Maps palette, click **Apply** to display the results in the model.

6.3 Line of Sight Analysis

Stakeholders are often concerned about how a project is expected to look from a specific view. More importantly, they want to know what they can or cannot see from a specific point of view. Residents from the surrounding community might want to know that traffic cannot see into their backyards. Stakeholders might also want to know that views of the surrounding landscape are not going to be lost because of the proposed project. In these cases, a line of sight study can be conducted to better understand what can be seen from a specific location.

A Line of Sight analysis is conducted by orienting the view to the angle and direction to be analyzed. Anything in the line of sight becomes selected in the model when you run the analysis, as shown in Figure 6–24. These objects remain selected even when the view changes, enabling you to see what is selected after moving the camera.

Figure 6–24

How To: Conduct a Line of Sight Analysis

1. In the model, set the view point and angle using the standard navigation tools.

2. In the In Canvas tools, click ![icon] (Build, manage, and analyze your infrastructure model)> ![icon] (Analyze your model)> ![icon] (Select Visible).

3. Press <Esc> to clear all of the selected features.

© 2017, ASCENT - Center for Technical Knowledge®

6.4 Measure the Model

To meet project constraints, you must ensure that everything is being created with the correct measurements. It is best to continually check the model and ensure that features are the correct distance from each other, and have the correct area and volumes. These checks help you to avoid having to recreate and edit objects later. Measurement tools are found in the In Canvas tools, under ▒ (Build, manage, and analyze your infrastructure model)> ▒ (Analyze your model). The available tools are as follows.

Icon	Purpose
▒ (Point to Point Distance)	Measures length, width, and height from one point to another along a straight line. Distance displays in the model similar to a dimension.
▒ (2D Distance & Slope)	Measures the slope between two points. Distance displays in the model similar to a triangle showing the 2D horizontal distance, vertical distance, and grade between two points.
▒ (Path Distance)	Measures length, width, and height along a polyline path. Distance displays in the model similar to a series of dimensions with individual values displayed for each segment, as well as the total distance. It can be used to display measurements across a terrain.
▒ (Range Finder)	Measures the distance of a target point from your current position. Distance displays in the model similar to a single point with a label indicating the distance, altitude, heading, and inclination from your position. You can set multiple target points in a session.
▒ (Terrain Statistics)	Measures the area and volume of a terrain by specifying the perimeter points.

How To: Measure Single Distances

1. In the In Canvas tools, click ▨ (Build, manage, and analyze your infrastructure model)>▨ (Analyze your model)> ▨ (Measure Point to Point).
2. Click the first point to start the measurement.
3. Click the second point where the measurement ends. The measured value displays similar to Figure 6–25.

Figure 6–25

4. Press <Esc> to remove the temporary dimension.

How To: Measure 2D Distance & Slope

1. In the In Canvas tools, click ▨ (Build, manage, and analyze your infrastructure model)>▨ (Analyze your model)> ▨ (2D Distance & Slope).
2. Click the first point to start the measurement.
3. Click the second point where the measurement ends. The measured value displays similar to Figure 6–26.

Figure 6–26

4. Press <Esc> to remove the temporary dimension.

© 2017, ASCENT - Center for Technical Knowledge®

How To: Measure a Series of Distances

1. In the In Canvas tools, click ![icon] (Build, manage, and analyze your infrastructure model)> ![icon] (Analyze your model)> ![icon] (Measure Path Distance).
2. Click the first point to start the measurement.
3. Click all of the subsequent points along the path as required. Double-click on where the measurement ends. The measured values display similar to those shown in Figure 6–27.

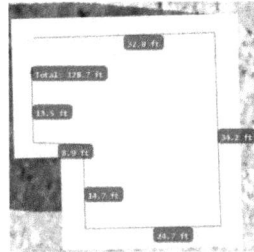

Figure 6–27

4. Press <Esc> to remove the temporary dimensions.

How To: Measure Ranges

1. In the In Canvas tools, click ![icon] (Build, manage, and analyze your infrastructure model)> ![icon] (Analyze your model)> ![icon] (Range Finder).
2. Click a point in the model. The range values display similar to those shown in Figure 6–28.

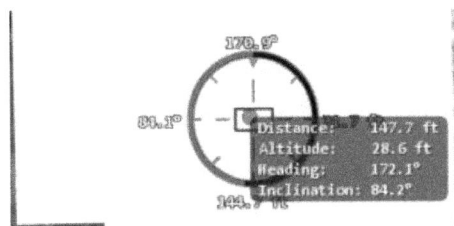

Figure 6–28

3. Press <Esc> to remove the temporary dimensions.

How To: Measure Terrain Statistics

1. In the In Canvas tools, click ![icon] (Build, manage, and analyze your infrastructure model)> ![icon] (Analyze your model)> ![icon] (Terrain Statistics).

2. Click the first point to start a boundary. The boundary defines the area to measure.

3. Click all of the subsequent points along the required boundary. Double-click on the point where the boundary should end. A boundary and its measure values display similar to that shown in Figure 6–29.

Figure 6–29

4. Press <Esc> to remove the temporary dimensions.

© 2017, ASCENT - Center for Technical Knowledge®

6.5 Analyze Shadows

Conducting a shadow study can help determine whether the project can expect to receive enough sunlight at specific times of day or throughout the year. During a shadow study, you can toggle shadows on or off, and set various sun and sky settings.

Visual Effects

To adjust the lighting and appearance of your model, change the View Style settings in the Utility Bar. In the Utility Bar, expand the View Style drop-down and click ⚙ (Configure current view). Then, change the settings on the Visualization stack of the View Settings asset card, as shown in Figure 6–30.

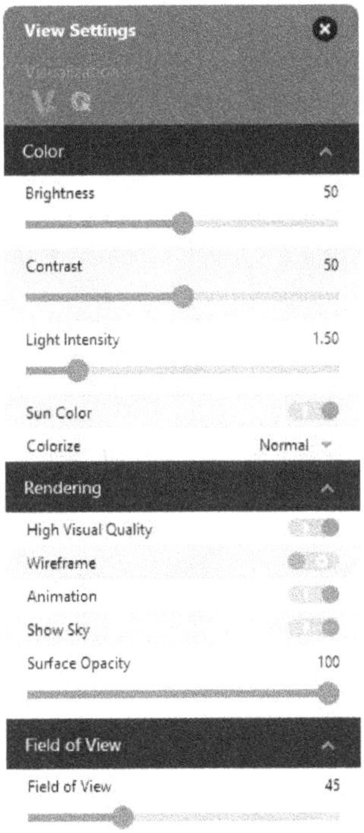

Figure 6–30

Toggle Shadows On/Off

Studying how shadows are cast in a model helps you to determine whether solar panels can be used to power a building. It can also help you to determine whether horizontal and vertical curves need to be modified along a transportation corridor to reduce the effects of shadows. For instance, too much shade on a road that is prone to snow and ice can create dangerous conditions for commuters.

In the Visual Effects asset card, you can toggle on shadows by toggling the **High Visual Quality** setting to **On**, as shown in Figure 6–31. Changing this setting to **Off**, toggles the shadows off.

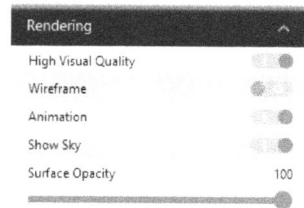

Figure 6–31

Brightness & Contrast

Both the brightness of the model and the contrast between light and dark can be controlled in the Visual Effects asset card, as shown in Figure 6–30. Additionally, you can change the color palette used by the model, selecting the normal, sepia, or grayscale palettes found in the Colorize drop-down list, as shown in Figure 6–32.

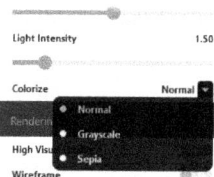

Figure 6–32

© 2017, ASCENT - Center for Technical Knowledge®

Field of View

The Field of View slider, found in the Visual Effects asset card, enables you to control how much of the model displays in the view as you zoom in and out.

Sun & Sky Settings

The time of year and time of day can both be set using the environment sliders in the Sun & Sky asset card, as shown in Figure 6–33. Additionally, you can set the amount of cloud coverage, wind speed/direction, and amount of cloud cover in the model. You can open the Sun & Sky asset card in the In

Canvas tools > ▨ (Build, Manage, and analyze your

infrastructure model)> ▨ (Analyze your model) > ☁ (Sun & Sky).

Figure 6–33

Practice 6c

Analyze the Model

Practice Objectives

- Analyze the model graphically by conducting a line of sight analysis and a shadow study.
- Analyze the model numerically by measuring the model.

Estimated time for completion: 10 minutes

In this practice you will conduct a line of sight analysis and measure the model to ensure that it meets the project requirements. You will then conduct a shadow study to ensure that the project receives enough sunlight and that shadows do not create any unforeseen issues.

Task 1 - Conduct a line of sight analysis.

In this task, you will conduct a line of sight analysis to determine whether certain homes can be seen from a specific point where you are considering putting a passenger loading station for the railway.

1. In the Home Screen, click [Open].

2. In the *C:\InfraWorks Fundamentals Practice Files\Analyze* folder, select **Analyze.sqlite** and click **Open**.

3. In the Quick Access Toolbar, expand *Switch Active Proposal* and select **C_Task1**.

4. In the Utility Bar, click [Bookmark you current location] and select **LOS**.

5. In the In Canvas tools, click [Build, manage, and analyze your infrastructure model)> [Analyze your model)> [Select Visible]. All of the objects displayed in this line of sight are selected and highlighted in yellow to display them clearly.

6. In the Utility Bar, click [Bookmark your current location] and select **New Neighborhood**. Homes and roads will be selected, as shown in Figure 6–34. Note: After changing the view orientation, the selected objects remain selected and can be reviewed more easily.

© 2017, ASCENT - Center for Technical Knowledge®

Figure 6–34

7. Press <Esc> to clear the selection.

___

Task 2 - Measure the model.

___

In this task, you will measure the church building to ensure that it meets the project requirements for capacity. You will then measure the length of road to a specific cul-de-sac to ensure that it meets emergency evacuation codes.

1. In the In Canvas tools, click ▮ (Build, manage, and analyze your infrastructure model)> ▢ (Analyze your model)> ⬌ (Measure Point to Point).

2. In the Utility Bar, click ▯ (Bookmark your current location) and select **Church**.

3. Measure the length and width of the main chapel of the church, as shown in Figure 6–35.

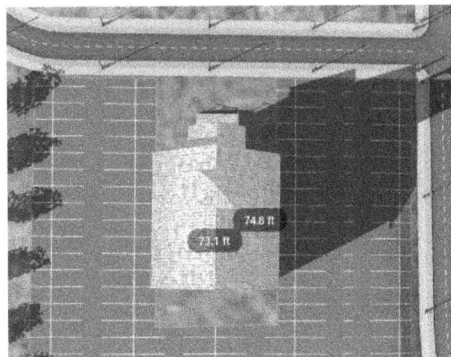

Figure 6–35

4. Press <Esc> to remove the temporary dimensions.

5. In the Utility Bar, click ⬛ (Bookmark your current location) and select **Bridge Elevation**.

6. In the In Canvas tools, click ⬛ (Build, manage, and analyze your infrastructure model)> ⬛ (Analyze your model)> ⬛ (2D Distance & Slope).

7. Click the first point to start the measurement near the start of the bridge, as shown in Figure 6–36.

8. Click the second point near the edge of the water. The measured value displays similar to Figure 6–36.

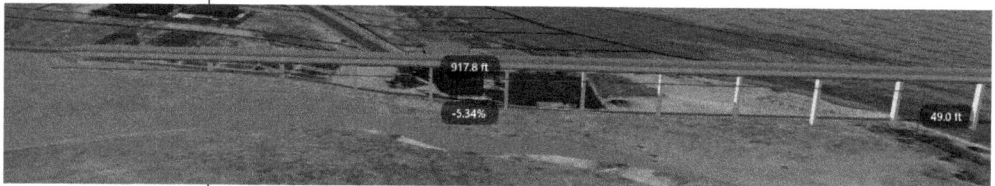

Figure 6–36

9. Press <Esc> to remove the temporary dimension.

10. In the Utility Bar, click ⬛ (Bookmark your current location) and select **New Neighborhood**.

11 In the In Canvas tools, click ⬛ (Build, manage, and analyze your infrastructure model)> ⬛ (Analyze your model)> ⬛ (Measure Path Distance).

12. Click the series of points shown in Figure 6–37 to measure the new roads from where they intersect Redwood Road, to where they end at the future cul-de-sac.

© 2017, ASCENT - Center for Technical Knowledge®

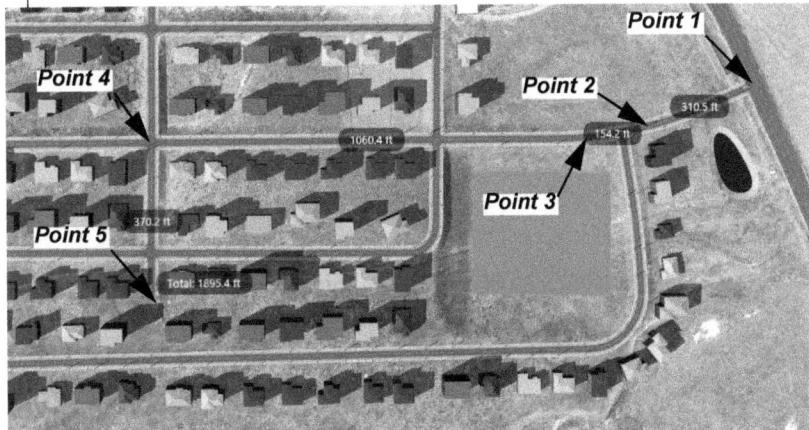

Figure 6–37

13. Press <Esc> to remove the temporary dimensions.

Task 3 - Conduct a shadow study.

In this task, you will conduct a shadow analysis to ensure that the new roads will not have increased numbers of accidents due to ice buildup on the roads that is caused by shadows.

1. In the Utility Bar, click ▯ (Bookmark your current location) and select **Church**.

2. In the Utility Bar, expand the View Style drop-down and click ⚙ (Configure current view).

3. In the View Style asset card, toggle on the **High Visual Quality**.

4. In the In Canvas tools, click ▯ (Build, manage, and analyze your infrastructure model)> ▭ (Analyze your model)> ☀ (Sun & Sky).

5. In the Sun & Sky asset card, set the *Date slider* to **January 1, 2017** and set the *Time slider* to **9:00 am**.

6. Continue moving the sliders to analyze the shadows over time.

7. Close the model.

Chapter Review Questions

1. Which of the following is not a theme that you can create in the model?

   a. Feature Theme

   b. Terrain Theme

   c. Point Cloud Theme

   d. Sky Theme

2. When conducting a Line of Sight analysis, the selected objects in the line of sight change when the view changes.

   a. True

   b. False

3. Which measurement tool would you use to determine the distance, altitude, or inclination of a point from the current camera viewpoint?

   a. (Measure Point to Point)

   b. (Measure Path Distance)

   c. (Range Finder)

   d. (Terrain Statistics)

4. Where can you find the measurement tools?

   a. (Create and manage your model)

   b. (Select model features)

   c. (Create conceptual design features)

   d. (Analyze your model)

5. How do you toggle shadows on in the model?

   a. In the View Settings asset card.

   b. In the Sun & Sky asset card.

© 2017, ASCENT - Center for Technical Knowledge®

6. How do you filter a data source in preparation for adding it to a suitability map?

   a. Select the features in the model first.

   b. Create a Terrain Theme.

   c. Create a Feature Theme.

   d. Create a subset of the data source in the Model Explorer.

Command Summary

Button	Command	Location
	2D Distance & Slope	• **In Canvas Tools:** Build, manage, and analyze your industry model>Analyze your model
	Create Subset	• **Model Explorer**
	Feature Themes	• **In Canvas Tools:** Build, manage, and analyze your industry model>Analyze your model
	Path Distance	• **In Canvas Tools:** Build, manage, and analyze your industry model>Analyze your model
	Point Cloud Themes	• **In Canvas Tools:** Build, manage, and analyze your industry model>Analyze your model
	Point to Point Distance	• **In Canvas Tools:** Build, manage, and analyze your industry model>Analyze your model
	Range Finder	• **In Canvas Tools:** Build, manage, and analyze your industry model>Analyze your model
	Select Visible	• **In Canvas Tools:** Build, manage, and analyze your industry model>Analyze your model
	Sky & Sun	• **In Canvas Tools:** Build, manage, and analyze your industry model>Analyze your model
	Suitability Maps	• **In Canvas Tools:** Build, manage, and analyze your industry model>Analyze your model
	Terrain Statistics	• **In Canvas Tools:** Build, manage, and analyze your industry model>Analyze your model
	Terrain Themes	• **In Canvas Tools:** Build, manage, and analyze your industry model>Analyze your model
	Visual Effects	• **In Canvas Tools:** Build, manage, and analyze your industry model>Settings and Utilities

© 2017, ASCENT - Center for Technical Knowledge®

Chapter 7

Collaborating with Others

In most projects, multiple design professionals or departments work on different elements of the design. For the architectural elements, architects often use the Autodesk® Revit® software to model buildings, while civil engineers and surveyors work on the detailed design phase using the AutoCAD® Civil 3D® software. The Autodesk® InfraWorks® software can communicate with other Autodesk software types, which enables you to take advantage of models created by other departments. Additionally, if you have purchased the Autodesk InfraWorks software, project files can be shared over the cloud to make accessing them much easier. In this chapter, you learn how to use the Autodesk InfraWorks 360 service to share files, import Autodesk Revit and AutoCAD Civil 3D files, and create scenarios for effective collaboration.

Learning Objectives in this Chapter

- Share design elements between Autodesk InfraWorks and AutoCAD Civil 3D.
- Import an Autodesk Revit model.
- Create a scenario that includes storyboards to share on the Internet.

7.1 Share Design Elements with AutoCAD Civil 3D

Autodesk InfraWorks models can be opened directly in the AutoCAD Civil 3D software. Therefore, you do not have to recreate these design elements for the detailed design phase of the modeling process. Additionally, AutoCAD Civil 3D drawing files can be imported into an Autodesk InfraWorks model to help communicate the final design to stakeholders by taking advantage of the high definition graphics. When you add an AutoCAD Civil 3D DWG data source, the following AutoCAD Civil 3D data objects are imported:

- Corridors

- Surfaces

This does not include pressure pipes at this time.

- Pipes

- Pipe Networks

When importing AutoCAD Civil 3D DWG files into an Autodesk InfraWorks model, you might want to start a new proposal and remove any roads that might end up duplicated before starting the import process. If you do not do this, your roads might display similar to that shown in Figure 7–1. The problem occurs when the software cannot determine which alignment to use, and tries to use both.

Figure 7–1

© 2017, ASCENT - Center for Technical Knowledge®

In order to import an AutoCAD Civil 3D DWG file directly, you must have the AutoCAD Civil 3D 2017 software installed on your computer.

How To: Import AutoCAD Civil 3D DWG Files

1. In the In Canvas tools, click [ ] (Build, manage, and analyze your infrastructure model) > [ ] (Create and manage your model> [ ] (Data Sources).

2. In the Data Sources palette, expand [ ] (Add file data source) and select **AutoCAD Civil 3D DWG**.

3. In the Select Files dialog box, browse to the AutoCAD Civil 3D DWG file, select it and click **Open**.

    *   Alternatively, you can drag and drop .DWG files into the Autodesk InfraWorks model from Windows Explorer. When you do, a DWG File Import dialog box displays that enables you to select what type of data source to use for the file, as shown in Figure 7–2. Select the **AutoCAD Civil 3D DWG** option and click **OK**.

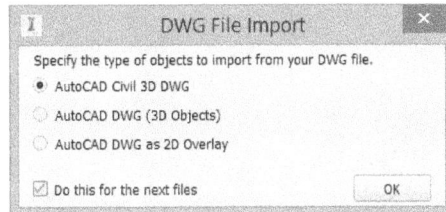

Figure 7–2

4. In the Choose Data Sources dialog box, select all of the AEC objects you want in the Autodesk InfraWorks model, as shown in Figure 7–3. Click **OK**.

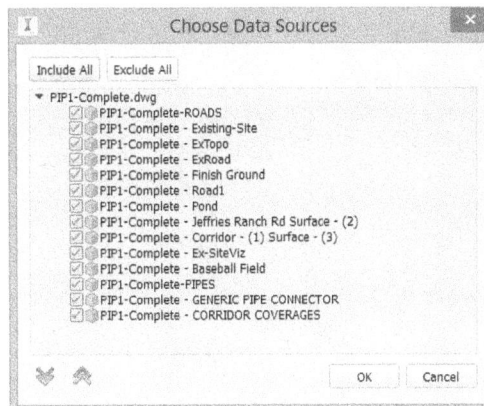

Figure 7–3

5. In the Data Sources palette, note that all of the imported AEC objects display under their appropriate source type and are selected, as shown in Figure 7–4. Click ⟲ (Refresh data source).

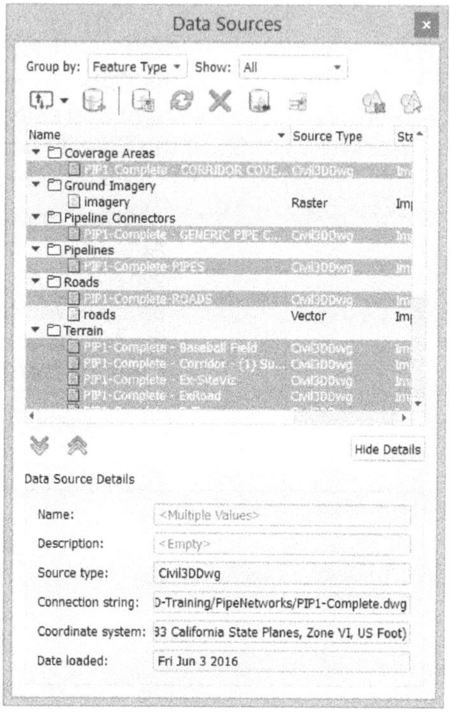

Figure 7–4

Drawing Overlays

When the AutoCAD Civil 3D DWG data source type is selected, only the AEC objects are imported into the Autodesk InfraWorks model. In order to import other linework (such as parcel lines and utilities other than pipe networks), you can use an *AutoCAD DWG as 2D Overlay* data source type. When working with terrain overlays, you can:

- Move

- Rotate

- Scale

- Control selectability

- Control transparency, as shown in Figure 7–5.

© 2017, ASCENT - Center for Technical Knowledge®

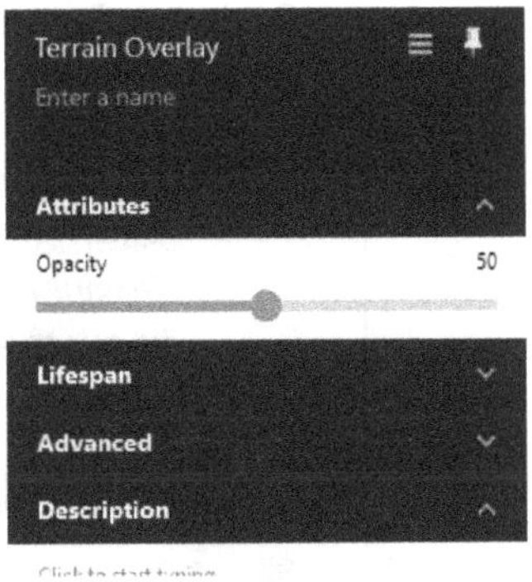

Figure 7–5

How To: Import AutoCAD Civil 3D DWG Files

AUTODESK® INFRAWORKS™ 360

To use this feature, access to the Internet and Autodesk® InfraWorks® 360 are required.

1. In the In Canvas tools, click (Build, manage, and analyze your infrastructure model) > (Create and manage your model> (Data Sources).
2. In the Data Sources palette, expand (Add file data source) and select **AutoCAD DWG as 2D Overlay**.
3. In the Select Files dialog box, browse to the AutoCAD DWG file, select it and click **Open**.
   - Alternatively, you can drag and drop .DWG files into the Autodesk InfraWorks model from Windows Explorer. When you do, a DWG File Import dialog box displays that enables you to select what type of data source to use for the file, as shown in Figure 7–6. Select the **AutoCAD DWG as 2D Overlay** option and click **OK**.

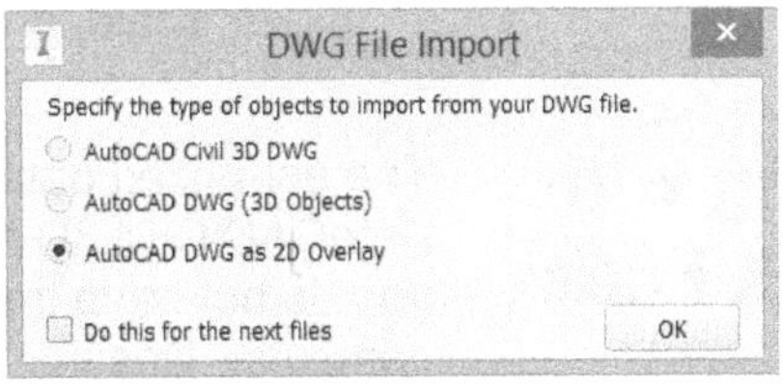

Figure 7–6

4. In the Data Import dialog box, when the following warning displays, click **Send**:
   - *This feature requires an Internet connection and an Autodesk 360 account. By clicking "Send", you will be transmitting data to InfraWorks 360 cloud-based services.*
5. In the Data Source palette, under *Terrain Overlays*, double-click on the imported DWG data source.

6. In the Data Source Configuration dialog box, adjust the **Scale** and **Rotation** as necessary. Click **Interactive Placing...** and double-click on a point in the model where the drawing should be located, as shown in Figure 7–7.

- Alternatively, you can set the coordinate system under *Position*. Then set the X and Y coordinate values if you know them. (These values can be found by hovering the cursor over the expected insertion point in the Autodesk InfraWorks model. Then take note of the coordinates in the bottom-left corner of the model window.)

Set the Coordinate System and location manually

Or

Place Interactively

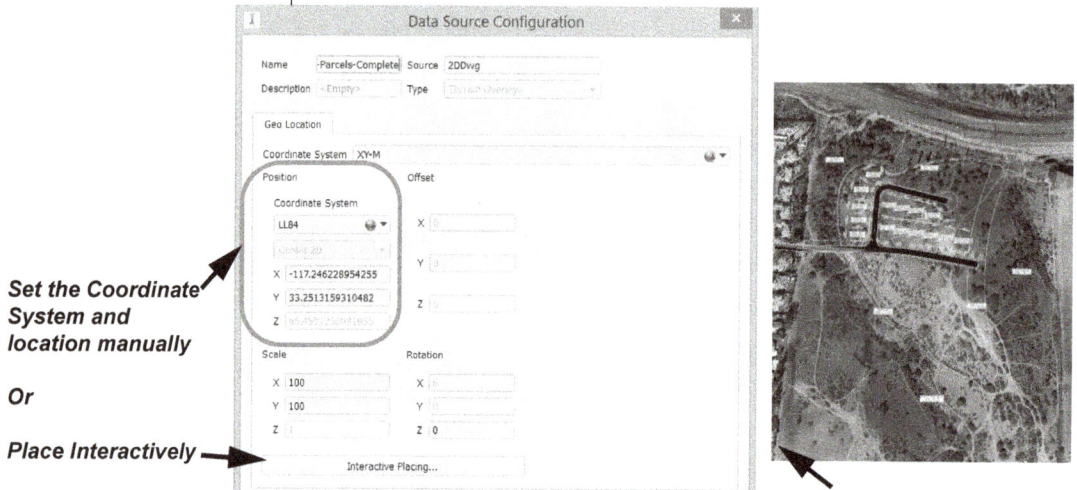

Figure 7–7

7. In the Data Source Configuration dialog box, click **Close & Refresh**.

8. In the model, select the overlay. Then use the gizmos to move, scale, or rotate the overlay as required.

Working with .IMX Files

The enhanced data exchange process makes it easy to import AutoCAD Civil 3D files directly. However, if any errors occur or if you do not have the AutoCAD Civil 3D software on your computer, files can also be transferred between the software packages using .IMX files. Alternatively, IMX files can be used to copy Autodesk InfraWorks features from one model to another.

© 2017, ASCENT - Center for Technical Knowledge®

Exporting .IMX Files

When exporting an .IMX file to be used in the AutoCAD Civil 3D software, you can export the entire Autodesk InfraWorks model, or a portion of the model. When you export an .IMX file, everything becomes part of the .IMX, including the existing conditions of features that were imported from other data sources. To reduce the file size and duplication of model elements in the AutoCAD Civil 3D software, it is recommended that you only export a portion of the model by using a bounding box or polyline. In addition to setting how much of the model to include in the .IMX file, you can also set the target coordinate system.

How To: Create an .IMX file

1. In the In Canvas tools, click ✖ (Settings and Utilities)> (Export IMX).
2. In the Export to IMX dialog box, set the model extents in the Defining Interactively drop-down list by selecting **BBox** or **Polygon** (as shown in Figure 7–8), or by selecting the **Use Entire Model** option.

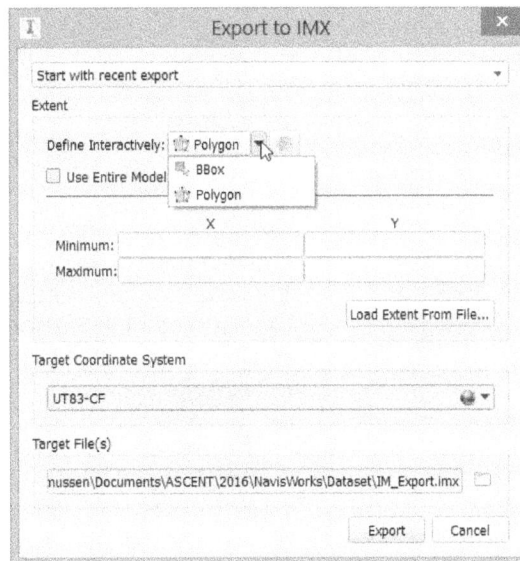

Figure 7–8

3. In the Export to IMX dialog box, set the target coordinate system and the target's directory and filename.
4. Click **Export**.

Importing .IMX Files

When importing .IMX files into an Autodesk InfraWorks model, you use the process that would be used to import any other data source. Importing files does not create a link to the file. Therefore, it is recommended that you create a new proposal before importing an .IMX file to ensure that you have a base model to revert to if anything changes. If the detailed design changes in the AutoCAD Civil 3D software, you have to create and import an updated .IMX file.

Only certain AutoCAD Civil 3D elements can be imported into the Autodesk InfraWorks software. These elements include surfaces, alignments and profiles, corridor models, and pipe networks. Each element must be configured separately. When you import an .IMX file with multiple objects, you must select which type of data to include. The Choose Data Sources dialog box enables you to select the data to import, as shown in Figure 7–9.

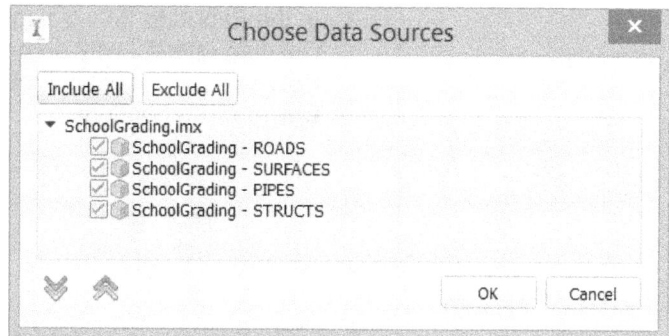

Figure 7–9

Once imported, each data type becomes its own data source in the Data Sources palette. Before they display in the model, the data source must be configured. The list below describes how each data source is handled and configured in the Autodesk InfraWorks software.

- **Surfaces:** Both existing ground and finish ground surfaces can be imported, becoming terrain surfaces. If a grid surface is imported, it is converted into a TIN surface. Only one surface can be displayed in the model at a time, so you must select which surface to import in the *IMX* tab in the Data Source Configuration dialog box, as shown in Figure 7–10.

© 2017, ASCENT - Center for Technical Knowledge®

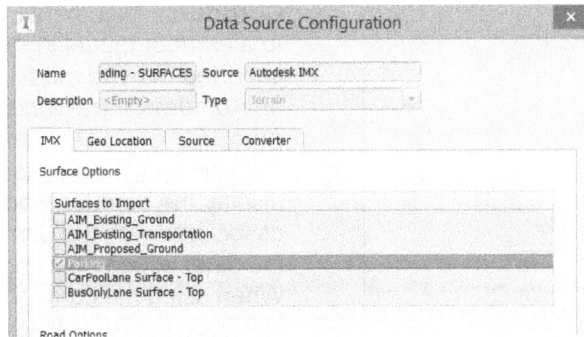

Figure 7–10

- **Alignments and Profiles:** Alignments and profiles are combined into one road feature. They are assigned a road style in the Data Source Configuration dialog box in the *Common* tab, in the *Style* area. Any alignments and profiles that are used to create a corridor model are imported separately. For any alignments that are not associated with a corridor model, you can set the style in the *Common* tab in the Data Source Configuration dialog box, as shown in Figure 7–11.

Figure 7–11

- **Corridors:** Alignments and profiles that have been assigned to a corridor model in the AutoCAD Civil 3D software can be imported into the model in a few different ways. You can use an Autodesk InfraWorks road style, or you can use the AutoCAD Civil 3D corridor surface or regions to display the road design. If the Autodesk InfraWorks styles are used to display the corridor model, only one centerline alignment associated with the corridor is used to stylize the road. All of the other alignments associated with the corridor are ignored. When using the corridor surface or regions to stylize the road, two options are available in the *IMX* tab in the Data Source Configuration Dialog Box, as shown in Figure 7–12.

Road Options

☑ Use Civil3D Corridor Regions (instead of native road styles)

☐ Use corridor regions instead of top surface

3D Model Options

☐ Tile

Figure 7–12

The two **Road Options** are as follows.

- **Use Civil 3D Corridor Regions (instead of native road styles):** If the corridor surface is used to stylize the road, the surface becomes a coverage area rather than a road feature. The road in Figure 7–13 uses the native road styles, while the road in Figure 7–14 shows the same road using the Civil3D Corridor Regions setting.

Native road style

Figure 7–13

Civil3D corridor regions

Figure 7–14

- **Use corridor regions instead of top surface:** This option creates a more detailed display of the road surface. The detail is sharp enough to display curbs, medians and other raised or lowered areas more clearly. Figure 7–15 shows the changes that occur to the road used in Figure 7–14 when with both Road Options are selected.

© 2017, ASCENT - Center for Technical Knowledge®

Figure 7–15

This does not include pressure pipes at this time.

- **Pipe Networks:** Pipes from the AutoCAD Civil 3D software become Pipes in the Autodesk InfraWorks software, while structures become Pipe Connectors. Pipes and Pipe Connectors display separately when a pipe network is imported from the AutoCAD Civil 3D software, as shown in Figure 7–16. When configuring the pipe networks, set the style in the *Common* tab in the Data Configuration dialog box.

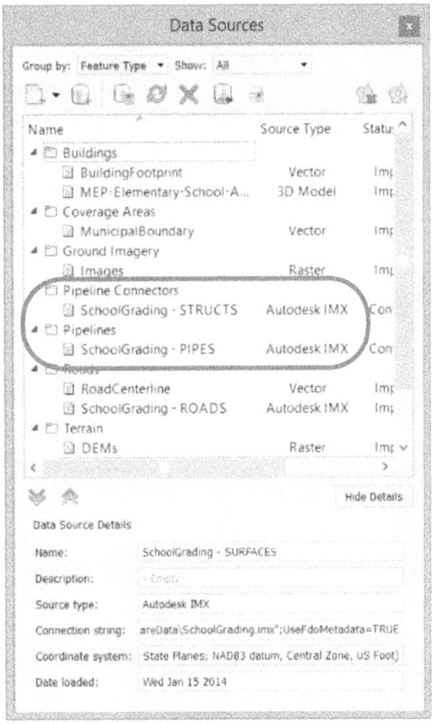

Figure 7–16

How To: Import an .IMX file

1. In the In Canvas tools, click ![icon] (Build, manage, and analyze your industry model)>![icon] (Create and manage your model)>![icon] (Data Sources).
2. In the Data Sources palette, expand ![icon] (Add file data source) and select **Autodesk IMX**.
3. In the Select Files dialog box, browse to the location of the file, select it, and click **Open**.
4. In the Choose Data Source dialog box (shown in Figure 7–17) select the AutoCAD Civil 3D objects that you want to import. Click **OK**.

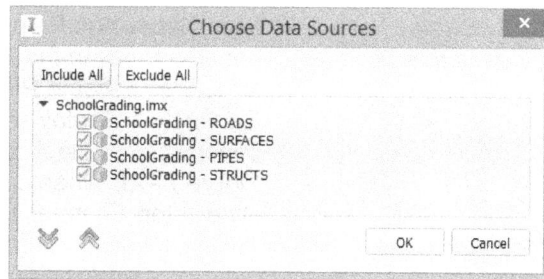

Figure 7–17

5. In the Data Sources palette, double-click on the .IMX files to configure them.
6. If it is a surface or corridor model, in the *IMX* tab, in the Data Source Configuration dialog box, select the required settings.
7. Click **Close & Refresh** to display the imported data in the model.

© 2017, ASCENT - Center for Technical Knowledge®

Practice 7a

Working with AutoCAD Civil 3D Users

Practice Objectives

- Import AutoCAD Civil 3D DWG files.
- Create .IMX files for sharing data with the AutoCAD Civil 3D software.
- Import .IMX files from the AutoCAD Civil 3D software to display the final design.

Estimated time for completion: 20 minutes

In this practice you will move data between the Autodesk InfraWorks software and the AutoCAD Civil 3D software.

Task 1 - Remove potential duplicate roads.

In this task, you will remove roads that are being imported from AutoCAD Civil 3D to avoid duplicates.

1. In the Home Screen, click **Open**.

2. In the *C:\InfraWorks Fundamentals Practice Files\ShareData* folder, select **Sharing.sqlite** and click **Open**.

3. In the Quick Access Toolbar, expand *Switch Active Proposal* and select **A_Task1**.

4. In the Utility Bar, click ▦ (Bookmark your current location) and select **New Neighborhood**.

5. In the model, select the roads and coverage shown in Figure 7–18.

Figure 7–18

6. Press <Delete>.

Task 2 - Import a drawing overlay.

In this task, you will import a drawing overlay in order to display the linework for a parking lot.

1. Continue working in the same model as the last task. If you did not complete the last task, in the Quick Access Toolbar, expand *Switch Active Proposal* and select **A_Task2**.

2. In the Utility Bar, click 🔲 (Bookmark your current location) and select **New Neighborhood**.

3. In the In Canvas tools, click 🔳 (Build, manage, and analyze your infrastructure model) > 🔲 (Create and manage your model> 🔲 (Data Sources).

4. In the Data Sources palette, expand 🔲 ▾ (Add file data source) and select **AutoCAD DWG as 2D Overlay**.

5. In the Select Files dialog box, browse to *C:\InfraWorks Fundamentals Practice Files\ShareData\Civil Files* folder, select **Site Layout - Base.dwg** and click **Open**.

6. In the Data Import dialog box, click **Send**.

7. Once you note that the Status is no longer showing *Processing,* in the Data Source palette, under *Terrain Overlays*, double-click on the **Site Layout - Base** data source.

8. In the Data Source Configuration dialog box, do the following, as shown in Figure 7–19.
    *   Under Coordinate System, expand the drop-down list and select **UT83-CF**.
    *   In the *X* field, type **1535406.6239**.
    *   In the *Y* field, type **7272355.4011**.
    *   Under Scale, for both the *X* and *Y* fields, type **12**.
    *   Click **Close & Refresh**.

*If **UT83-CF** is not in the drop-down list, click*

🔵 *(Choose Coordinate System) and search for it.*

© 2017, ASCENT - Center for Technical Knowledge®

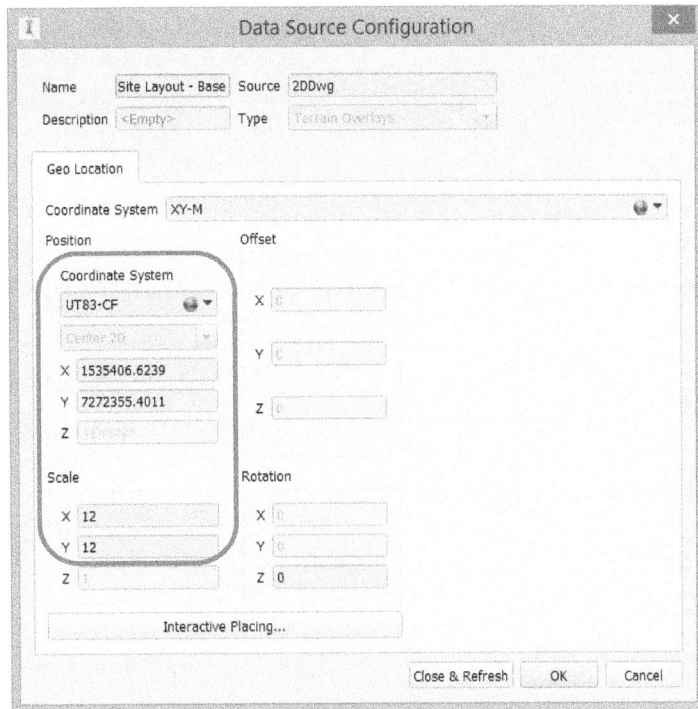

Figure 7–19

9. In the Utility Bar, click (Control visibility, display, and selectability of features).

10. In the Model Explorer palette, under Overlays, to the right of

   Site Layout - Base, click 🔒 (Selectable/ Unselectable) to lock the new overlay.

Task 3 - Import AutoCAD Civil 3D Data.

In this task you will import the AutoCAD Civil 3D surfaces, pipes, and roads from the detailed design phase of the project.

1. Continue working in the same model as the last task. If you did not complete the last task, in the Quick Access Toolbar, expand *Switch Active Proposal* and select **A_Task3**.

2. In the Utility Bar, click (Bookmark your current location) and select **School**.

3. In the Data Sources palette, expand ⬜ ▾ (Add file data source) and select **AutoCAD Civil 3D DWG**.

   - If the Data Sources palette is not open, in the In Canvas

     tools, click ▮ (Build, manage, and analyze your

     infrastructure model)> (Create and manage your

     model)> (Data Sources).

4. In the Select Files dialog box, browse to the *C:\InfraWorks Fundamentals Practice Files\ShareData\Civil Files* folder, select **Site Layout-wPipes.dwg**, and click **Open**.

5. In the Choose Data Sources dialog box, select the objects shown in Figure 7–20. Click **OK**.

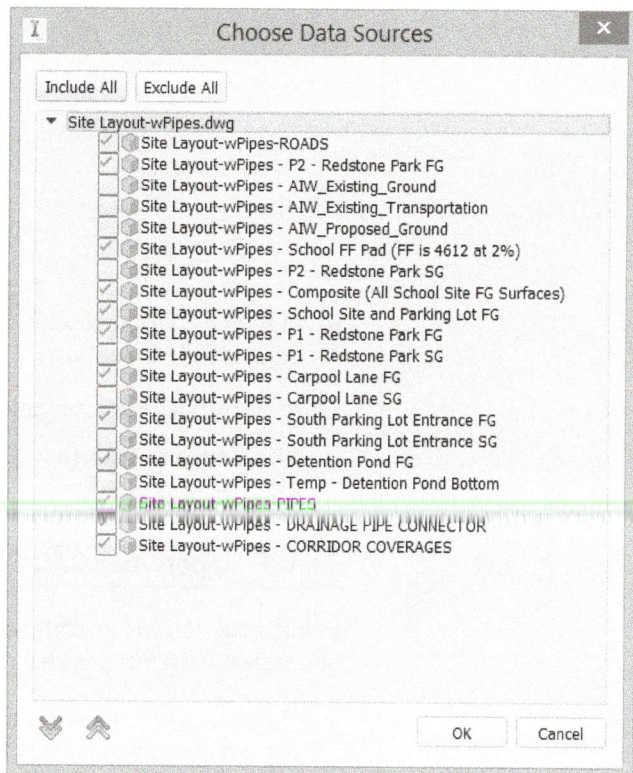

Figure 7–20

6. In the Data Sources palette, click ↻ (Refresh).

7. Once the Status no longer displays *Processing*, in the Data Source palette, under *Roads*, double-click on the **Site Layout-wPipes-Roads** data source.

© 2017, ASCENT - Center for Technical Knowledge®

8. On the *Common* tab of the Data Source Configuration dialog box, next to Rule Style, click ✎ (Style chooser), as shown in Figure 7–21.

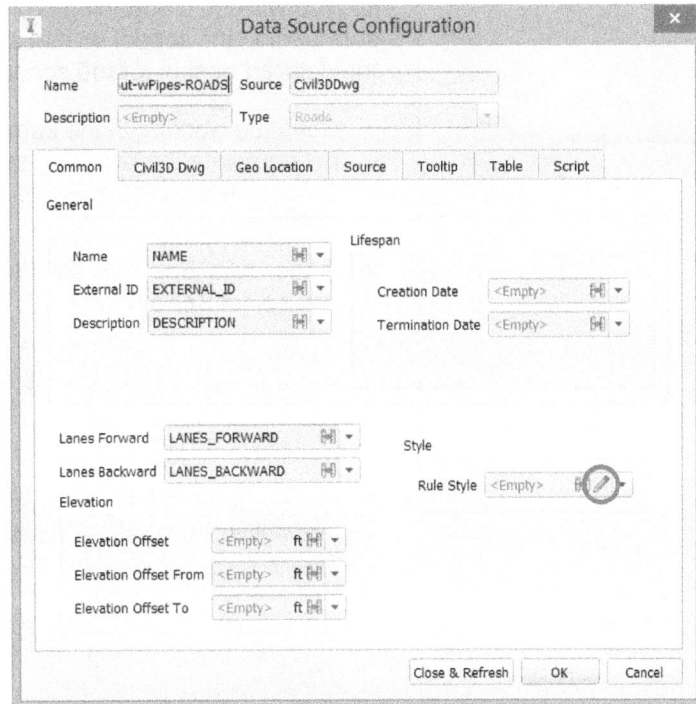

Figure 7–21

9. In the Select Style dialog box, select **Sidewalks with Lamps** and click **OK**.

10. In the Data Source Configuration dialog box, click **Close & Refresh**.

11. In the Utility Bar, click ⊞ (Bookmark your current location) and select **Pond**.

Note the road going around the pond. This road is included in the model because alignments and corridors were used to create the pond grading in the AutoCAD Civil 3D software.

12. Select the road and press <Delete>.

This may not work depending on which version of the software you are using.

Task 4 - Export an .IMX file.

In this task, you will export part of the model to send it to the AutoCAD Civil 3D software for the detailed design phase. To do so, you will use a bounding box to select the information surrounding the school so that another team member can create the detailed design for the school's grading plans.

1. Continue working in the same file as the last task. If you did not complete the last task, in the Quick Access Toolbar, expand *Switch Active Proposal* and select **A_Task4**.

2. In the Utility Bar, click [II] (Bookmark your current location) and select **School**.

3. In the In Canvas tools, click [X] (Setting and Utilities)> [icon] (Export IMX).

4. In the Export to IMX dialog box, expand the Define Interactively drop-down list and select **BBox**, as shown in Figure 7–22.

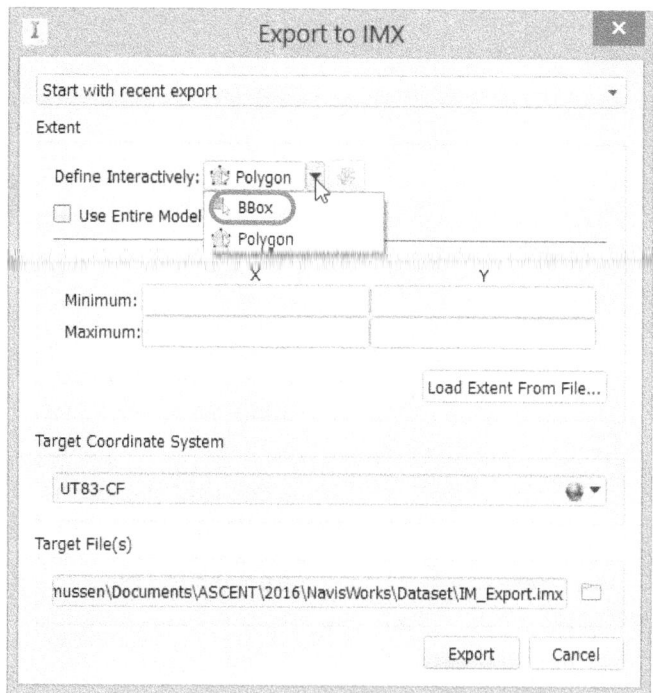

Figure 7–22

© 2017, ASCENT - Center for Technical Knowledge®

5. In the model, create the bounding box shown in Figure 7–23. Single-click the bottom left corner, and then double-click the top right corner.

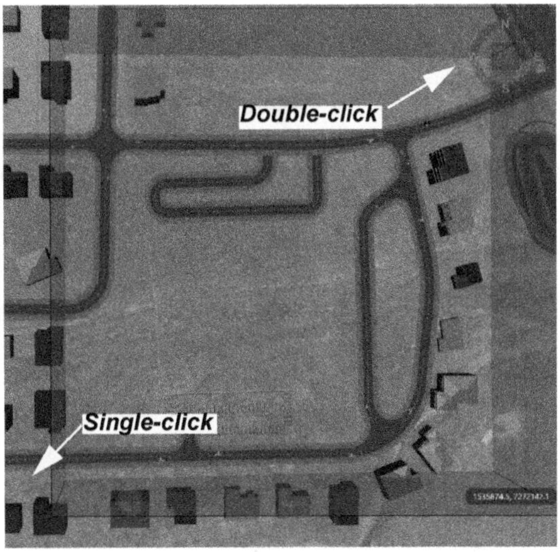

Figure 7–23

6. Ensure that the *Target Coordinate System* is **UT83-CF**, and set *Target File* to **C:\InfraWorks Fundamentals Practice Files\ShareData\IM_Export.imx**.

7. Click **Export**.

7.2 Working with Autodesk Revit Models

AUTODESK
INFRAWORKS 360

To use this feature, access to the Internet, a Navisworks Manage license or the cloud, and Autodesk® InfraWorks® 360 are required.

Determining how a building is going to look in its surrounding environment is valuable for gaining stakeholder buy-in. Until recently, the best an architect could do was to approximate what the ground surface looked like using basic tools in the Autodesk Revit software. At the same time, civil professionals could only create basic 2D line work or a basic 3D model of the building in the AutoCAD Civil 3D software to simulate where the building was to be located. Using the Autodesk InfraWorks software, architects, MEP engineers, and civil professionals can bring their models together into one model to better communicate how an entire project should look when construction is complete. Figure 7–24 shows an Autodesk Revit MEP model of a building that has been imported into an Autodesk InfraWorks model.

Figure 7–24

The tools used to import an Autodesk Revit model are the same as those used to import existing conditions data sources. The biggest difference in the importing process is that a coordinate system has not been assigned to most Autodesk Revit models. Therefore, you either have to know the exact coordinates of where to place the building, or you have to interactively place the building in the model. When importing an Autodesk Revit model, you can preview the model being imported and make any required corrections before placing it in the model. The Data Source Configuration dialog box is shown in Figure 7–25.

© 2017, ASCENT - Center for Technical Knowledge®

Models larger than 100 megabytes in size can negatively affect performance. It is recommended that you simplify large 3D models in their source applications before importing them. The import fails if the 3D model is larger than a gigabyte in size.

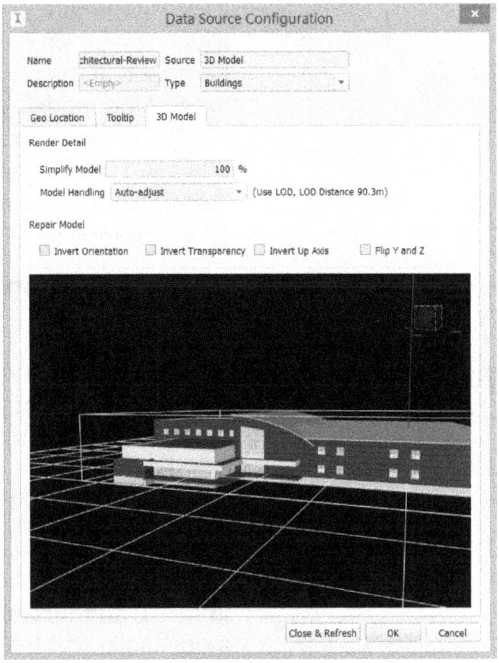

Figure 7–25

Render Detail

How the model renders in the Autodesk InfraWorks model can be controlled using the Model Handling drop-down list in the *3D Model* tab of the Data Source Configuration dialog box. The options used to adjust the model are as follows.

- **Auto-adjust:** The Autodesk InfraWorks software determines the settings for the 3D model. If the automatic setting applies a Level of Detail (LOD), you can change the *LOD Distance* setting by selecting the **Use LOD** option, and adjusting the *LOD Distance*.

- **Direct Display:** The **Repair Model** options and settings for Simplify Model are applied to the 3D model, but they do not adjust how the model is rendered. Use this setting if the model uses a small number of triangles to define its shape. For example, a house with little detail.

The LOD Distance setting is found in the Model Explorer. Higher level of detail settings enable you to see greater detail from a greater distance.

- **Use LOD:** Level of Detail settings generate a series of simplifications, assigning the best one based on viewing distance. If you select this option, ensure that you also set the *LOD Distance*.

- **Tile:** Permanently attaches the 3D model to multiple display tiles. When a single object spans multiple tiles, its display can be erratic. If the object is on the periphery of the displayed area of the model, it might not display at all, or might only display when you zoom in closer to the object. Permanently attaching the 3D model to multiple display tiles helps avoid these issues. This is especially helpful if the model is large or spans several model units (such as a bridge).

- **Use Dynamic LOD:** Sets the LOD dynamically.

Repair Model

When a model does not display as expected in the model, you might need to make slight adjustments to the model. The following five adjustment options can be used to repair the imported model.

- **Invert Orientation:** Inverts the direction of the *Face Normals* that form each surface of the model.

- **Invert Transparency:** Makes the transparent areas of the model solid and the solid areas transparent.

- **Invert Up Axis:** Flips the model upside-down.

- **Flip Y and Z:** Controls whether the *up* axis runs along the Y- or Z-axis since some applications use the Y-axis as the *up* direction, rather than the Z-axis.

How To: Import an Autodesk Revit Model

1. Sign in to the Autodesk InfraWorks 360 service.
2. In the In Canvas tools, click ![icon] (Build, manage, and analyze your industry model)> ![icon] (Create and manage your model)> ![icon] (Data Sources).
3. In the Data Sources palette, click ![icon] (Add file data source) and select **Autodesk Revit**.

AUTODESK
INFRAWORKS 360

To use this feature, access to the Internet, a Navisworks Manage license, and Autodesk® InfraWorks® 360 are required.

© 2017, ASCENT - Center for Technical Knowledge®

4. In the Select Files dialog box, browse to the required Autodesk Revit file and click **Open**.

   • If the Data Import dialog box shown in Figure 7–26 opens, click **Send**.

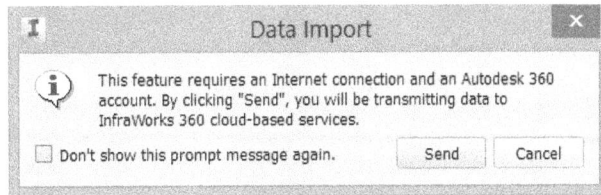

Figure 7–26

   • If the Transfer Navisworks Files message displays (as shown in Figure 7–27), click **Transfer**.

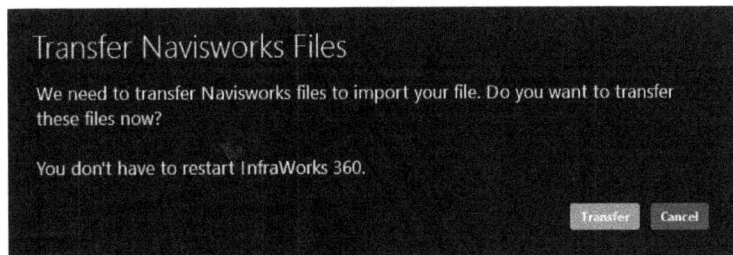

Figure 7–27

5. In the Data Sources palette, double-click on the Autodesk Revit model data source that you just imported.
6. In the common area, the **Type** can be set, as shown in Figure 7–28. By default, the *Type* is set to **Buildings**.

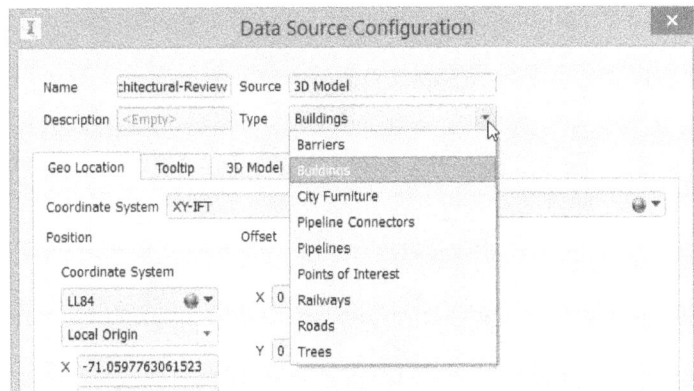

Figure 7–28

*This displays because you need a Navisworks Manage license to import Autodesk Revit files unless you clear the selection of the application option **Navisworks based Local Import** on the Data Import page.*

Only change the Type if the imported model is not a building.

7. In the *Geo Location* tab, set the X, Y, and Z values under *Position* or click **Interactive Placing**, as shown in Figure 7–29.

If provided, the Autodesk InfraWorks software can automatically read the location data from the Revit file.

Figure 7–29

© 2017, ASCENT - Center for Technical Knowledge®

8. Preview the model in the *3D Model* tab, as shown in Figure 7–30.

   - Select an appropriate *Model Handling* option to set the Level of Detail (LOD).

   - Make any necessary adjustments to the model under the Model Repair area.

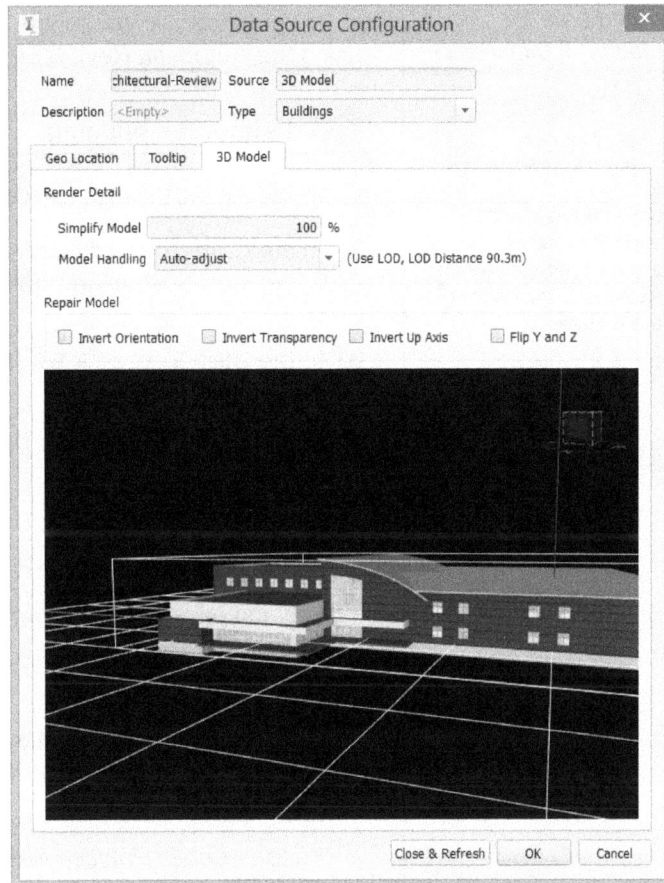

Figure 7–30

9. Click **Close & Refresh** to complete the import process and display it in the model.

Practice 7b

Import an Autodesk Revit File

Practice Objective

- Import an Autodesk Revit model and note how it fits with other design elements.

In this practice you will import a school model that was created using the Autodesk Revit MEP software.

Estimated time for completion: 5 minutes

AUTODESK INFRAWORKS 360

To complete this practice, access to the Internet, a Navisworks Manage license, and Autodesk® InfraWorks® 360 are required.

Task 1 - Import a building.

1. In the Home Screen, click **Open**.

2. In the *C:\InfraWorks Fundamentals Practice Files\ShareData* folder, select **Sharing.sqlite** and click **Open**.

3. In the Utility Bar, click ⬜ (Bookmark your current location) and select **School**.

4. In the Utility Bar, expand *Switch Active Proposal* and select **B_Task1**.

5. In the In Canvas tools, click ⬛ (Build, manage, and analyze your industry model) > ⬛ (Create and manage your model)> ⬛ (Data Sources).

6. In the Data Sources palette, click ⬜ (Add file data source) and select **Autodesk Revit**.

7. In the Select Files dialog box, browse to the *C:\InfraWorks Fundamentals Practice Files\ShareData* folder, select **MEP-Elementary-School-Architectural-Review.rvt** and click **Open**.

   - If the Data Import information dialog box displays (shown in Figure 7–31), click **Send**.

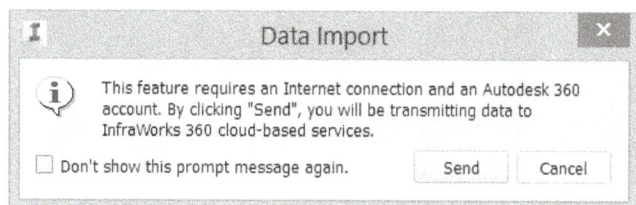

   Figure 7–31

© 2017, ASCENT - Center for Technical Knowledge®

- If the Data Import warning dialog box displays (as shown in Figure 7–32), click **OK**.

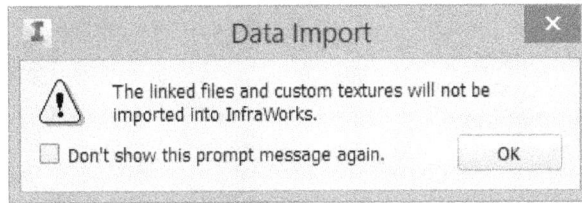

This dialog box prompts you that the custom textures that were part of the Autodesk Revit model will be ignored. Custom textures cannot be imported into the Autodesk InfraWorks software.

Figure 7–32

8. In the Data Sources palette, in the *Building* folder, double-click on the **MEP-Elementary-School-Architectural-Review** model data source that you just imported.

   Note: You might have to wait for the model to finish processing. You will know it is done when *In Progress* is replaced with *Imported* in the Status column, as shown in Figure 7–33.

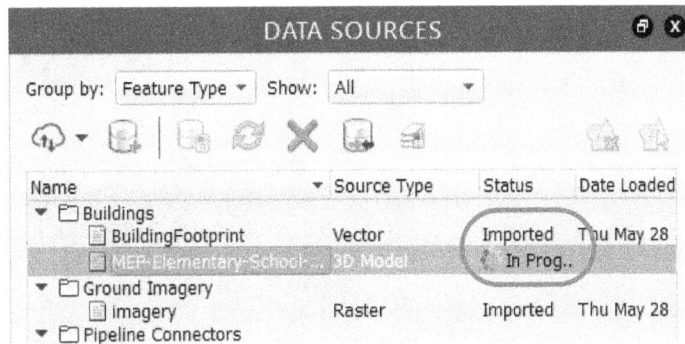

Figure 7–33

9. In the Data Source Configuration dialog box, ensure that the *Type* is set to **Buildings**.

10. In the *Geo Location* tab, click **Interactive Placing**.

If changes are made to the original Autodesk Revit model, you will need to import the updated model.

11. In the model, double-click to place the school model on the coverage, as shown in Figure 7–34.

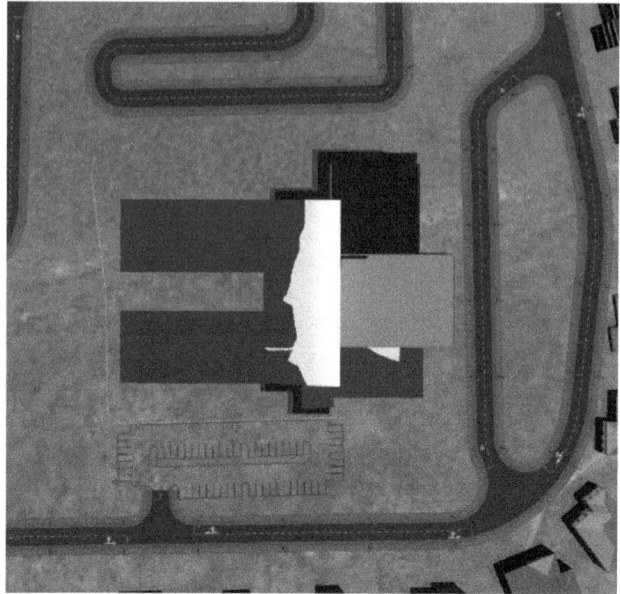

Figure 7–34

12. In the Data Source configuration dialog box, click **Close & Refresh** to update the model. The Autodesk Revit model now displays in the Autodesk InfraWorks model.

13. In the model, select the building. Then use the ⬦ (Move Gizmo) to reposition the model as required.

© 2017, ASCENT - Center for Technical Knowledge®

7.3 Share Files Using the Autodesk InfraWorks 360 Service

Autodesk InfraWorks 360 is a cloud service used to store and share models over the Internet. Once you have signed into your Autodesk InfraWorks 360 account, you can share models, proposals, and scenarios.

The following is an example of how the Autodesk InfraWorks 360 service can be used to share and collaborate on files:

- A group is created by your team's administrator, and you and your team are invited to join the group.

- An architect publishes a model to the group.

- You download and make changes to the architect's Autodesk InfraWorks model.

- You synchronize your local changes with the online version.

- The architect synchronizes with the online model and notes how the changes affect the model.

- You and your team continue to make changes and synchronize your versions to the model in the cloud. Any conflicts are automatically resolved throughout the process.

Sign In

When you first start Autodesk InfraWorks 360, you should be asked to sign into your Autodesk Account. If you do not have an account, click **Need an Autodesk ID?** in the Autodesk Account Sign In screen to create a new account. Once signed in, your login information is saved for 14 days and determines what tools are available to you. You should not see the Autodesk Account Sign In screen for 14 days unless you manually sign out.

How To: Sign In to Autodesk InfraWorks 360

1. In the Autodesk Account Sign In screen, type your user name and click **NEXT**, as shown in Figure 7–35. Type your password and click **Sign In**.

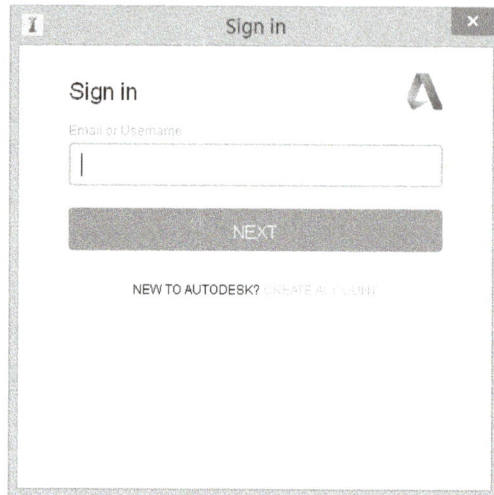

Figure 7–35

Manage Group Memberships

Models are shared using groups to ensure that you can control who is able to access the model. To create groups and assign people to them, you must be a group administrator.

Users Roles

Anyone can create a free account and become an Autodesk InfraWorks 360 user. You do not need to own a copy of the software in order to create an account. Therefore, each person inside a firm and all of the firm's clients can create an account. The key is knowing the user rights level that each individual should be assigned. User rights fall into four roles, as listed below.

- **Admin:** Initially, only one administrator is assigned to an account. However, the admin can give Admin rights to any user's account. Admins have the ability to create groups, add users, and download/upload or synchronize models to the cloud.

- **Author:** Authors can only download and synchronize models that they have downloaded, to the cloud. They cannot upload new models to the cloud.

© 2017, ASCENT - Center for Technical Knowledge®

- **Publisher:** Publishers can upload/download, and synchronize models to the cloud. They can also upload scenarios to the cloud.

- **Reader:** Readers can only download and view models from the cloud. They cannot upload updates or new models to the cloud.

How To: Manage Group Memberships

If 👥 is not displayed,

click 👤 (Manage groups and cloud models) to expand it.

1. In the Home Screen, click 👥 (Manage group memberships).

2. In the Manage Group Memberships dialog box, *in the Administer Groups* tab, select the account the groups should be applied to, and then click ➕ (Add Group), as shown in Figure 7–36.

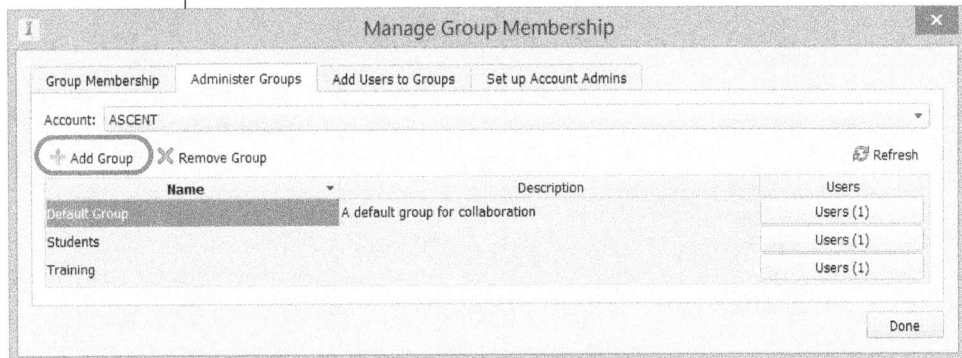

Figure 7–36

3. In the Add Group dialog box, type a name and description in the respective fields. Click **OK**.
4. Next to the new group, click **Users** to add users to the group.
   - This automatically switches to the *Add Users to Group* tab.
   - Alternatively, you can select the *Add Users to Group* tab manually.
5. In the *Assign User to Groups* tab, select the group to work with at the top, and then click ➕ (Add User).

The Administrator is automatically added to the group with an assigned role of Admin.

6. In the new row, type the email address that is connected to the user's Autodesk InfraWorks 360 account. Then assign them the role of Author, Publisher, or Reader, as applicable. Click **OK**.

How To: Assign Admin Rights

1. In the Home Screen, click 👥 (Manage group memberships).
2. In the Manage Group Membership dialog box, select the *Set up Account Admins* tab.
3. Select the account that you want to add to the admin rights group in the Account drop-down list.

A list of users for the account displays.

4. In the Admin column, check the email address for the users that should obtain admin rights, as shown in Figure 7–37.

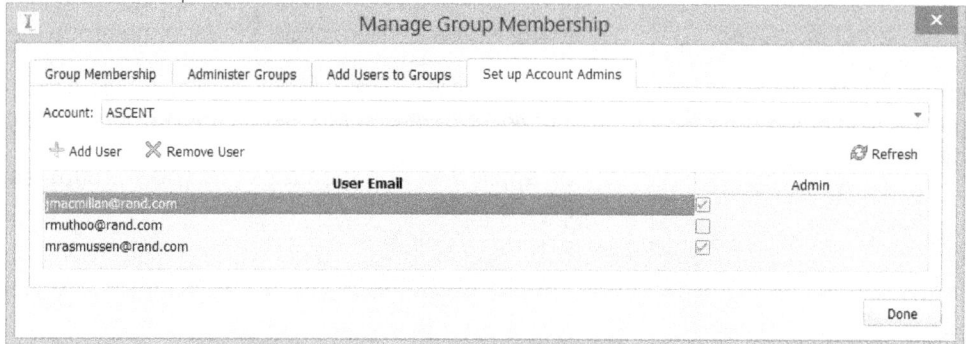

Figure 7–37

5. Click **OK**.

Working with Models

Publishing Models

When you publish a model, you make it available to others to see the selected proposals. By default, only the master proposal and common resources are published. Additional proposals can be published by selecting them in the Publish Model dialog box. You can also determine who has access to the model by selecting a group that has been created for you by a group administrator.

How To: To Publish a Model

1. Open the model you want to publish.

2. In the Utility Bar, click 🔄 (Publish this model to InfraWorks 360).

3. In the Publish Model dialog box, select the Group that you want to share the model with from the Group drop-down list.

© 2017, ASCENT - Center for Technical Knowledge®

4. Select the proposals you want to share in the *Select Resources* area, as shown in Figure 7–38. Type any Publishing Notes to describe what is included in this version of the model. Click **Publish**.

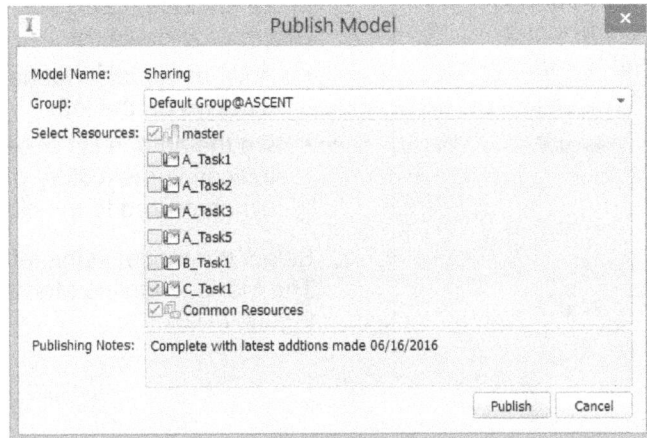

Figure 7–38

Accessing Online Models

Once a model has been shared, others that are invited can access it by selecting the model on the Home Screen, as shown in Figure 7–39. Click the appropriate thumbnail to download and open the model.

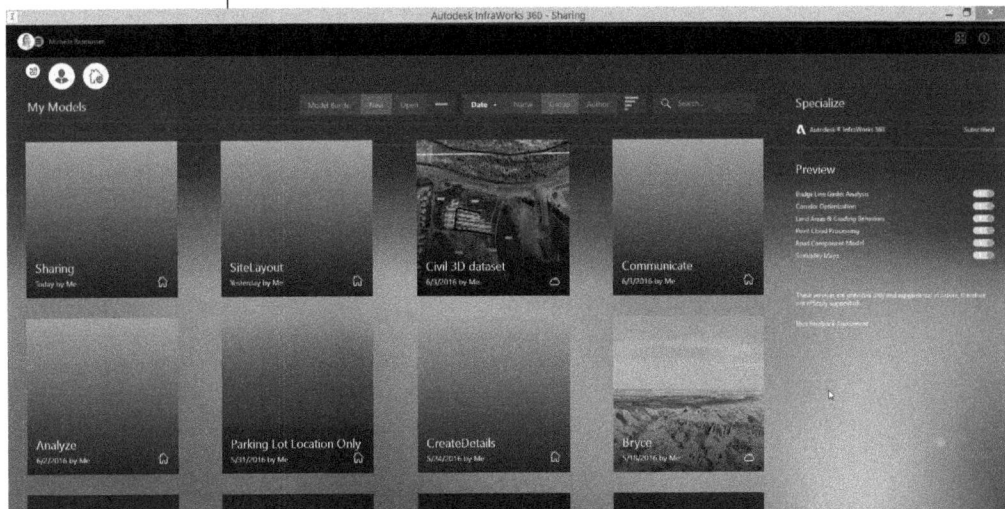

Figure 7–39

If the model does not display in the thumbnails on the Home screen, they can download it from the cloud.

How To: Download Models from InfraWorks 360

If 👥 *is not displayed,*

click 👤 *(Manage groups and cloud models) to expand it.*

1. On the Home screen, click 👥 (Manage online models and scenarios).
2. In the Manage dialog box, select the model's group in the Group drop-down list.
   - A list of models that have been published to the cloud displays on the left.
   - On the right, a list of each model's history displays indicating the history of when the model was synchronized to the cloud.

3. Select the model in the left column and click ⬇ (Download). The Manage Online Models dialog box is shown in Figure 7–40.

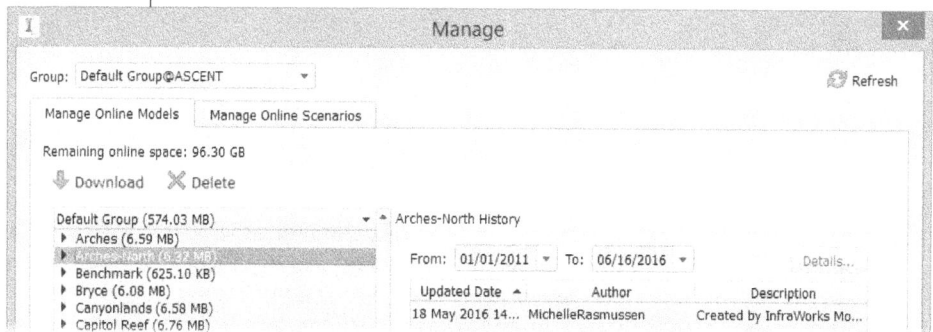

Figure 7–40

4. In the Download As dialog box, select the location in which the model is going to be saved on your computer, as shown in Figure 7–41.

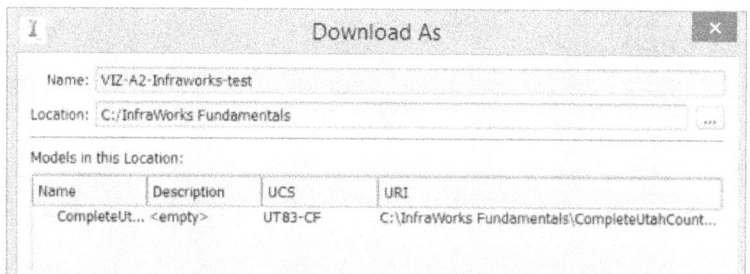

Figure 7–41

- If you no longer want to share a model, click ✖ (Delete) in the Manage dialog box to remove it from the group in the cloud.

© 2017, ASCENT - Center for Technical Knowledge®

Synchronizing Models

Synchronizing a model enables you to share your latest changes with others through the cloud, review changes others have made to the model, and resolve any conflicts between local and shared versions of the files. Conflicts are resolved automatically and you do not have any control over how they are resolved. The last local change usually takes precedence over a conflicting change from the online group, and deletions take precedence over updates.

It is extremely important that all members of a team use the same version of the Autodesk InfraWorks software. If one team member upgrades a model, the shared, cloud model also updates. Any changes that are not synced to the cloud before upgrading a model are lost. Communication is key to sharing models and upgrading them. It is best to sync changes frequently when working in a team environment.

*If you do not have the required permissions to edit the model, **Sync** is grayed out in the Synchronize Model dialog box.*

In the Synchronize Model dialog box, the *Local Last Changed* column indicates the last time you made changes to the model on your computer. The *Online Last Changed* column indicates when the model was last changed in the cloud. If ⚠ displays next to a file or proposal, the local file or proposal has not been shared with the cloud. Figure 7–42 shows the Synchronize Model dialog box.

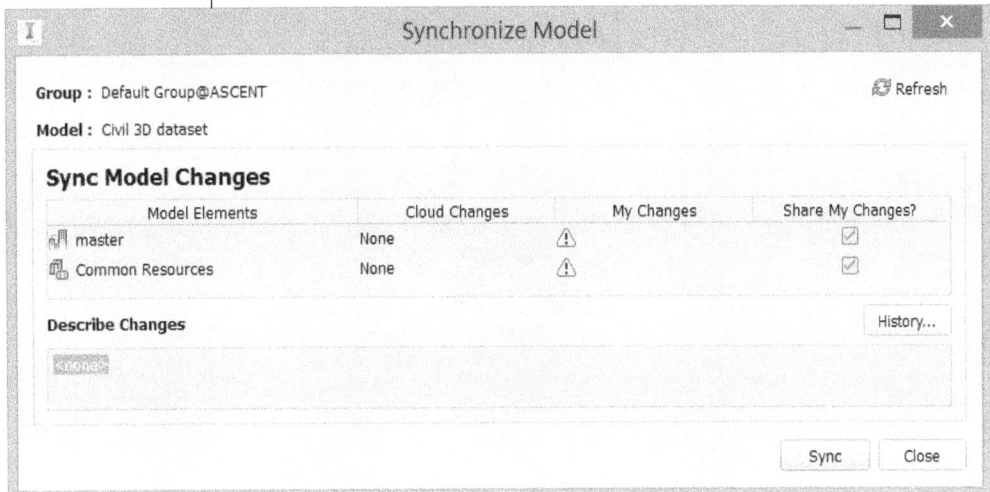

Figure 7–42

7.4 Working With Scenarios

Scenarios require the Autodesk InfraWorks 360 online service since they publish to the cloud when the model is synchronized.

Scenarios are packages that include all or part of a model for others to view on the Internet or on an Apple® device (e.g., an iPad® or iPhone®). Scenarios eliminate the need to have the Autodesk InfraWorks software installed on a computer to review a project. Scenarios can be published to the Autodesk InfraWorks 360 service for sharing with the public or a project team. Figure 7–43 shows the Scenario palette.

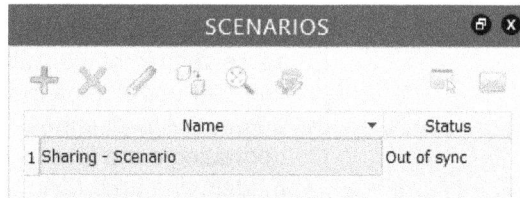

Figure 7–43

Scenario Palette

The Scenario palette provides tools to create, remove, modify, and share scenarios. The *Status* column communicates whether the scenarios is still generating, ready for viewing, or out of date. The tools found at the top the Scenario palette are as follows:

Icon	Description
	Add a new scenario.
	Remove the selected scenario(s).
	Edit the selected scenario.
	Duplicate the selected scenario.
	Zoom to the extents of the selected scenario(s).
	Edit the AOI (Area of Interest) of the selected scenario.
	Open in web browser.
	Email URL.

© 2017, ASCENT - Center for Technical Knowledge®

Scenario Asset Card

Name and Proposal

When creating a scenario, the *Name & Proposal* area describes the contents of the file. The *Name* and *Description* fields should never be left blank. This is where you select which proposal to share with others over the cloud.

Area of Interest

The *Area of Interest* area enables you to define the model extents, and to set the initial view that displays when the file is opened. Figure 7–44 shows the Scenario Editor asset card with the *Area of Interest* area expanded.

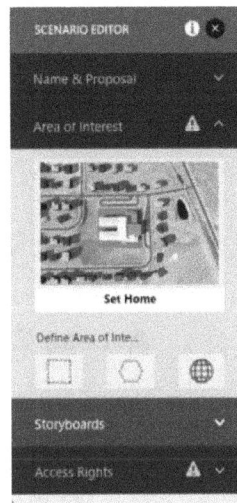

Figure 7–44

Define Area of Interest

The ⊕ **Entire Model** option shares everything that is modeled. If only a portion of the model is to be shared, select the ▢ (Bounding Box) or ⬡ (Polygon) option as required, and select the required area in the model.

Set Home Position

Setting the home position enables users to quickly navigate back to a set view. The view can be created by zooming the model to the location for the home view (this can be done while the Scenario Editor asset card displays). Then click **Set Home**, which saves the view as the home position.

Storyboards

Storyboards are saved presentations that help communicate the design to stakeholders. Including a storyboard in a scenario enables users to display the storyboard without installing the Autodesk InfraWorks software. Figure 7–45 shows the Scenario Editor asset card with the *Storyboards* area expanded.

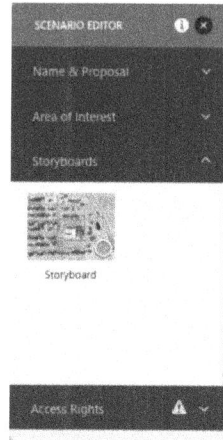

Figure 7–45

Access Rights

The *Access Rights* area displays which group has the ability to view the scenario. The group is set when publishing the model to the cloud. In addition to the group, you can toggle on the option to make the scenario available to the public, as shown in Figure 7–46.

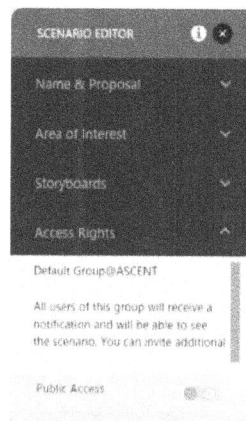

Figure 7–46

© 2017, ASCENT - Center for Technical Knowledge®

How To: Create a Scenario

1. In the In Canvas tools, click ▣ (Create and conduct infrastructure design presentations)> 🖼 (Scenario Browser).
2. In the Scenarios palette, click ✛ (Add a new scenario).
3. In the Create Scenario asset card, in *the Name & Proposal* area, type in the name and a description for the scenario. Then select which proposal to make available to others.
4. In the Scenario Editor asset card, in *the Define Area of Interest* area, select the type of boundary required, then define the extents boundary, if required.
5. In the model, navigate to the view you would like to set as the home view.
6. In the *Area of Interest* area, click **Set Home** to set the home view of the scenario to your current view of the model.
7. In the Scenario Editor asset card, in the *Storyboards* area, select the storyboards that you want to include.
8. In the *Access Rights* area, toggle Public Access on or off, as required.
9. In the Utility Bar, click, 🔄 (Sync model changes to InfraWorks 360) to make the model available to others. Once the web views of the model are ready, an email is sent to you with a link.

You can continue working in the model even when an asset card displays.

Practice 7c

Share the Model Using a Scenario

Practice Objective

- Create a package that includes storyboards, points of interest, and watermarks to share on the Internet using scenarios.

Estimated time for completion: 10 minutes

In this practice you will create a scenario to be posted on the Internet.

Task 1 - Create a scenario.

1. In the Home Screen, click **Open**.

2. In the *C:\InfraWorks Fundamentals Practice Files\ShareData* folder, select **Sharing.sqlite** and click **Open**.

3. In the Utility Bar, expand *Switch Active Proposal* and select **C_Task1**.

4. In the Utility Bar, click ▣ (Bookmark your current location) and select **School**.

5. In the In Canvas tools, click ▣ (Create and conduct infrastructure design presentations)> ▣ (Scenario Browser).

6. In the Scenarios palette, click ╬ (Add a new scenario).

7. In the Scenario Editor asset card, note that the scenario name is automatically derived from the model name with **- Scenario** appended to the end (e.g., Sharing - Scenario). For the *Proposal to Publish*, select **C_Task1**.

8. In the *Area of Interest* area, click ▢ (Bounding Box) to define the scenario extents.

© 2017, ASCENT - Center for Technical Knowledge®

9. In the model, click points to set the scenario extents shown in Figure 7–47.

Remember to double-click on the last point to end the selection.

Figure 7–47

10. In the Utility Bar, click (Bookmark your current location) and select **SchoolEntrance** to orient the model view to that shown in Figure 7–48. In the Scenario Editor asset card, click **Set Home** to define the home view of the scenario.

Figure 7–48

11. In the Scenario Editor asset card, leave all of the other settings as their defaults

12. In the Utility Bar, click, (Publish model to InfraWorks 360) to make the model available to others.

Chapter Review Questions

1. Anyone can create groups and add members to them in the Autodesk InfraWorks 360 service.

   a. True

   b. False

2. When importing an Autodesk Revit model, which of the following is not one of the five adjustment options that can be used to repair the imported model?

   a. **Invert Orientation**

   b. **Flip Y and Z**

   c. **Flip X and Z**

   d. **Invert Up Axis**

3. Which type of file can be used to exchange design data between the Autodesk InfraWorks software and the AutoCAD Civil 3D software or between two Autodesk InfraWorks models?

   a. .IMX

   b. .FBX

   c. .PNT

   d. .TIN

4. You can drag and drop .DWG files into an Autodesk InfraWorks model from Windows Explorer.

   a. True

   b. False

5. How do you share a model with someone who does not have InfraWorks?

   a. Create watermarks

   b. Duplicate the model

   c. Create saved views

   d. Create a scenario and publish the model

© 2017, ASCENT - Center for Technical Knowledge®

Command Summary

Button	Command	Location
	Data Sources	• **In Canvas Tools:** Build, manage, and analyze your infrastructure model> Create and manage your model
	Manage group memberships	• **Home Screen**
	Manage Online models and scenarios	• **Home Screen**
	Publish this model to InfraWorks 360	• **Utility Bar**
	Scenario Browser	• **In Canvas Tools:** Create and conduct infrastructure design presentations
N/A	**Sign In to InfraWorks 360**	• **Home Screen**
	Sync model changes to InfraWorks 360	• **Utility Bar**

© 2017, ASCENT - Center for Technical Knowledge®

Chapter

8

Communicate the Design to Stakeholders

The most important part of any project is the approval process. Without buy-in from all of the stakeholders a project can be delayed, which can impact the project's timeline and budget. To ensure buy-in from all of the stakeholders, proper communication must take place. You need to ensure that everyone involved knows how the project is expected to look once it has been built. In this chapter you learn how to create high-end visualizations to help communicate the design intent. Images and storyboards are created to make this possible.

Learning Objectives in this Chapter

- Present a simple image of the model using a snapshot.
- Create a visual style for viewing the model in various ways.
- Present a slide-show of the design to stakeholders by creating storyboards.
- Publish scenarios of the model to the cloud for others to review.

8.1 Creating Images

The Autodesk InfraWorks software enables you to create images of varying quality. You can create quick snapshots or realistic renderings of the model to communicate to stakeholders exactly how a project is expected to look when construction is finished.

Snapshots

A snapshot is a quick, low-resolution image of the current model view. Figure 8–1 shows an example of a snapshot. The image looks like the current view, and uses the current visual effects settings. Therefore, if shadows are toggled off in the model, they do not display in the snapshot. The quality of the image can be adjusted using various settings, such as the level of detail (LOD), style, and snapshot resolution settings.

Figure 8–1

© 2017, ASCENT - Center for Technical Knowledge®

How To: Create a Snapshot

1. In the In Canvas tools, click 🖥️ (Create and conduct infrastructure design presentations)> 📷 (Create Snapshot).
2. In the Camera Snapshot dialog box, set the required resolution for the image, as shown in Figure 8–2. Click ⬚ (Browse) to set the path and filename for the image.

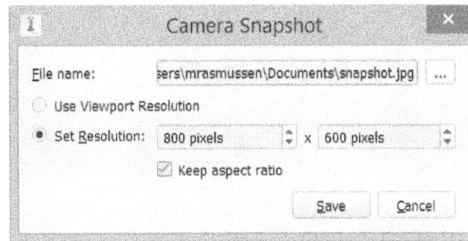

Figure 8–2

Snapshot images can be saved as .JPG, .PNG, or .TIFF images.

3. In the Select Image File dialog box, in the expanded Save As Type drop-down list, select the image type that you want to create, as shown in Figure 8–3. Enter the required filename and location and click **Save**.

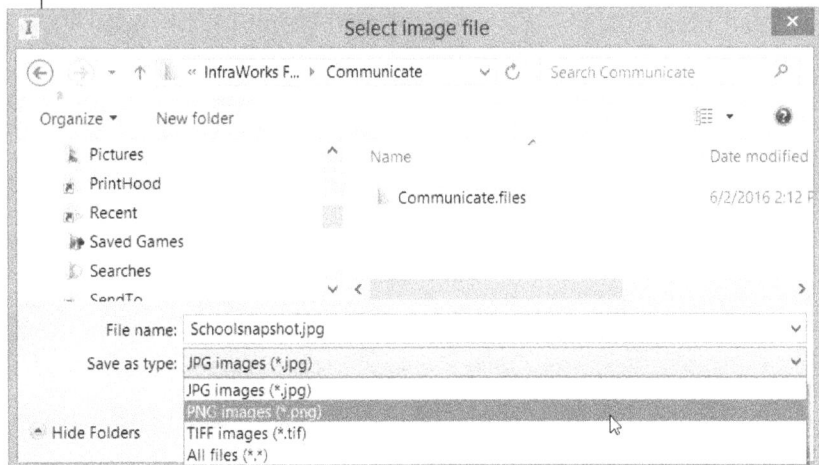

Figure 8–3

4. In the Camera Snapshot dialog box, click **Save**.
5. To display the image, use Windows Explorer to open it from the saved location.

Visual Styles

When working with Snapshots, what you see in the model when you snap the image is how the image displays. This is controlled by the Visual Style. The Utility Bar enables you to change the current visual style. New visual styles can be created to highlight various aspects of the model, as shown in Figure 8–4.

Wireframe toggled on in the View Settings, Visualization palette

Wireframe toggled off in the View Settings, Visualization palette

Figure 8–4

Different view settings can be assigned to each visual style. Visual styles and view configurations are saved locally, so that they are available in every model that you open. All of the view setting options can be found in one of two tabs in the View Settings panel.

© 2017, ASCENT - Center for Technical Knowledge®

Visualization Tab

The *Visualization* tab controls a range of lighting effects.

- Color
  - **Brightness**: Adjusts the amount of black in the model's colors.
  - **Contrast**: Adjusts the definition between areas of differing values to provide more image depth.
  - **Light Intensity**: Adjusts the overall brightness and intensity of colors uniformly.
  - **Sun Color**: Adds a tint to simulate sun position.
  - **Colorize**: Select between normal, gray scale, or sepia color schemes.
- Rendering
  - **High Visual Quality**: Toggles shadows for high or rough resolution model display.
  - **Wireframe**: When on, reduces features to 3D skeletons, displaying only lines and vertices.
  - **Animation**: Toggles water wave and cloud movement.
  - **Show Sky**: Toggles the display of the sky background.
  - **Surface Opacity**: Adjusts the transparency of the ground surface.
- Field of View
  - **Field of View**: Adjusts feature flatness, similar to a wide-angle lens on a camera.

Interaction Tab

The *Interaction* tab controls the visibility of certain tools and other interaction settings.

- Feedback
  - **Status Bar**: Toggles the cursor's coordinates on the bottom left of the model window.
  - **Tooltips**: Toggles the text, images, links, or model property values that display when you hover over a command or feature.
  - **Links**: Toggles the display of feature links to external data stores, tooltips, or maps.
  - **Edit mode**: Toggles the ability to make changes to model features.

- Navigation
  - **View Cube**: Toggles the display of the ViewCube.
  - **Proximity**: Toggles the display of tooltips when the proximity distance is reached.
  - **Automatic Zoom To Selection**: Toggles the automatic zoom on selected features.
  - **Highlight Sketched Features**: Toggles the linework that highlights sketched features when in drawing mode.
  - **Lock Mouse Above Ground**: Toggles the ability to view features below the surface.
  - **Show Statistics**: Toggles the display of feature statistics while in edit or draw mode.

How To: Create a New Visual Style

1. In the Utility Bar, expand the View Style drop-down and click **Add**.
2. In the Utility Bar, expand the View Style drop-down and click ⚙ (Configure current view).
3. On the *Visualization* tab, make the required changes to adjust the model display, as shown in Figure 8–5.

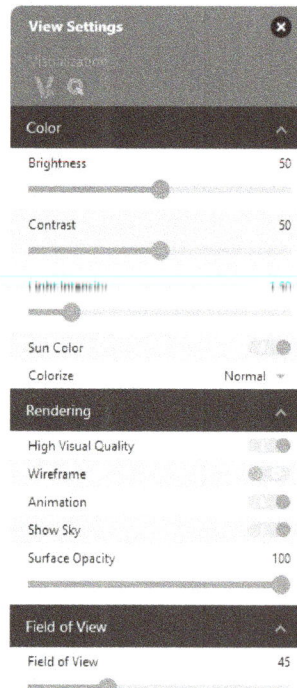

Figure 8–5

© 2017, ASCENT - Center for Technical Knowledge®

4. In the View Settings panel, click ⬜ (Change navigation and application feedback settings) to open the *Interaction* tab.
5. Set the required toggles to the right to toggle them on or left to toggle them off, as shown in Figure 8–6.

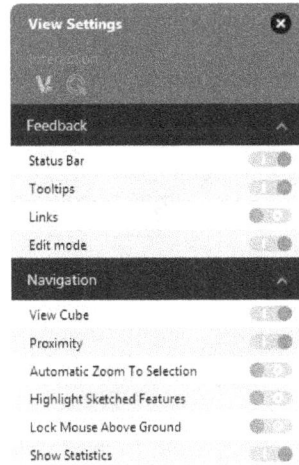

Figure 8–6

Practice 8a

Communicating the Design Using Images

Estimated time for completion: 10 minutes

Practice Objective

- Communicate the design intent to stakeholders using images.

In this practice you will create a snapshot using a bookmark orientation. You will also render an image of the same view.

Task 1 - Create a snapshot.

1. In the Home Screen, click **Open**.

2. In the *C:\InfraWorks Fundamentals Practice Files\ Communicate* folder, select **Communicate.sqlite** and click **Open**.

3. In the Utility Bar, click ▉ (Bookmark your current location) and select **StudentDropOff**. Ensure that **A_Task1** is the current proposal in the Utility Bar.

4. In the Utility Bar, for the Visual Style, select **Engineering View**. Then switch it back to the **Conceptual View** and note the differences.

5. In the In Canvas tools, click ▣ (Create and conduct infrastructure design presentations) > ▣ (Create Snapshot).

6. In the Camera Snapshot dialog box, ensure that the resolution is set to the default, as shown in Figure 8–7. Click (Browse) to set the path and filename for the image.

Figure 8–7

© 2017, ASCENT - Center for Technical Knowledge®

7. In the Select Image File dialog box, expand the Save as type drop-down list, and select **PNG Images**, as shown in Figure 8–8. Enter the required filename and location and click **Save**.

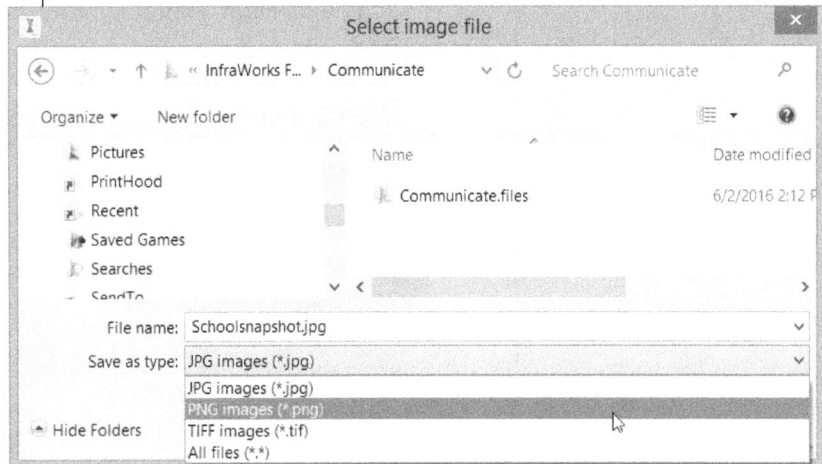

Figure 8–8

8. In the Camera Snapshot dialog box, click **Save**.

9. To display the image, use Windows Explorer to open it from the saved location.

Task 2 - Create a Visual Style.

1. In the Utility Bar, expand the View Style drop-down and click **Add**.

2. In the Utility Bar, expand the View Style drop-down and click ⚙ (Configure current view).

3. On the Visualization tab, make the following changes, as shown in Figure 8–9.

   - Set the *Brightness* and *Contrast* both to **50**.
   - Set the *Light Intensity* to **3**.
   - Toggle off **High Visual Quality**, **Animation**, and **Show Sky**.
   - Toggle on **Wireframe**.
   - Set the *Surface Opacity* to approximately **50**.

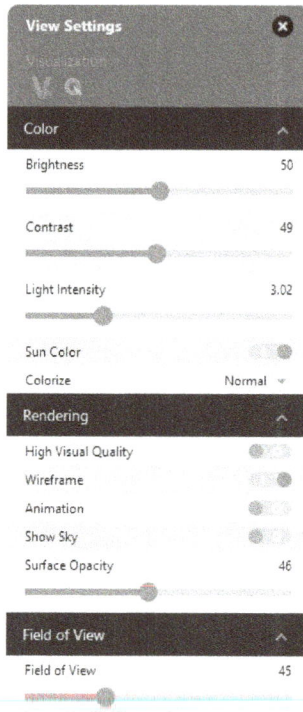

Figure 8–9

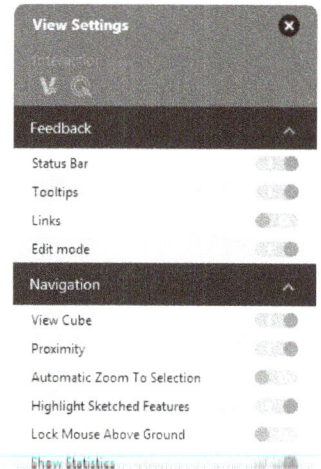

Figure 8–10

4. In the View Settings panel, click ⬛ (Change navigation and application feedback settings) to open the *Interaction* tab.

5. Toggle on **Highlight Sketched Features**, as shown in Figure 8–10, above.

6. Close the View Settings panel.

© 2017, ASCENT - Center for Technical Knowledge®

8.2 Working with Storyboards

Storyboards are a collection of elements or keyframes that are combined together in a slide show to tell a compelling story about the design. The keyframes in a storyboard are generated from animations. These animations are either Path or Camera animations. Still images can also be incorporated using a Still Motion Camera animation.

Using storyboards, you can simulate driving through the model, get a birds-eye view of the model, or explore the model. Figure 8–11 shows the Storyboard palette.

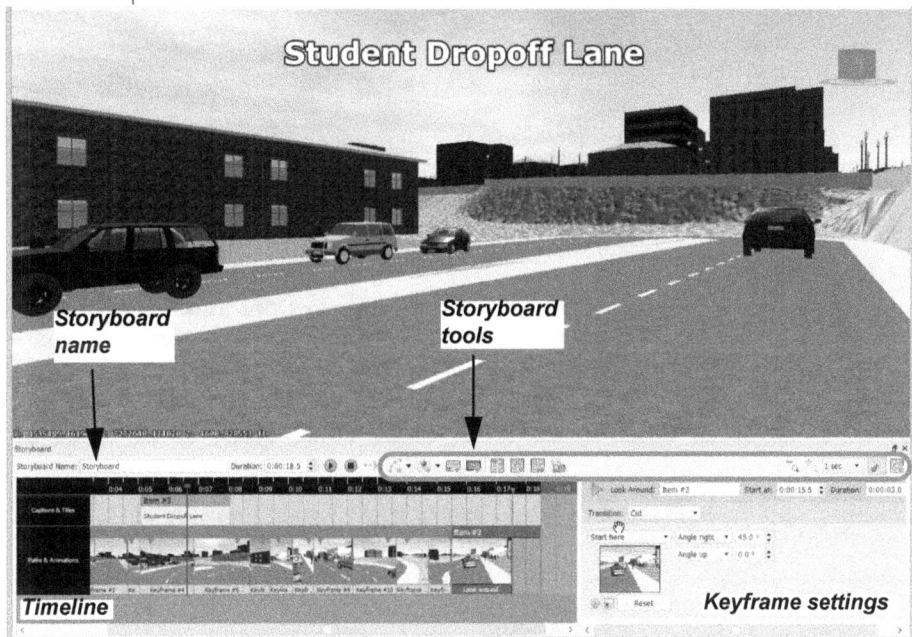

Figure 8–11

- **Storyboard Name:** Displays the name of the current storyboard and enables you to edit the name as required.

- **Timeline:** Indicates when specific elements display and how long they remain in the view before changing to the next element.

- **Storyboard Tools:** Contains tools for creating elements and managing the storyboard.

- **Keyframe Settings:** Provides settings that can be specified for the active (selected) keyframe element.

Working with the Timeline

The Timeline identifies the sequence of the keyframes and details approximately how long each keyframe displays in the presentation. Keyframes can be an image, camera animation, or path animation.

Figure 8–12 shows a storyboard timeline and describes its contents. You can drag and drop keyframes to new locations in the timeline to change the order in which they display. You can also drag the right side of a keyframe to change its duration.

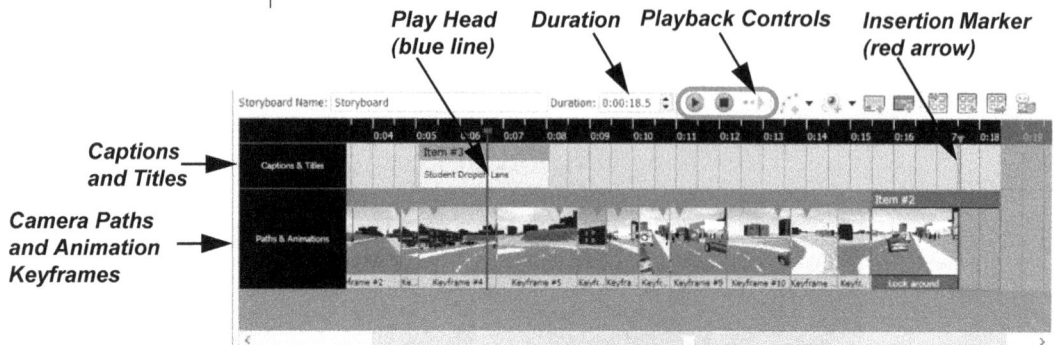

Figure 8–12

- **Play Head (blue square and line):** Indicates where play stops and resumes during playback. Double-click on the timeline to move the play head to a specific location.

- **Duration:** Lists the total time (i.e., start to finish) of the storyboard.

- **Playback Controls:** Starts and stops the presentation at the play head location. It also enables you to control whether the model view follows the storyboard position.

- **Captions and Titles:** Enables you to label specific views in the model to draw attention to points of interest.

- **Camera Paths and Animation Keyframes:** Thumbnails used to indicate what is presented at specific times along the timeline. You can drag and drop the thumbnails to change their order or duration.

- **Insertion Marker (red triangle and line):** Indicates where new elements display in the model when you add them. Click and drag the insertion marker to a location in the timeline to insert the next storyboard feature.

© 2017, ASCENT - Center for Technical Knowledge®

Playback Controls

The following playback controls can help you to view and navigate through the presentation.

Icon	Description
⏵ / ⏸ (Play/Pause)	Starts playing the storyboard from the location of the play head. Once in Play mode, the button displays as a pause button, which enables you to stop the animation without moving the play head from its current position in the timeline.
⏹ (Stop)	Stops playing the storyboard and causes the play head to return to its original position in the timeline.
(Follow Storyboard Position)	Causes the model view to change according to the current keyframe being played in the storyboard.

Adding Keyframes

The keyframes in a storyboard are generated from animations, which are either Path or Camera animations. In each animation category there are multiple animation types. All of the path and camera animation types are added from the Storyboard palette, as shown in Figure 8–13.

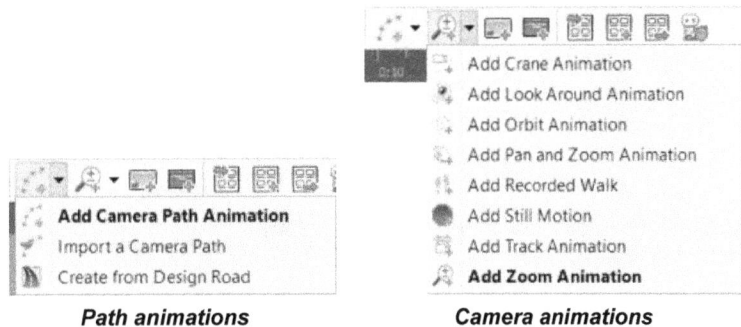

Path animations   *Camera animations*

Figure 8–13

Path Animations

Path animations can be used to automatically create a series of camera positions/angles along a path. There are three path animation options:

- **Add Camera Path Animation:** Creates a series of views starting at one view, which is manually set and ending at another view, which is also manually set.

- **Import a Camera Path:** Imports a saved path which is found in a point feature file (i.e., .DB, .SHP, .SDF, or .SQLITE files).

- **Create from Design Road:** Creates a path along the centerline of a design road.

Hint: Create from Design Road

When you create a path animation from a design road, you can set the horizontal and vertical offsets for both the camera and the target. You can also set the speed, direction of travel, and the keyframe density, as shown in Figure 8–14.

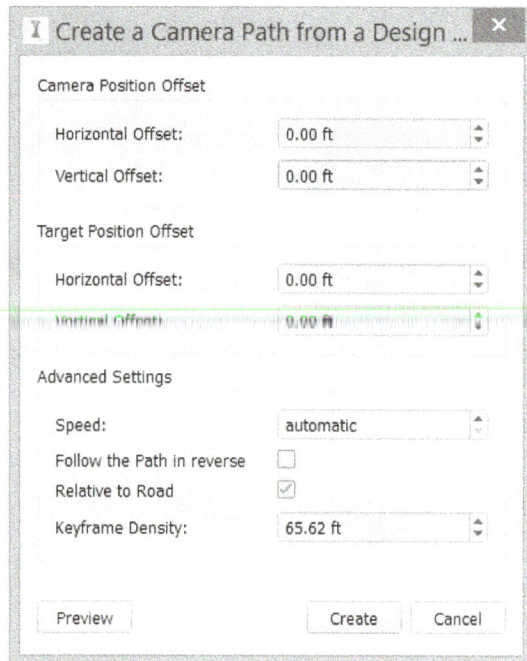

Create a Camera Path from a Design ...

Camera Position Offset

Horizontal Offset: 0.00 ft

Vertical Offset: 0.00 ft

Target Position Offset

Horizontal Offset: 0.00 ft

Vertical Offset: 0.00 ft

Advanced Settings

Speed: automatic

Follow the Path in reverse ☐

Relative to Road ☑

Keyframe Density: 65.62 ft

Preview   Create   Cancel

Figure 8–14

© 2017, ASCENT - Center for Technical Knowledge®

Camera Animations

Camera animations start the transition from a specific camera view, and end at another camera view, which is determined by the storyboard keyframe settings. There are eight camera animation options:

- **Crane Animation:** Moves the camera up and away from or down and towards the camera view.

- **Look Around Animation:** Rotates the view while the camera remains in a fixed position.

- **Orbit Animation:** The camera rotates around a fixed focal point in the shape of a sphere.

- **Pan and Zoom Animation:** The camera pans and zooms simultaneously. The effect is a zooming motion along a path that is determined by distance values and zoom percentages.

- **Recorded Walk:** The camera jumps directly to a shot and then plays a recording that you create. It highlights specific design elements from set angles, rather than by panning or zooming.

- **Still Motion:** Transitions the camera to a still motion shot. The camera does not move for the duration of this shot.

- **Track Animation:** Moves the camera to the left or right of the original camera view.

- **Zoom Animation:** The camera moves closer to or further away from the original focal point of the camera view.

Keyframe Settings

Each keyframe that you add to a storyboard has its own set of properties that can be set to control how the camera moves in the model. Figure 8–15 shows the settings for a Look Around Camera Animation keyframe.

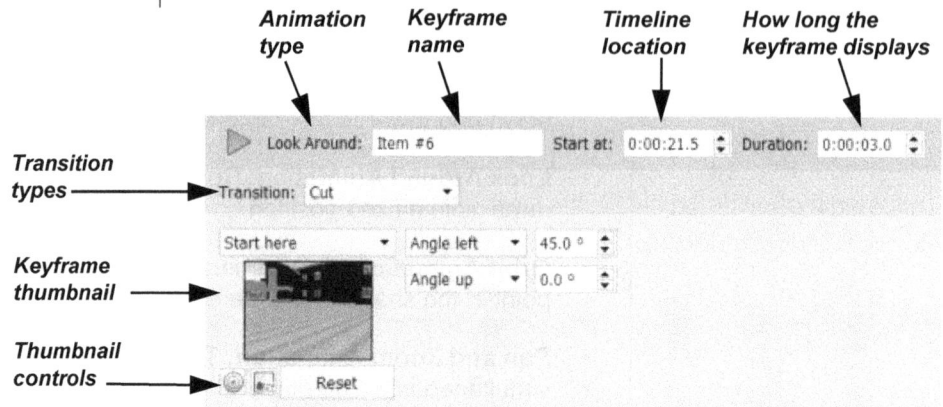

Figure 8–15

The following are areas of the Keyframe settings that are used in multiple animation types.

- **Animation Type:** Lists the type of animation that was used to create the keyframe.

- **Transition Types:** Enables you to set the transition type when entering and exiting the keyframe. There are three transition types:
  - **Cut:** Moves directly to the current keyframe view.
  - **Fade from black:** After the previous keyframe, the view displays as black. It then fades into the current keyframe over a duration that you set using the setting to the right of the Transition drop-down list, as shown in Figure 8–16.

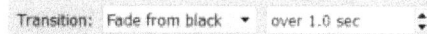

Figure 8–16

- **Fade from white:** After the previous keyframe, the view displays as white. It then fades into the current keyframe over a duration that you set using the setting to the right of the Transition drop-down list, as shown in Figure 8–16.

© 2017, ASCENT - Center for Technical Knowledge®

- **Thumbnail Controls:** Enables you to change the model view or thumbnail view. The following options are available for all of the animation types.

  - ⊙ **(Go To Location):** Quickly sets the model view to be the location of the thumbnail.

  - 🖼 **(Refresh):** Refreshes the thumbnail of the keyframe from the current scene content.

  - **Reset:** Changes the keyframe view to the current model view.

How To: Add a Path Animation

This procedure uses the Camera Path Animation as an example. The process is similar for the other Path animations.

1. In the Storyboard palette, move the Insertion Marker (red triangle and line) to the location on the timeline where you want to insert the new path animation.
2. Navigate to the view that you want to use as the starting point of the animation.
3. In the Storyboard palette, expand the Camera Animations

   drop-down list and click 🎬 (Add Camera Path Animation), as shown in Figure 8–17.

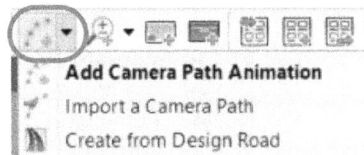

Figure 8–17

Note that the first keyframe displays as a thumbnail in the timeline, as shown in Figure 8–18.

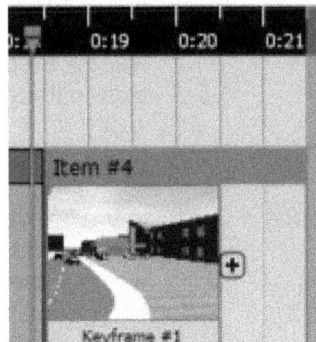

Figure 8–18

4. In the *Storyboard Keyframe Settings* area, set the options in the Transition and Interpolate drop-down lists and the **Camera speed control** option, as shown in Figure 8–19. The settings displayed are applied to the currently selected keyframe.

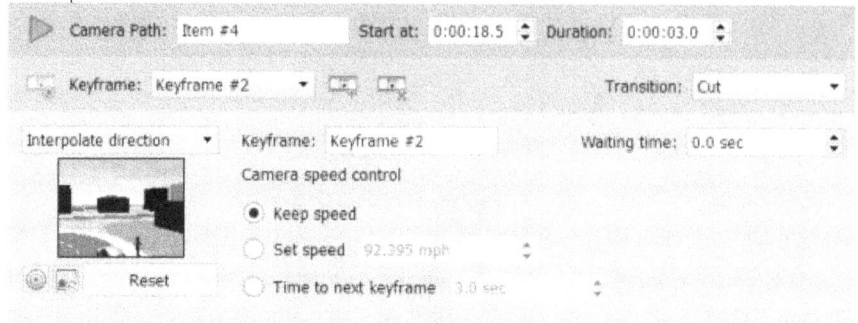

Figure 8–19

Hint: Camera Path Settings

You can select one of three focal points for the camera view, set the camera speed, and determine the type of transition. The Camera Focal Point drop-down list contains options for setting the camera to **Look Along Path**, **Interpolate Direction**, or **Interpolate Focus Point**. The Camera Speed control options enable you to keep the camera speed as it is set by the current start time and duration, set a specific speed, or set the time until the next keyframe.

5. In the model, navigate to the required view to prepare the next keyframe in the camera path.
6. In the Storyboard timeline, click ⊕ (Add Keyframe) to the right of the first Keyframe's thumbnail.
7. Repeat Steps 4 to 6 to add additional camera positions to extend the path as required.

How To: Create a Camera Animation

This procedure uses the Pan and Zoom Animation as an example. The process is similar for the other camera animations.

1. In the Storyboard palette, move the Insertion Marker (red triangle and line) to the location on the timeline where you want to insert the new camera animation.
2. Navigate to the view that you want to use as the starting point of the animation.

© 2017, ASCENT - Center for Technical Knowledge®

3. In the Storyboard palette, expand the Camera Animations drop-down list and click (Add Pan and Zoom Animation), as shown in Figure 8–20.

Figure 8–20

4. In the *Storyboard Keyframe Settings* area, set the options in the Transition, Distance, and Zoom drop-down lists, as shown in Figure 8–21. The settings apply to the currently selected keyframe.

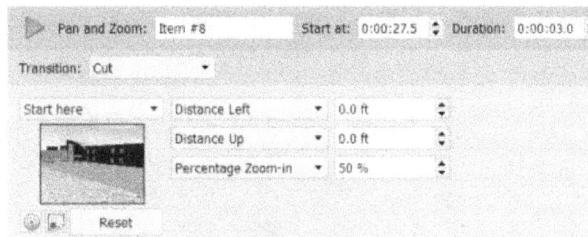

Figure 8–21

Add Captions and Titles

Captions and titles are located in the storyboard palette. These tools enable you to place labels, text, and images into multiple keyframes in the storyboard. An example of captions and titles is shown in Figure 8–22.

Figure 8–22

Captions

Captions are labels that overlay keyframes in the storyboard presentation. You can add multiple captions, which become stacked vertically, based on their assigned location. Click

🔲 (Add a new Caption) to create a caption in the model view. Use the caption settings to edit the caption's text, font, size, and transition settings.

Titles

Titles can include text and images to introduce the entire story, individual chapters of the story, or to display credits and

acknowledgments. Click 🔲 (Add a new Title) to create a caption in the model view. Use the caption settings to edit the title's text, font, size, and transition settings.

Reusing Storyboards

If a storyboard is created in another model, you can reuse it by importing it into the current model. All of the camera positions and transitions from the previous model remain the same, but the current model's elements display in the keyframes.

- 🔳 **(Export Current Storyboard):** Creates a .JSON file for sharing storyboards between Autodesk InfraWorks models.

- 🔳 **(Import Existing Storyboards):** Imports a .JSON file from another model.

Create & Share Storyboard Videos

Storyboards are most useful when you can share them with others. Unfortunately, most stakeholders do not have the Autodesk InfraWorks software. Exporting a storyboard to a video enables anyone to display the presentation. Storyboards can be exported to a number of different encoders. The encoders that can be used when creating a video are as follows.

You can also use any DirectShow compatible encoders that are installed on your computer.

Format	Properties
Uncompressed Video	A generic .AVI format that does not have any properties that can be specified.
Windows Media® Video	Video compression format developed by Microsoft. You can select Windows Video Media 9 or Windows Video Media 9 Advanced Profile from Properties, and set the bitrate (kilobits per second).

© 2017, ASCENT - Center for Technical Knowledge®

DV Video Encoder	An .AVI format that encodes an uncompressed video stream into digital video (DV). You can set the video format, DV format, and resolution in the properties. Video formats include: • NTSC (National Television System Committee standard) • PAL (Phase Alternating Line)
MJPEG Compressor	An .AVI format that compresses an uncompressed video stream using motion JPEG compression. It does not have any properties that can be specified.

How To: Record a Video

1. To create a video from a storyboard, in the Storyboard Tools palette, click 🎥 (Export Storyboard to Video).
2. In the Export Storyboard dialog box (shown in Figure 8–23), select the required encoder, filename, frame rate, and resolution.

Figure 8–23

3. Click **Record**.

Additional Storyboard Tools

Additional storyboard tools are used to create and manage storyboards and control the display of the timeline. The following tools are available.

Icon	Description
(Add New Storyboard)	Creates a new, empty storyboard.
(Zoom Out/In)	Zooms the timeline to display a longer or shorter presentation duration in the timeline viewing area.
2 sec ▼ (Zoom Resolution)	Sets the amount of time by which the timeline zooms in and out.
(Hide/Show Item Detail)	Displays or hides details connected to the currently selected item in the timeline viewing area.
(Show Storyboard Library)	Displays a list of storyboards associated with the current model and their duration.

© 2017, ASCENT - Center for Technical Knowledge®

Practice 8b

Estimated time for completion: 30 minutes

Communicating the Design Using a Storyboard

Practice Objective

- Communicate the design intent to stakeholders using a storyboard.

In this practice you will add path and camera animations to create a storyboard.

Task 1 - Create a storyboard.

In this task you will create a presentation to show how parents will use the carpool lane to pick up and drop off students. You will use a camera path animation to simulate driving up to the drop off location. You will then add camera path animations to get a bird's eye view of the school.

1. In the Home Screen click **Open**.

2. In the *C:\InfraWorks Fundamentals Practice Files\ Communication* folder, select **Communicate.sqlite** and click **Open**.

3. In the Utility Bar, select **Conceptual View** for the Visual Style.

4. In the In Canvas tools, click [icon] (Create and conduct infrastructure design presentations)>[icon] (Storyboard Creator).

5. If a blank storyboard is not available, in the Storyboard palette, click [icon] (Add New Storyboard).

6. In the Storyboard palette, rename the new storyboard as **Carpool**.

7. In the Utility Bar, click [icon] (Bookmark your current location) and select **1-Carpool**.

8. In the Storyboard palette, click [icon] (Add Camera Path Animation). The first view displays as a thumbnail in the timeline, as shown in Figure 8–24. The default duration is 3 seconds.

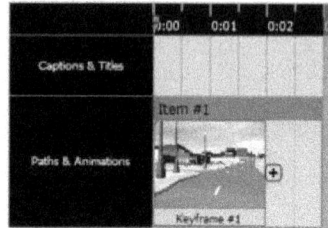

Figure 8–24

9. In the *Storyboard Keyframe Settings* area, do the following, as shown in Figure 8–25:

   - Expand the *Transition* drop-down list and select **Cut**.
   - Expand the *Interpolate* drop-down list and select **Interpolate Direction**.
   - For *Time to next keyframe*, accept the default.

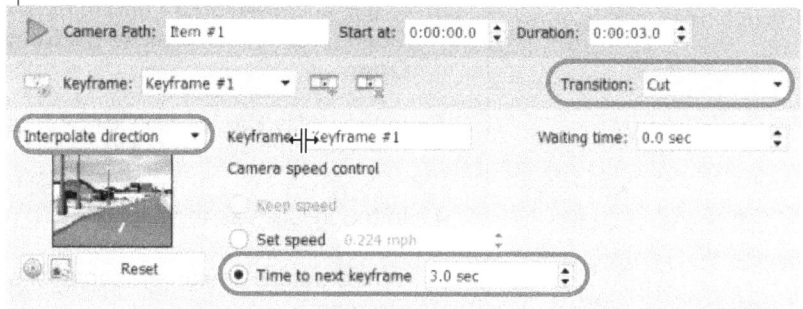

Figure 8–25

10. In the Utility Bar, click [icon] (Bookmark your current location) and select **2-Carpool**.

11. In the Storyboard timeline, click [icon] (Add Keyframe), which displays to the right of the first Keyframe.

© 2017, ASCENT - Center for Technical Knowledge®

12. Repeat Steps 10 and 11 to add more camera positions and extend the path. Bookmarks have been created that will enable you to quickly move from one view to another along the path a car should follow to pick up students. Use the bookmarks in sequential order (3-Carpool, 4-Carpool, ..., 7-Carpool). When you have finished, the last keyframe view and the timeline should display as shown in Figure 8–26. The Camera Path Animation (Item#1) consists of these seven keyframes.

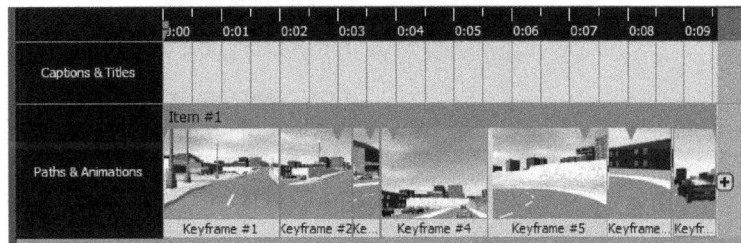

Figure 8–26

13. Move the Insertion Marker (red line) to the end of the storyboard.

14. In the Storyboard palette, expand the Camera Animations drop-down list and click 🕭 (Add Pan and Zoom Animation). The timeline displays as shown in Figure 8–27. This keyframe sets the camera to pan and zoom simultaneously as the driver looks for a student.

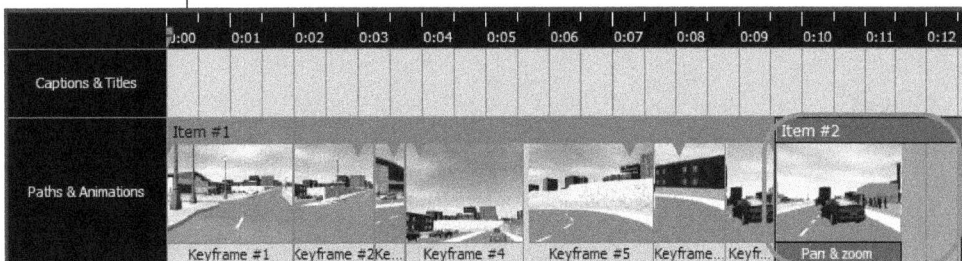

Figure 8–27

15. Ensure that the last keyframe is selected. In the keyframe settings, select **Distance Right**, type **15** for the distance measurement, and set the *Percentage Zoom-in* to **100%**, as shown in Figure 8–28.

	Pan and Zoom:	Item #2	Start at: 0:00:19.7	Duration: 0:00:03.0
Transition:	Cut			
Start here	Distance Right	15.0 ft		
	Distance Up	0.0 ft		
	Percentage Zoom-in	100 %		
	Reset			

Figure 8–28

16. In the Storyboard palette, click ▶ (Play the current storyboard).

17. Move the Insertion Marker (red line) to the end of the storyboard.

18. In the Storyboard palette, expand the Camera Animations drop-down list and click 📷 (Add Crane Animation). The timeline displays as shown in Figure 8–29.

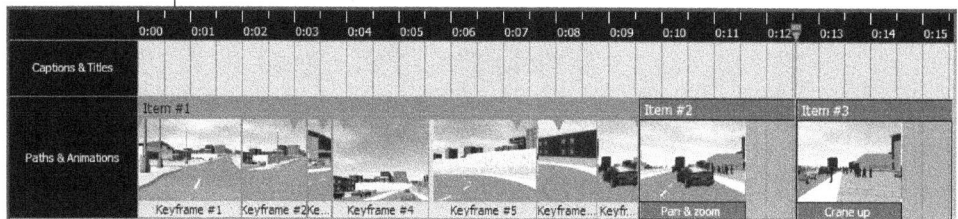

Figure 8–29

19. In the keyframe settings, in the *Distance Up* field, enter **50**. In the *Distance Back* field, enter **50** again. Clear the **Lock camera on center-of-interest** option, as shown in Figure 8–30.

	Crane:	Item #3	Start at: 0:00:22.7	Duration: 0:00:03.0
Transition:	Cut			
Start here	Type:	Crane up		
	Distance Up:	50.0 ft		
	Distance Back:	50.0 ft		
	Distance Left	0.0 ft		
	Reset	☐ Lock camera on center-of-interest		

Figure 8–30

© 2017, ASCENT - Center for Technical Knowledge®

20. Move the Insertion Marker (red line) to the end of the storyboard.

21. In the Storyboard palette, expand the Camera Animations drop-down list and click ⚹ (Add Orbit Animation). The timeline displays as shown in Figure 8–31.

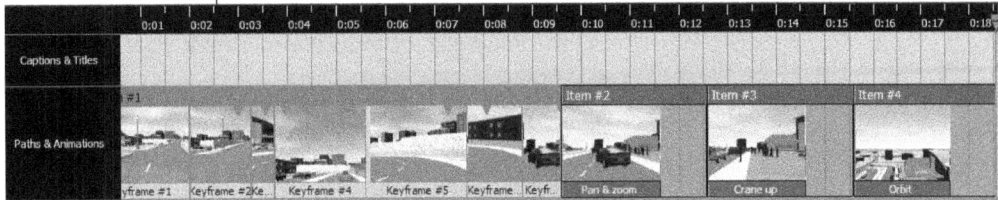

Figure 8–31

22. In the keyframe settings, in the *Angle left* field, type **90**, and in the *Angle up* field, type **45**, as shown in Figure 8–32.

Figure 8–32

23. In the Storyboard palette, click ⏺ (Play the current storyboard).

Task 2 - Export the storyboard to video.

---

1. In the Storyboard palette, click 📹 (Export Storyboard to Video).

2. In the Export Storyboard dialog box, next to the *Filename* field, click ⬚ (Browse).

3. In the Select Video File dialog box, enter the required filename and location and click **Save**.

4. In the Export Storyboard dialog box, click **Record**.

5. Using Windows® Media Player®, open and play the video you just created.

Task 3 - Create a storyboard from a design road.

If you have design roads in your model, you can create a storyboard much quicker than the process used in the first task. In this task you will create a new storyboard and use the car pool lane to create a path animation.

1. In the Utility Bar, click ▣ (Bookmark your current location) and select **StudentDropOff**.

2. In the Storyboard palette, click ▦ (Add New Storyboard).

3. In the Storyboard palette, rename the new storyboard as **Design Road**.

4. In the Storyboard palette, expand ⁺ (Add New Camera Path Animation) and select **Create from Design Road**.

5. In the model, select the car pool design road which was followed manually in Task 1.

6. In the Create a Camera Path from a Design Road dialog box, set the following, as shown in Figure 8–33.
   - *Camera Position Horizontal Offset*: **5**
   - *Camera Position Vertical Offset*: **5**
   - *Target Position Horizontal Offset*: **5**
   - Click **Create**

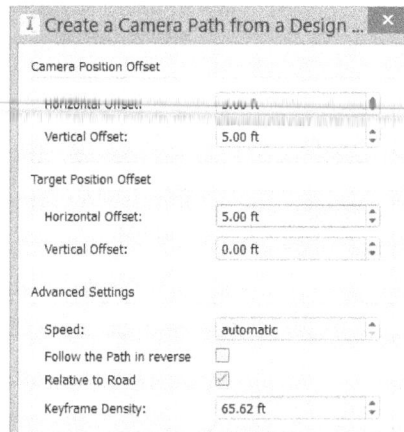

Figure 8–33

7. In the Storyboard palette, click ▶ (Play the current storyboard).

© 2017, ASCENT - Center for Technical Knowledge®

Chapter Review Questions

1. When creating a snapshot, in which file format(s) can the image be saved?

   a. JPG images (*.JPG)

   b. PNG images (*.PNG)

   c. TIFF images (*.TIF)

   d. All of the above.

2. When adding a title to a storyboard, which of the following can be included?

   a. Text only.

   b. Text and an image.

   c. An image only.

3. Which camera animation would you use to move the camera up and away from the current view?

   a. **Look Around Animation**

   b. **Still Motion**

   c. **Crane Animation**

   d. **Zoom Animation**

4. Which of the following is not a transition option?

   a. **Fade from Center**

   b. **Cut**

   c. **Fade to Black**

   d. **Fade to White**

5. Which of the following can be used as keyframes in a storyboard? (Select all that apply.)

   a. Snapshots

   b. Rendered images

   c. Path animations

   d. Camera animations

Command Summary

Button	Command	Location
	Create Snapshot	• **In Canvas Tools:** Create and conduct infrastructure design presentations
	Storyboard Creator	• **In Canvas Tools:** Create and conduct infrastructure design presentations
	Storyboard Player	• **In Canvas Tools:** Create and conduct infrastructure design presentations

© 2017, ASCENT - Center for Technical Knowledge®

Example of a GIS Data Source

This appendix is an example of a Geographic Information System (GIS) data source, showing the GIS layers of Utah County[1]. This GIS was obtained from the GIS Division of the Utah County Information Systems department.

---

1. (Department, GIS Division of the Utah County Information Systems, 2013)

Utah County GIS Layers – Presented by the GIS Division of the Utah County Information Systems Department

For more information go to www.utahcountyonline.org

Road Centerlines

Tags

Roads, Transportation, Spillman

Summary

Road segments representing centerlines of all roadways or carriageways in the vicinity of Utah County. Data schema reflects ESRI's Local Government Data Model with additional fields pertinent for local Utah County processes and applications.

Description

Road segments representing centerlines of all roadways or carriageways in the vicinity of Utah County. Typically, this information is compiled from orthoimagery or other aerial photography sources. This representation of the road centerlines support address geocoding and mapping. It also serves as a source for public works and other agencies that are responsible for the active management of the road network. Data schema reflects ESRI's Local Government Data Model with additional fields pertinent for local Utah County processes and applications.

Credits

The GIS Division of Utah County's Information Systems Department.

Use limitations

While there are no constraints or warranties with regard to the use of this dataset, users are encouraged to attribute content to the GIS Division of Utah County Information Systems Department.

Scale Range

Maximum (zoomed in)   1:5,000
Minimum (zoomed out)   1:500,000

Extent

West -112.313967   East   -110.850577
North 40.681317   South 39.679831

Spatial Reference

NAD 1983 StatePlane, Utah Central Zone, FIPS 4302, US Survey Feet

© 2017, ASCENT - Center for Technical Knowledge®

Utah County GIS Layers – Presented by the GIS Division of the Utah County Information Systems Department

For more information go to www.utahcountyonline.org

Field	DataType	Length	AliasName	Description
OBJECTID	Object ID		ObjectID	Sequential unique whole numbers that are automatically generated.
GLOBALID	Global ID		GlobalID	Global Identifiction number (Needed for replication)
CENTERLINEID	Text	20	Centerline ID	A unique id for the road centerline segment
FROMLEFT	Long		Left From Address	Lowest address range on left side of the road
TOLEFT	Long		Left To Address	Highest address range on left side of the road
FROMRIGHT	Long		Right From Address	Lowest address range on right side of the road
TORIGHT	Long		Right To Address	Highest address range on right side of the road
ROADPREDIR	Text	2	Road Prefix	The directional prefix of the address
ROADNAME	Text	50	Road Name	Primary street name. If a numbered street (i.e. 200 WEST) also has another well known name like "FREEDOM" BLVD. "FREEDOM" would generally be designated the primary name and "200 WEST" the alternate name
ROADTYPE	Text	4	Road Type	The type of road (Street, Road, Avenue, etc...)
ROADPOSTDIR	Text	2	Post Direction	Suffix Direction
FULLNAME	Text	125	Full Road Name	The full primary name of the road including any prefix and/or suffix and street type
ALTROADNAME	Text	30	Alternate Road Name	The secondary or alternative name of the road. A numbered street name, such as 200 WEST, would generally be listed as the alternate name while "FREEDOM" in FREEDOM BLVD would be the road's primary name.
ALTROADTYPE	Text	4	Alternate Road Type	Alternate street type (Street, Road, Avenue, etc...)
ALTROADNAME2	Text	30	Alt Road Name2	Second alternate street name
ALTROADTYPE2	Text	4	Alt Road Type2	Second alternate street type
MUNILEFT	Text	30	Municipality on Left	The municipality on the left side of the road. "Unincorporated" if in Utah County but not within a municipality.
MUNIRIGHT	Text	30	Municipality on Right	The municipality on the right side of the road. "Unincorporated" if in Utah County but not within a municipality.
ZIPLEFT	Text	5	Zip on Left	Zip code on left side of the road
ZIPRIGHT	Text	5	Zip on Right	Zip code on right side of the road
FEDROUTE	Text	10	Federal Route	The federal route name. Used to populate the number within the highway marker shield
FEDRTETYPE	Text	20	Federal Route Type	A functional classification of route that can be used to symbolize the route if detail beyond what is provided in ROADCLASS is needed
AFEDROUTE	Text	10	Alternate Federal Route	The alternate federal route name. Used to populate the number within the highway marker shield
AFEDRTETYPE	Text	20	Alternate Federal Route Type	A functional classification of route that can be used to symbolize the route if detail beyond what is provided in ROADCLASS is needed
STROUTE	Text	10	State Route	The state route name. Used to populate the number in the state highway marker shields
STRTETYPE	Text	20	State Route Type	A functional classification of route that can be used to symbolize the route if detail beyond what is provided in ROADCLASS is needed
ASTRTE	Text	10	Alternate State Route	An alternate state route name. Used to populate the number in the state highway marker shields
ASTRTETYPE	Text	20	Alternate State Route Type	A functional classification of route that can be used to symbolize the route if detail beyond what is provided in ROADCLASS is needed
CTYROUTE	Text	10	County Route	County route name. Currently Utah County does not designate county route numbers, therefore, this field is not used
FAEROUTE	Text	10	FEA Route Number	Federal aid eligible route number (a null value indicates not federal and eligible road)
PROJECTID	Long		UC Project ID	Internal Utah County Project ID for B road segments
SURFACE	Text	20	Surface	Road Surface Type
CONDITION	Text	20	Condition	Condition of the road
ROW_WIDTH	Short		ROW Width	Right-of-way width in feet
ROADCLASS	Text	20	Road Class	Functional classification of roads based on type of service
RDCLASS_UHJCA	Text	5	UHJCA Class	Road classification based on Utah's Highway Jurisdiction & Classification Act (A = State, B = County, C = Municipalities, D = Public thoroughfares.
CFCCCODE	Text	3	CFCC Code	CFCC Code (Census Feature Classification Code)
OWNEDBY	Short	2	Owned By	Indicates which organization owns the asset
MAINTBY	Short	2	Maintained By	Indicates which organization maintains the asset
DCLASSID	Text	4	D Road ID	Internal Utah County ID number for D Class road segments
RS2477	Text	3	RS2477	Indicates whether the road segment is designated a RS2477 road
COUNTYNAME	Text	20	County Name	The county name the road segment is located in
CULDESAC	Text	5	Cul de sac	A flag that indicates whether the road segment depicts a cul-de-sac circle
ONEWAYDIR	Text	10	One Way Indicator	A code that indicates whether the traffic flows with, or against, the direction of the vertices
ROADLEVEL	Long		Above or Below Grade	A code that indicates whether the traveled roadway is above or below grade
INWATER	Text	5	In Water	A flag that indicates whether the segment of the road is crossing water
SOURCEFEATUREID	Text	20	Source Feature ID	ID of the segment that may be related to another source database
DATASOURCENAME	Text	100	Data Source	Name of the source of this data
LASTUPDATE	Date		Last Update Date	Last date the road segment was edited
LASTEDITOR	Text	100	Last Editor	Last person's username that edited the road segment
ISVISIBLE	Text	5	Is Visible	Flag indicating if the segment should be visible on a map
EDITCOMMENTS	Text	250	Edit Comments	Comment Field

© 2017, ASCENT - Center for Technical Knowledge®

Index

© 2017, ASCENT - Center for Technical Knowledge®

© 2017, ASCENT - Center for Technical Knowledge®

www.ingramcontent.com/pod-product-compliance
Lightning Source LLC
Chambersburg PA
CBHW080709220326
41598CB00033B/5358